The Death of a Christian
The Order of Christian Funerals

*Studies in the Reformed Rites
of the Catholic Church,
Volume VII*

Revised Edition

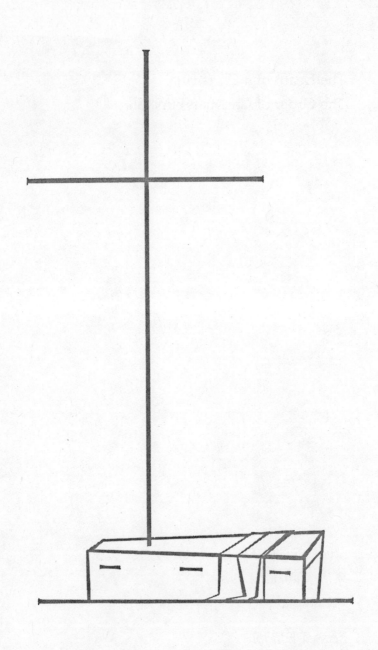

Richard Rutherford, C.S.C.
with Tony Barr

The Death of a Christian:
The Order
of Christian Funerals

A PUEBLO BOOK

The Liturgical Press   Collegeville, Minnesota

Design: Frank Kacmarcik

Copyright © 1980 by Pueblo Publishing Company, Inc.
Copyright © 1990 by The Order of St. Benedict, Inc., Collegeville, Minnesota. All rights reserved.

Printed in the United States of America

ISBN 0-8146-6040-1

In Memoriam
THOMAS C. ODDO, C.S.C.
1944–1989

priest
leader
brother
friend

Contents

The Reformed Order of Christian Funerals

Introduction

In the quarter century since the promulgation of the *Constitution on the Sacred Liturgy,* few works of liturgical renewal have had the extensive impact and welcome reception enjoyed by the reformed funeral liturgy. Belief in the paschal mystery is unquestionably the principal metaphor of contemporary Catholic faith in face of death. As such, it formed the renewal mandate of Vatican Council II and the central focus of liturgical reform of funeral rites. The latter took shape in the *Ordo Exsequiarum* both as presented by the Roman Congregation for Worship in 1969 and as "received" by the Universal Church in vernacular rituals. After two decades of pastoral experience with the provisional English edition, the *Rite of Funerals,* and after widespread consultation and further revision, the International Committee on English in the Liturgy (ICEL) has prepared a superbly pastoral book of funeral rites, the *Order of Christian Funerals* (1989). The English-speaking episcopal conferences served by ICEL have approved this edition for use in their national churches. Through the tireless work of the Secretariat for the Liturgy, the *Order of Christian Funerals* has been published in its entirety for use in the United States by authority of the National Conference of Catholic Bishops.

Essential to the centrality of the paschal mystery in all this is to recognize that death, not only resurrection, is at the heart of the mystery. Belief in the resurrection of Jesus and hope that our Christian Initiation gives us a participation in that risen life, even beyond the limitations of our mortality, offer the faithful a means to make sense of death, the greatest threat to our identity as living beings. Indeed, the paschal mystery is about death *and* resurrection. But death is what we know; resurrection is what we believe in and hope for. With sensitive respect for the full impact of death, its sadness and grief, the Christian dares to celebrate the funeral liturgy. Such is the paschal character of Christian death, and in the Catholic tradition, the Order of Christian Funerals is its liturgy.

That liturgy is the topic of this book, and its celebration today motivates this revised study of its origins (Chapter One), its development in history (Chapters Two and Three), and its present form and expression (Chapters Four and Five). Further pastoral reflections on contemporary usage and some future agenda constitute Chapter Six, while several appendices review the editorial history of the new *Order* and offer a more detailed reflection on four topics of pastoral concern. By sharing the fruit of liturgical research and hundreds of pastoral conversations, this book hopes to render the revised funeral liturgy and its expression of the paschal character of Christian death ever more accessible.

Many people have contributed to the revision of this book. Although most remain silent partners, several deserve very special thanks. The first is Tony Barr. As patient collaborator in the writing and constant mentor of pastoral, musical breadth, and greater international sensitivity, he well deserves his share of recognition on the title page of this volume. The timely completion of this revision to accompany the appearance of the *Order of Christian Funerals* would not have been possible without the discreet, though generous, cooperation of John Page, Peter Finn, and James Schellman of ICEL and of the Secretariat for the Liturgy of the NCCB, particularly John Guerrieri, the past director, Ronald Krisman, Alan Detscher, and Kenneth Jenkins. Among the many hidden motivators over the years have been my students at the University of Portland, University of Notre Dame, and St.

John's University (Collegeville, Minn.), whose pastoral commitment in ministry provided fresh insights and an essential complement of reality testing. Special gratitude is due my Holy Cross Community in Portland, my mother, Margaret; my sister Gail and her family Richard and Ralph; friends Patsy Ross and Alan Helyer—all of whom contributed generous financial and personal support to enable completion of this task in the midst of ordinary daily labors. University of Portland staff Kay McEwen, Brenda Tharp, and their assistants are the heroines whose editorial and technical expertise transformed the work into a book.

All these persons have taught me never again to read lightly over citations of gratitude. Truly, without them, this revised edition would never have seen the light of day. I alone, however, bear the responsibility for what has become of their gift in these pages.

Richard Rutherford, C.S.C.
Easter 1990

Evolution of the Order

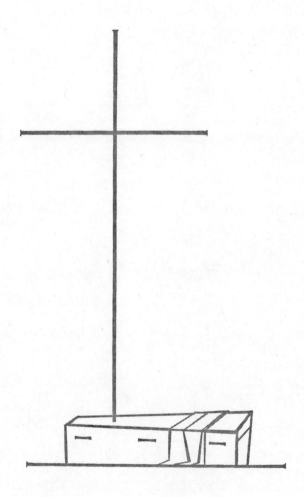

Chapter One

Origins

Long before medieval theologians began to write their
tracts on the four last things, Christians had been expressing their beliefs about death and life after death
in the way they cared for their dead. The followers of
Jesus, taking reverent care of the bodies of their dead
and holding their memory in honor, were simply continuing the customs of the culture into which the
Church of Christ was born. Funeral ritual belongs to
the very heritage of the human community. Speaking
with the authority of scholarly consensus, the anthro-
pologist Margaret Mead once said, "I know of no people for whom the fact of death is not critical, and who
have no ritual by which to deal with it."[1]

CULTURAL AND RELIGIOUS ROOTS
In the Mediterranean world of the first century A.D.,
the many different nations embraced by the vast
Greco-Roman culture observed funeral rites consisting
of both their own ancient heritages and elements
found elsewhere in the contemporary empire. Although customs differed widely from people to people, the funeral rites carried out by ordinary Roman
citizens were sufficiently widespread to give us an example of the kind of funeral first-century Christians
would have known.[2]

Culturally, apprehension seems to have been the primary inspiration for funerary ritual. Personal emotions
of loss and grief certainly played their part, but fear

3

far more than hope, aversion more than affection, motivated pagan rituals at death. It was generally believed that the dead were inclined to be resentful and quick to take revenge. Funerary rites served to appease them. Burial, it was held, guaranteed a certain peace; otherwise one's shade might be doomed to everlasting, restless wandering, to be a source of dread in the world of the living. For this reason, burial of the dead was regarded as the minimum of ritual concern. Even the dead stranger was to be given a ritual burial. Both Greek and Roman literature attest how deeply rooted in popular religious sensibility this last honor paid to the dead was.[3]

The other primary influence on the early Christian funeral was, of course, its Judaic roots. In the history of Israel, burial of deceased members of the community was an obligation and a work of mercy. Burial in their own land (Genesis 23) and with their ancestors (Genesis 49; 50; Joshua 24:32–33) were noteworthy values ascribed to patriarchs, judges, and kings (Judges 8:32; 12:7; 16:31; II Kings 9:28). Enemies, too, were accorded some form of burial, if only a mound of stones (Joshua 8:29; 10:26; II Samuel 21:13–14). The deuterocanonical book *Tobit* illustrates the importance of this practice in the life of a devout Jew, who was tested and rewarded by God. In postexilic times, rabbis taught that the obligation to care for the dead extended not only to relatives and friends but to any deceased Jew. They repeatedly insisted that this duty of fraternal love likewise included the dead outside Judaism.[4]

Jewish funerary rites seem always to have reflected the realism and simplicity that characterize present-day "Justification of Judgment" (*Tzidduk Ha-din*) liturgy. Although this liturgy dates from the ninth century and does not document first-century practice as such, it is believed to reflect Jewish liturgical expres-

4

sion that would have been familiar to the earliest Christians.[5]

Besides these two predominant influences, the religious syncretism of the times brought still other active cultural forces to bear. Imperial Rome was strongly attracted to the mystery cults from the East and to the religious beliefs and practices of Egypt.[6] One consequence of all this diversity contributes much to our understanding of the first-century milieu.

In summary it can be said that "during the late Republic and throughout the Empire . . . belief in the survival after death of personal individuality prevailed and views on the nature of the life that awaited the soul beyond the grave were, in the main, optimistic. Both literature (to some extent) and funerary art (to a high degree) do, in fact, reveal that there was in this age a deepening conviction that the terror and power of death could be overcome and that richer, happier, and more godlike life than that experienced here was attainable hereafter, under certain conditions, by the souls of the departed."[7]

Optimistic interest in life hereafter and ritual care for the dead were thus something Christians shared with the world around them as part of their human cultural heritage. Nevertheless, early Christian eschatology and the early Christian funeral were peculiarly Christian. It would be a mistake to deny that the cultures in which the Church took root influenced the experiential faith of Christians; yet one cannot fail to acknowledge the reciprocal influence that the faith had on the way those Christians lived their lives. "The world of Early Christendom," it has been documented, "is one which must be understood from within. It is not the prevailing form—which is usually that of late Classical times—but the Christian content which plays the determining role."[8] It is important not only to uncover the

5

cultural and religious roots of Christian funerary rites
but also to interpret them as the rituals of believing
Christians.

THE CHURCH OF THE MARTYRS (A.D. 30–313)
During the first three centuries of the life of the
Church, aptly called the Church of the Martyrs, the
earliest witnesses to Christian care of the dead are the
cemeteries themselves. These were public cemeteries
and not, as popular piety once believed, secret burial
places of persecuted Christians. Very few date from
before the fourth century, and they reveal that Christians and pagans were buried in a similar manner,
sometimes even side by side in the same cemetery.
Only the decorative representations and inscriptions indicate any distinction between these early graves. Certain apparently neutral pagan motifs continued to appear with Jewish and Christian ones on the same
grave.[9] Even these early decorations proclaimed in
their pristine manner that for the Christians their dead
"were no mere shades whom they remembered with
sadness and resignation. These were the ones who
had gone before to the Paradise of the Shepherd, to
the 'place of refreshment, light and peace.' During the
funeral meal [which Christians initially continued to
celebrate as something quite ordinary], they linked the
'refreshment' with another meal, that of the Eucharist,
the Food of Life. That is why, in the chamber of the
funeral meal [in the catacomb of St. Priscilla, Rome],
we see, on the arch above the center couch, the pic-
ture of the meal with loaves and fishes and on the
walls that of the deliverance and the rebirth from the
water."[10] Such funerary decorations preserved for us
the symbolic motifs in which those early Christians
gave expression to their faith in face of death, a faith
that speaks not of death but of life. Far from denying
physical death, this proclaims the belief that the life
entered at baptism and nourished at the eucharist is of

6

a different order, which is in no way affected by physical death. Its only paradigm is the life of the Lord Jesus, dead and risen, as symbolized by Christian initiation. Its food is the body of the Lord Jesus, broken and given as the bread of life. For those reborn to this life in the waters of baptism and fed at the Lord's eucharistic banquet in union with his Church, the idea that physical death might terminate such life simply has no place in the categories of the faith. This is not to say that physical death itself, as well as its harsh consequences for bereaved survivors, was not real. But in the face of grief, of painful human loss and separation, Christians found consolation in the promise of life. They had every hope that the life they once shared together in the eucharist would be theirs again in the eschatological kingdom. Ignatius of Antioch, writing to the Ephesians, reminded erring Christians what it meant "to share in the one common breaking of bread—the medicine of immortality, and the sovereign remedy by which we escape death and live in Jesus Christ for evermore."[11]

Since those first sad hours on the hillside of Calvary, Christians have been recognized as a "nightwatch people."[12] The handful of disciples gathered at that empty tomb to celebrate the birth of the Church and the new hope for the future.[13] Each week when sabbath drew to a close and the new week began, at sunset on Saturday evening, those same disciples gathered to keep watch all night long, anticipating the dawn of the first day of the week, waiting in hope for the return of the risen Lord. The months, years, and decades following the resurrection saw this liturgical nightwatch assembly formulating its faith that the risen Lord returns whenever his disciples gathered in vigil to share the good news that Jesus had risen and was Lord for ever. This was done by proclaiming the Scriptures, pouring the waters of baptism, breaking bread, and transmitting the power of the Spirit through the laying on of hands.

In Christian antiquity, vigils were far more dynamic than one might think today. They were certainly not merely peaceful, reflective occasions for contemplation and growth in holiness. On the contrary, they were highly charged activities involving the whole assembly. In the crucible of vigil, the assembly forged the roots of gospel tradition. In the intensity of vigil, the Church made its first hesitant steps away from Judaism into a world not yet charted; and as always, the unique occasion for gathering was the celebration of Jesus dead and risen with its repercussions on the entire assembly. Gospel tradition emerged as a catechesis for discipleship because of a no-longer-dead person, the Christ.[14]

The faith on which this discipleship was founded was stronger even than the consequence of physical death, whether by natural causes or destruction by beasts or ill fortune. At the promised resurrection, all things would be restored by the all-powerful God, Lord of all nature, for belief in an everlasting life in Christ pertained not to the soul only.[15] The climax of redemption belongs both to spirit and to flesh; hence, Christians paid care and respect to the mortal remains of the faithful dead while they remembered their souls in prayer.

The epitome of participation in Christ's redemptive death and resurrection was martyrdom, for such a death was believed to bear perfect witness to Christ and thus to enjoy the immediate reward of paradise with him. The tombs of the martyrs very early became places of vigil and special devotion. Simple shrines or memorials (*memoriae*) were erected at their tombs, some as adjacent crypts in the catacombs, others above ground nearby or in the homes of the martyred saints. Many of these precious places were to be the sites of future churches. Gradually, lists of local martyrs, with the dates of their death, were compiled to guide the annual commemorations by the faithful. The cult of the martyrs so preserved indicates the kinds of commemorative rites that were held for the dead. Moreover, such annual commemorations mirrored the rituals of the burial itself.[16]

These few examples from church life, together with the earliest Christian iconograpy, demonstrate the spirit of prayer that characterized Christian burial and commemorations. The redeemed soul is shown with hands upraised in prayer to its Redeemer. Similarly, as we have seen, the conception of "refreshment" is frequently depicted as a banquet including the gospel motif of the loaves and fishes. This is an allusion to both the celestial banquet and the eucharist, which already in the Church of the Martyrs was becoming the Christian funeral meal *par excellence*. Funerary inscriptions also have preserved this attitude of prayer. The words "life" or "in peace," for example, express the *confidence* in faith that the deceased Christian actually is in peace and enjoys everlasting life, as well as the *petition* for these blessings.

In addition to references to the celebration of the eucharist and the singing of psalms, there are explicit allusions to other funerary prayers on the part of individuals and the community. The belief that prayer was appropriate to Christian care for the dead was taken for granted. Those early Christians needed no explanations to understand what their homilies, funerary inscriptions, and iconography meant.

The same may be said for Christian ritual at the time of burial. As we have seen above, what can be gathered from scattered impressions shows that Christians followed the basic funerary customs of their neighbors. Only those practices believed to be contradictory to the faith were rejected.[17] Usages that survive through the centuries involve washing and laying out of the corpse, prayer, lighted tapers or candles and the burning of incense, carrying the deceased to burial, and final disposition in grave or tomb. Lighted torches, necessary when ancient Roman funerals were traditionally conducted at night, came to be carried before the body in the funeral processions of historical times, even when most funerals took place in the daytime.[18]

Tertullian's assertion in his Apology[19] that Christians do not buy incense for use in idolatrous worship of pagan gods has been interpreted to imply that incense played no role in the Christian funeral of the second and third centuries. An opposite opinion argues that incense could well have been used in the care of Christian dead both for fumigation and as a simple form of embalming but without any religious significance.[20] In time, when burning incense would no longer be associated with idolatry and apostasy, western Christians would begin to follow eastern practice (where incense was a sign of entering God's presence and a call to purification) and adopt it as a token of esteem for ecclesiastical dignitaries or ministers. Still later, it would be used to honor the actions, objects, or places associated with the presider, such as walking in procession, the gospel book, the altar. It was natural that the burning of incense, once a practical means of fumigation pertaining to the care of the dead, would embrace this religious significance and become part of Christian funeral rituals.

In the Jewish temple, incense has been a sign of coming into God's sight; "Shekinah" was the glory of God hidden in the cloud. It became the symbol of approaching a God obscured in the cloud of smoke, because gazing on God's face was not possible. At the same time, the smoke symbolized purification, the burning away of impurity, the relinquishing of all ownership through burnt sacrifice. Incense thus became a sign of respect for the dead person, hallowing that person in the eyes of the assembly. It also symbolizes the rising of our prayers to God on his or her behalf (Psalm 141).

The guiding spirit of the funeral in Christian antiquity was the same perduring motif of "life" that permeated early funerary iconography. Sources pertaining to the funeral of heroic martyrs and famous personages have been preserved in detail, and they illuminate what was specifically Christian about their manner of burial: above all, an attitude of prayerful joy. That joy is at once realistic in the face of human grief and expression of the Christian faith that redemption unto life in Christ is not affected by physical death. An apologist of the mid-second century, Aristides of Athens, defended the way Christians behaved at the death of a "just" Christian; they "rejoice and give thanks and accompany the corpse, for he has emigrated from one place to another."[21] A century later in North Africa, Cyprian urged with pastoral concern that his people not fall back into pagan ways of mournful despair at the death of dear ones.[22]

It was Cyprian who also declared that the martyrdom of constant Christian commitment should be a source of deepest consolation to the living when so many fellow Christians were dying in the plague. Eusebius cited a pastoral letter describing Alexandrian Christians in similar straits a century later:

"With willing hands they raised the bodies of the saints to their bosoms; they closed their eyes and mouths, carried them on their shoulders and laid them out; they clung to them, embraced them, washed them, and wrapped them in grave-clothes. Very soon the same services were done for them, since those left behind were constantly following those gone before."

The author of that letter, according to Eusebius, did not hesitate to assert that "death in this form, the result of great piety and strong faith, seems in every way equal to martyrdom."[23]

Evidence such as this assures us that when the peace of Constantine opened the way for the established Church of the Empire,[24] the fundamental spirit and structure of future Christian funeral liturgy were already tradition. From the beginning, Christians had buried their dead as an act of faith in the redemption promised by their baptism into the death and resurrection of Jesus. They imbued everything surrounding burial with this faith; even the most human activities, such as the washing and anointing of the dead, and the tomb itself became symbols of liturgy. To the spiritual inheritance of psalms, they added Christian hymns; the eucharistic banquet came to supersede the memorial funeral meal; Jewish and pagan funerary art inspired new Christian representations expressing the mystery of redemption. The Christian experience of burial as an occasion of praise and thanksgiving acquired its own proper ritual expression. Favorite psalms and hymns came to be sung more frequently; certain prayer formulas were found to be especially fitting; repeated ritual practices became characteristic. This attitude of faith and the increasingly familiar ways in which Christians translated that faith into worship constituted the origin of a Christian funeral liturgy.

THE CHURCH OF THE EMPIRE (A.D. 313–600)
During the four centuries following the Edict of Milan, church life became increasingly more complicated. The pristine faith once manifested in worship at the burial of a Christian could no longer always be taken for

12

granted. Following Constantine's emancipation of the Christians, new masses of converted peoples began entering the Church. Their budding experience of the faith did not know the fervor of the primitive community of the Lord's own companions, nor that new sense of mission as a "third race" in a world of pagans and Jews. Accounts of living faith sealed by the martyrs' blood were past history to these new Christians. Furthermore, they were themselves "conquerors," bringing with them cherished funerary customs that were bound to have an effect on the developing Christian liturgy of burial. During these centuries, the Church was becoming a church of the masses, and its liturgy, even something as personal as the funeral, tended more and more to become highly formalized rites performed by a specialized clergy. Nevertheless, the impressions one gets of church life during this era point to a funeral liturgy that had grown from the seeds of primitive Christian tradition.

Once again, Christian cemeteries have preserved art and epitaphs that provide valuable evidence from the width and breadth of the Constantinian Empire. From the fourth century alone, some 1,000 sarcophagi, entire or in fragments, are the best preserved monuments of the period. Of them it can be said, "The old symbols: shepherd, fisherman, banquet, have disappeared. The unveiled figure of Christ makes its appearance, most in the representations of the miracles of Christ, with Old Testament prefigurations alongside. Small historical and symbolical cycles develop: the passion of Moses-Peter and the childhood of Christ. As a series, the 'deliverance' motifs hold their own the longest."[25]

Among the miracles of Jesus, the healing of the blind man and the raising of Lazarus from the dead, both symbols of baptism, continue the theme of "life" that death cannot destroy. Peter's denial "at the crowing of the cock" was seen as the dawn of new life after the forgiveness of sins. Nearly all known Christian cemeteries dating from after A.D. 313 show the continued practice of decorating the resting places of the dead with Old Testament scenes of divine deliverance: the sacrifice of Isaac, Daniel among the lions, Jonah freed from the sea monster, the three young men in the furnace, Susanna rescued from the "dirty old men," and Job delivered from misery.

Fifth-century sarcophagi indicate a new, purely symbolic decoration. They show, for example, the late classical cliché of vine and branches, now inseparably intertwined with the XP of Christ's monogram. Such a composition could not fail to remind Christians of their life in Christ the vine and of the fruit of that life untouched by physical death (John 15). Although varying in styles and motifs, funerary representations from all parts of the late Roman Empire continued to preach symbolically the kerygma pure and simple: redemption through Christ Jesus the Lord.[26]

Patristic Authors of the early Empire
With its freedom, the Church of the Empire became more vocal. Sermons and writings explicitly intended to teach the Christian faith also bear witness to Christian liturgical practice. These literary witnesses confirm without a doubt the central motif of Christian teaching concerning death: the belief, proclaimed from the beginning in word, liturgy, and art, that life in Christ is not undone by physical death. Nor is there any groping or hesitation here, as if something new were emerging with the emancipation of the Church. Rather, the freedom to speak out reveals simultaneous agreement among authors from all corners of the Empire on the centrality of this belief. Ambrose (d. 397), for example, grounding his teaching on the very promise of Jesus, summarized the tradition: " 'Do not fear,'

that is, do not fear because of this world, do not fear because of the iniquities of the world, do not fear because of the waves of bodily passions: I am the remission of sins. Do not fear because of darkness: I am the light. Do not fear because of death: I am the life. 'Whoever comes to me will not see death forever,' because he is the fullness of divinity, and honor, and glory, perpetuity is to him forever from the beginning of time both now and always and forever and ever."[27]

Ambrose's expression of belief in deliverance through God's mercy echoed the familiar theme of contemporary iconography. Similarly, the prayer for the faithful dead revealed faith in Jesus's promise of life without end for those who, believing in him, live the Christian life. Those who died outside communion with the Church were believed beyond the help of prayer. For Ambrose, "church" embraced the faithful, living and dead. Augustine, too, elaborated on this notion of communion of saints living and dead.[28]

A closely related belief also enjoyed universal adherence in patristic writings. Final resurrection and restoration of the body was imperative, for the perfect life in Christ was unthinkable without the reunion of the complete person, understood as union of soul and body.

In Christian funeral orations, one is struck by the way in which faith in life and resurrection declares *mourning* practices unchristian whereas it respects the genuine *grief* of the bereaved. In fact, this faith becomes the greatest source of consolation for that grief.[29] Mourning the deceased in pagan culture flowed from *despair*. One mourned emotionally, on the one hand, because death for the ordinary person was believed to be the absolute and definitive end of any really true life; religiously, on the other, because fear led to appeasing the dead in their miserable lot of half-life. For the Christian, mourning of this kind, with its drastic expressions of personal physical mutilation and dramatic wailing, had no meaning. Grief, however, had its place and was a respected emotion, a natural movement of the heart and soul of the bereaved at such loss.[30]

Grief was not to flow from despair, nor was it to take expression in the mourning practices of nonbelievers. Although, as we shall see, some of these mourning customs would survive to plague and eventually become reconciled with Christian practice, devout Christians had developed their own appropriate expression of grief in their rites of burial. Instead of wailing in despair, they sang psalms and hymns, expressing from the depth of their grief both their confidence in God and their solemn joy in the belief that Christ's promise of life would indeed be fulfilled for their deceased. Thus, Christian grief found consolation in the same hope that iconography depicted.

Prayer, too, expressed itself at this time in the same symbols as funerary art. "Light," "rest," and "deliverance" characterized the hereafter, according to Ambrose in his funeral address in memory of the Christian Emperor Theodosius. Ambrose prayed on that occasion: "Give perfect rest to Thy servant Theodosius, that rest which Thou hast prepared for Thy saints. Let his soul return there, whence it descended, where he cannot feel the sting of death, where he knows that this death is not the end of nature but of error. For in that he died, he died to sin; so that now there can be no place for sin; but he will rise again in order that his life may be restored perfectly by renewed gifts."[31]

The popular image of the "bosom of Abraham" remained a manner of concretizing the meaning of such "rest." Far from localizing a place of rest, Ambrose interpreted its meaning as follows: "The just are said to rest in the bosom of Abraham, for they rest in his

16

grace, in his rest, in his calm peace, who had put on faith like unto his and who transformed one and the same will into good works."[32] Elsewhere he referred to Abraham's bosom in the context of living faith as the holy patriarch's cloak of good deeds. This "cloak" embracing the saints was to become the distinguishing mark of Abraham in medieval art.[33]

It is above all Augustine who impresses upon us the way symbolic images of the faith defy definition. Using this scriptural image, he writes of a dead friend, "Now he lives in the bosom of Abraham. Whatever is signified by that bosom, thereby Nebridius lives, that sweet friend of mine."[34]

Another contemporary prayer, this one taken from the so-called *Euchologion* of Bishop Serapion, exemplifies well how faith in the fourth century took expression in symbolic language, the only language capable of rendering the inexpressible things of God.

Notice the realism of the faith that prays not only for the deceased but also for the consolation of the bereaved and for the community present: ". . . we beseech thee for the repose and rest of this thy servant or this thine handmaiden: given rest to his soul, his spirit, in green places (Psalms 23:2), in chambers of rest with Abraham and Isaac and Jacob and all thy Saints: and raise up his body in the day which thou hast ordained, according to thy promises which cannot lie (Titus 1:2), that thou mayest render to it also the heritage of which it is worthy in thy holy pastures. Remember not his transgressions and sins: and cause his going forth to be peaceable and blessed. Heal the griefs of those who pertain to him with the spirit of consolation, and grant unto us all a good end through thy only-begotten Jesus Christ, through whom to thee [is] the glory and strength in holy Spirit to the ages of the ages. Amen."[35]

Many other patristic writings illustrated these aspects of faith and practice at the Christian funeral. Among them, Augustine recounted the Christian death and funeral of Monica, his mother; Chrysostom explained the Christian name "cemetery"; Jerome described a joyful funeral procession in Jerusalem where the chanting of psalms and alleluia reverberated off the gilded roofs.[36]

Augustine's many references confirming "the practice of the universal Church" constitute a special source of impressions. For example, his short treatise entitled *The Care to Be Taken for the Dead* explained the value of the customary Christian care for the dead, especially of prayer on their behalf. It was not the place of burial, or even the fact of burial itself, but prayer that was advantageous for the deceased.[37] Augustine argued also that the value of such prayer depended on the good or evil of one's life before death, according to Scripture, and this is consistent with his own prayer for Monica.[38] It is not for us to distinguish who is helped or not, and thus, none of the faithful dead are to be excluded, according to Augustine.[39]

Furthermore, however good one's life had been, Augustine believed that no one except the martyrs died without sin. Thus, the precise nature of the help accorded the faithful dead through the prayer of the Church was the forgiveness of certain sins remaining after death. Through the intercession of the saints and the prayer of the Church, God in mercy and justice could forgive such remaining sins or at least grant a more tolerable damnation.[40] It was to be considered a duty in Christian charity to plead with God on behalf of the dead. This included the hope that one would receive the same care when death came. Augustine was insistent therefore that prayer, almsgiving, and especially offering the eucharist were efficacious for the dead. Moreover, burial and commemorative practices demonstrate respect for the body that once housed and served the soul, not in the manner of some decoration but pertaining to human nature itself. They reflect God's own care for humanity and point to a strong belief in the resurrection. But above all, they serve to assure continued prayerful remembrance by the living of those who have gone before.

We have devoted more space than usual to these impressions, for it was Augustine more than any other single influence who set the course and interpretation that "the practice of the universal Church to pray for the dead" would take in Medieval Europe.[41]

Aurelius Prudentius Clemens
The poet Prudentius (d. ca. 405), a layman, has left a rare and exceptional mirror of the Christian faith in the resurrection of the body and the impact of this belief in the life of the Church. His hymn on funerals, *God, the Blazing Fountain of Souls*,[42] considered a masterpiece of its kind in literature, was composed with a literary audience in mind and presumably reflected the faith of lettered Roman Christians of the fourth and fifth centuries.[43] Prudentius proclaims in verse the same kind of faith in the resurrection as found in contemporary patristic writings.

The natural, mortal condition of creatures flows from creation, the poem commences, and yet resurrection of the body is the Godgiven remedy for death. This is why Christians care for their dead (verses 1–16). Next, Prudentius ponders the mystery of death and resurrection (verses 57–112). Death is the suffering one must go through—the giving up of life—to truly live and appreciate life. The hymn closes with an exhortation and a commendation-like prayer at burial (verse 113–172).

For Prudentius, the care Christians showed their dead and their burial customs were signs that took their meaning from Christian faith in the resurrection of the body. Ritual practices noted in the poem did not differ much from those of the Empire generally at that time. Yet, one senses a Christian spirit which gives special meaning to them. For example, Prudentius refers to a vigil of some kind where the Christian homilist placed greater emphasis on the imminent restoration of life than on life's end or on the accomplishments of the deceased. Other customs such as the attention given tombs, the funeral procession, the manner of wrapping in white linen and preserving the body with myrrh, the final and even the regular decoration of graves with flowers and perfume, and the honor of burial itself all make sense, according to the poet, because the body thus cared for is believed to be "asleep" until called forth to life beyond death. Thus one understands why the wailing and disruptive mourning practices of the pagans were inappropriate among Christians. Death, already so natural and familiar, had become the path to unending life, the path that had been symbolized in the experience of the elder Tobias and laid open by the crucified Lord for all to follow. At a time when more fearful concerns began to preoccupy extant funerary references in literature, it is important to recognize that there was always a continuity of the belief of the earlier tradition.[44]

Pseudo-Dionysius the Areopagite
In the sixth century, Pseudo-Dionysius wrote a commentary on funeral liturgy common to his Syrian Church.[45] Although practice there differed in liturgical detail from certain customs in the West, one recognizes a common faith and a common understanding of that faith.

In summary, Dionysius describes the funeral as follows: The body of the deceased was brought to the church where the bishop first offered a prayer of thanksgiving to God. Then selections from Scripture about the promise of resurrection were read, and psalms on the same theme were sung. When the catechumens had been dismissed, the names of those who had already died in the faith were proclaimed, including that of the deceased, and all present were exhorted to pray that they themselves might receive ultimate happiness in Christ. Next, the bishop prayed over the body and gave the deceased a final kiss of peace; the other ministers and all the faithful followed suit. Then holy oil was poured over the body by the bishop. Finally, after a prayer for all the faithful departed, the bishop laid the corpse to rest in holy ground.

Bringing the body of the deceased to the church, Pseudo-Dionysius explains, symbolized one's place in everlasting life as a follower of Christ according to divine justice. To celebrate this justice, the bishop opened the funeral liturgy with a great prayer of thanksgiving. Chanting psalms and reading the divine promises both signified the kind of happiness and peace that awaited the blessed and exhorted the living to pursue that same goal. To Pseudo-Dionysius, this liturgy was at once both symbolic experience and exhortation.

In the prayer that followed, the bishop prayed that God in divine goodness would remit all the sins committed by the deceased because of human frailty and welcome her or him into the light and the place of the living, the bosom of Abraham, Isaac, and Jacob, where there is no sorrow, sadness, or tears. Here again, we recognize the traditional Christian images of life beyond physical death as well as the prayer of the Church for the forgiveness of sins.

In an eloquent reflection on the nature of petition and on the role of the bishop in the Church as revealer of

21

divine promises and judgments, Pseudo-Dionysius resolves the apparent inconsistency between the bishop's prayer for the remission of sins and biblical faith that one's lot after death is determined by the fruits of one's life (II Corinthians 5:10). The prayer for the dead is compared to any petition which God grants only to the deserving and only when the object is for their good. The analogy is obvious: God's goodness knows the hearts of the deceased, their strengths and frailties during life, and will respond to prayer on their behalf with divine justice. Such a prayer, the author argues, is likewise in accord with the bishop's revelatory role. To pray over the faithful dead for the forgiveness of sins and the reward of a place in the company of the patriarchs is to proclaim the promise of unending life to those who love God.

The final kiss of peace, according to Pseudo-Dionysius, is a desirable Christian gesture toward one who has lived a truly Christian life. The greeting that Christians regularly exchange among themselves is now shared with the deceased, a fitting sign of communion between the living and this dead Christian. He insists that although this kiss is a final gesture toward the body, it is not a "farewell," for life in Christ knows no farewell. This ancient explanation rings true both throughout the earlier tradition and today where it is applied by the late Cardinal Lercaro to the final commendation and farewell in the General Introduction to the *Ordo Exsequiarum* 1969.[46]

Especially significant is the explanation Pseudo-Dionysius gives for the anointing with oil in the context of the deceased's initiation as a Christian. At the time of Christian initiation, the anointing with oil called the one to be initiated into sacred combat; now, the poured oil proclaims that the deceased, having fought that sacred fight, has died victorious. The body receives an honorable burial among the other faithful departed, for it continues to participate in the glory of the soul. God, who joined the body and soul, rewards or punishes both as partners in good or evil. This funeral liturgy proclaims the unity of the Christian person, body and soul, before God.

What Prudentius expressed in poetry, Pseudo-Dionysius saw celebrated in Christian funeral liturgy. The influence of his writings on the development of Christian thought, from Gregory the Great through Thomas Aquinas and on into the 16th century, renders his reflections on funeral liturgy an especially significant mirror of liturgical tradition and continuity.

Although ritual practices and prayers continued much the same into the next century, an unmistakable shift was taking place in the understanding of how those rites and prayers functioned in the life of the Church. Canons of local synods and councils regularly mention certain burial practices that were prohibited by ecclesiastical authority.[47]

For example, the abusive practice of giving the holy communion to a corpse plagued the medieval Church. Similarly, altar cloths and other linens used in the celebration of Mass were employed in superstitious rites, either as shrouds or a type of talisman. The place of burial was also an issue. Interment near the principal altar, where the eucharist was celebrated, and in the baptistery had become widespread. An inordinate desire to be buried there gave rise to another practice: the multiple occupancy of one and the same grave site.

All these abuses shared a common motivation: securing protection for the soul of the deceased after death. It is noteworthy that all of them focus on the eucharist, whether it be holy communion itself, the linens on which the eucharist is celebrated, or a final resting place near the altar of celebration. By now, the eucharist as *viaticum* had become the sacrament of protection for the dying; popular preoccupation with the lot of the dead likewise took eucharistic expression. The writings of Pope Gregory the Great embody the incorporation of this religious mood into evolving liturgical theology—a union that shaped medieval funeral liturgy.

Gregory the Great

At the turn of the seventh century, the *Dialogues* of Gregory the Great reveal a perception of funerary and commemorative liturgy founded on an already developed theology of expiation.[48] With Augustine as their most notable master, Gregory and others explained the earlier emphasis on the effectiveness of prayer for the dead. The prayer of the Church, they taught, brought about the liberation of the faithful dead from the purifying fire of expiation for sin. Before long, this fire would become localized as "purgatory" and the tradition of prayer for the release of the "poor souls" its complement in popular piety.

Thus the religious sensibility of the times represented the eucharist and prayer for the deceased in a new way. They were formerly seen as reflecting the Church's evangelical trust in God's mercy toward the faithful departed, according to the divine promises and mysterious plan. Now this trust was becoming more and more a fear of God's judgment. Optimistic faith began to tend toward pessimistic fate. Belief that "the just God is merciful and therefore forgiving" shifted to mean that "the merciful God is just and therefore demands expiation."

This prevailing pessimism about the living had its effect on the attitude toward the lot of the dead. With the advent of severe penitential discipline, being Christian became a preoccupation with sin; care for the dead Christian became, in turn, a preoccupation with the wages of sin. Thus, to Gregory and his contemporaries, even the faithful Christian was presumed a sinner whose immediate lot after death was at best one of purification. It was the exceptional saint who escaped. Expiation for unrepented serious sin was presumed impossible and punishment for eternity its just retribution. Lesser sins of everyday life, however, could be forgiven, and the soul could be cleansed through purification by fire, as precious metals in a furnace. In that regard, the prayers of the Church, and especially the Mass, were believed to benefit the dead.

Implicit in Gregory's teaching is a new sense of something approaching the automatic, as if by performing so many prayers and Masses, the release of soul from the purifying fire would be achieved, provided the deceased had earned the right to such help during life. To be sure, Pope Gregory does not specify a *quid pro quo* theology, but such was nevertheless the attitude that soon came to characterize prayer for the dead in the Middle Ages.

An example of this attitude is the story that is believed to recount the origin of the so-called Gregorian Masses, a popular practice both throughout the Middle Ages and well into the 20th century. The story goes that Justus, a monk of Gregory's monastery, fell ill. During his illness, it was discovered that the monk had hidden three gold pieces in his cell, contrary to the *Rule*. In order to teach a lesson, Gregory was extremely severe. He ordered that no one offer consolation to the dying monk in his last moments, and furthermore, when he had died, the monks were to throw his gold pieces into the grave after him, crying: "May your money be with you in perdition." Brother Justus died repentant. Nevertheless, for 30 days, Gregory refused to allow prayers to be offered for him. Finally, he took pity on the deceased monk, whom he described as suffering in the fire, and ordered that

Mass be celebrated for Justus on 30 consecutive days. At the end of that time, Justus appeared to Gregory and told him that until then, he had been suffering, but now he was well because on that day he had been received into heaven. Gregory explains that his release coincided exactly with the Mass on the 30th day, clear proof that Justus had been freed through the offering of the Mass.[49]

There is no doubt that the *Dialogues* of Gregory the Great, with such marvelous stories illustrating his theology, contributed to the widespread success in Western Europe of the practice of celebrating the eucharist for the liberation of souls in purgatory. The attitude of those times, which Gregory thus shared and articulated in theology and liturgical practice, revealed the shift away from the ecclesial eschatology of the earlier tradition to an eschatology of the individual. Before long, this view attained universal acceptance in the West, and the writings of Pope Gregory remained its most authoritative champion.

Columba the Elder
One last witness affirms how thorough was that shift. The hymn *In Praise of the Father*, attributed to Columba the Elder of Iona (d. ca. 597), devotes its final seven stanzas to the day of judgment, the second coming of Christ, and the retribution of the damned and elect. In those verses, one already recognizes the themes and imagery that would take lasting form in the sequence Dies irae:

The day of the Lord,
the most righteous King of kings,

is near. That will be
a day of wrath and revenge,

a day of clouds and darkness,
a day of marvelous thundering

and a day of distress,
of mourning and of sadness.

It will be a day on which will stop
the love and desire for women,

the contentions of all men
and the cupidity of this world. (R)

We will stand in fear
before the tribunal of the Lord

and we will render to him
an accounting of all we have done.

Then will we see
all of our evil deeds.

At this time the records
of our consciences

will be opened in front of our eyes.
Then will we weep the bitterest tears

because no longer will we have
the materials needed for work. (Q)[50]

In contrast to the hymn by Prudentius, Columba's
work is preoccupied with the lot of the dead approaching judgment. Prudentius took for granted that the
just dead included the ordinary faithful Christian for
whom final judgment meant life with Christ.
Columba, on the other hand, was skeptical whether
anyone could survive the Lord's judgment unscathed.
Confidence founded on faith in the resurrection had
given way to fear and near despair.

Although there are no indications that his hymn ever
belonged to funeral liturgy as such, the presence of an
antiphon in certain manuscripts and a collect prayer in
others does suggest that it might have been part of a
public office in some churches or communities. In the
ninth century, a long part of the hymn was incorpo-

rated into a still longer poem by Rabanus Maurus entitled *Aeterne rerum conditor* (not the morning hymn of the same title by St. Ambrose). Its popularity as a private prayer is attested by a gloss praising its powers, including, among many others, protection "against every death save death on pillow," i.e., against tragic and untimely death.[51] Such a preoccupation with fear of death and the lot of the dead had thus become a familiar theme in medieval Church life.

CONCLUSION

The various opinions gathered in this chapter, despite cultural, geographic, and temporal influences, are elements of the religious treasury of living, believing people. They are not, as it were, entirely isolated and independent logs adrift in a fathomless sea of possible attitudes and expressions of belief. Rather, they continue to affect the living practice of the Church.

In summary, these opinions leave us with two distinct, though related, attitudes of faith in face of death. One is hopeful, reflecting what tradition presents as the pristine Christian attitude toward dying, i.e., "going to Christ." The other is threatening and pessimistic and reveals a shift whereby death is seen as a summons to judgment and inevitably to punishment for sin. Both of these attitudes appear to have existed side by side in differing degrees of emphasis from the earliest Christian times, and the first written texts of the funeral services indicate as much. The later development of Christian funeral liturgy in the West is a continuous story of the tense relationship between the same two attitudes.

NOTES

1. Margaret Mead, "Ritual in Social Crisis," in *Roots of Ritual*, ed. James Shaughnessy (Grand Rapids, Mich.: Eerdmans,

1973), pp. 89–90. See also Robert W. Habenstein and William M. Lamers, *Funeral Customs the World Over* (Milwaukee: Bulfin, 1960).

2. Jocelyn Toynbee, classicist and archeologist, provides a thorough description of this *funus translaticum.* Its ritual moments offer a good point of comparison with the early Christian funeral. See J.M.C. Toynbee, *Death and Burial in the Roman World* (Ithaca, N.Y.: Cornell University Press, 1971), pp. 43–51, and Richard Rutherford, *The Death of a Christian: The Rite of Funerals* (New York: Pueblo, 1980), pp. 4–5. Cf. Donna C. Kurtz and John Boardman, *Greek Burial Customs* (Ithaca, N.Y.: Cornell University Press, 1971).

3. Toynbee, *Death and Burial,* p. 43. See also Cyril Bailey, *Religion in Virgil* (Oxford: Clarendon, 1935), pp. 287–291. Cf. Virgil, *Aeneid* 6, 212–235, and Homer, *Iliad* 23, 109–256.

4. Tobit 1–2 and 12. See Rutherford, *Death* p. 31, note 4, for interpretations of burial obligations for both Jewish and gentile dead according to the *Babylonian Talmud:* Sotah 14a; B. Megillah 3b; b.Gittin 61a.

5. See Geoffrey Rowell, *The Liturgy of Christian Burial,* Alcuin Club Collections, No. 59 (London: SPCK, 1977), pp. 3–8. For an especially helpful collection of essays, consult *Jewish Reflections on Death,* ed. Jack Riemer (New York: Schocken, 1974).

6. Toynbee, *Death and Burial,* pp. 38–39; Siegfried Morenz, *Egyptian Religion,* (Ithaca, N.Y.: Cornell University Press, 1973; German original, 1960), pp. 183–213, 226–231; C. J. Bleeker, *Egyptian Festivals* (Leiden: Brill, 1967), pp. 124–140; J. Zandee, *Death as an Enemy According to Ancient Egyptian Conceptions* (Leiden: Brill, 1960), pp. 102–108.

7. Toynbee, *Death and Burial,* p. 38.

8. Frits van der Meer and Christine Mohrmann, *Atlas of the Early Christian World* (London: Nelson, 1966; Dutch original, 1958), p. 5.

Although there will be occasion in the course of this book to refer to many articles and studies on specific topics, the following books are indispensable guides to funeral practices during these earlier centuries. See Bibliography for references and abbreviations.

Alfred C. Rush, *Death and Burial in Christian Antiquity*, The Catholic University of America Studies in Christian Antiquity, 1 (Washington, D.C.: Catholic University of America Press, 1941). The is an excellent collection and analysis of data available in 1941 and pertinent to a doctoral dissertation. The work utilizes a comprehensive bibliography of earlier studies that is especially valuable to the later researcher. Rowell, *Christian Burial*, pp. 19–30, updates and concisely summarizes this vast data.

Joseph Ntedika, *L'Evocation de l'au-delà dans la prière pour les morts: Etudes de patristique et de liturgie latines, IVe-VIIIe S.*, Recherches Africaines de Théologie, 2 (Louvain-Paris: Nauwelaerts and Beatrice-Nauwelaerts, 1971). Particularly valuable for its collection of primary sources as well as extensive indices and a very complete bibliography, this work is most helpful in its treatment of patristic material. With regard to the liturgy, the author's literary method is less appropriately applicable, and his conclusions should be used with this in mind.

An excellent companion work for the interaction of archeological and homiletic sources is Victor Saxer, *Morts, Martyrs, Reliques en Afrique Chrétienne aux Prèmiers Siècles* (Paris: Editions Beauchesne, 1980).

Damien Sicard, *La liturgie de la mort dans l'église latine des origines à la réforme carolingienne*, Liturgiewissenschaftliche Quelle und Forshungen, No. 63 (Münster: Aschendorff 1978). Finally, especially worthwhile for its theological reflection on impressions gathered from earlier Christian times in ecumenical context, is Bruno Bürki, *Im Herrn entschlafen*, Beitrage zur praktischen Theologie, 6 (Heidelberg: Quelle & Meyer, 1969).

9. Van der Meer-Mohrmann, *Atlas*, pp. 47–55. For further details concerning structure, layout, and types of burial places, see Toynbee, *Death and Burial*, especially for Christian cemeteries, pp. 234–244.

10. Van der Meer-Mohrmann, *Atlas*, pp. 48–49.

30

11. Ignatius, *Ep. ad Ephesios* 20, trans. Maxwell Staniforth, *Early Christian Writings. The Apostolic Fathers* (Baltimore: Penguin, 1972), p. 106. See also Irenaeus, *Adv. Haer.* IV, 18, 5 (PG 7, 1029).

12. The earliest written accounts of the resurrection describe the women keeping watch at the tomb of the Lord "as the sun was rising" (Mark 16:2), "towards dawn on the first day of the week" (Matthew 28:1). Luke tells us that the disciples gathered at the tomb as the body of Jesus was placed inside "while the evening lamps of the sabbath were being lit" (Luke 23:50–56), a liturgical reference to the commencement of Erev Shabat (the evening ritual of welcoming new sabbath at sunset). Later, these same women returned after the sabbath "at the first sign of dawn" to gather at the tomb (Luke 24:1). The latest written account, John, describes that "it was still dark when those women came to the tomb" (John 20:1).

13. This theme is discussed from a scriptural viewpoint in Edward Schillebeeckx, *Christ the Experience of Jesus as Lord* (New York: Crossroad, 1980), pp. 468–514. The birth of the Church, the resurrection, is central to the proclamation made over the blessed water at the baptismal liturgy of Easter. See *Rite of Christian Initiation of Adults* (Washington, D.C.: USCC, 1988).

14. For a fuller treatment of the vigil see, for example, Gregory Dix, *The Shape of the Liturgy* (New York: Seabury, 1945, 1982), p. 325; Paul Bradshaw, *Daily Prayer in the Early Church*, Alcuin Club Collections, No. 63 (London: SPCK, 1981), *passim*; Herman Wegman, *Christian Worship in East and West*, trans. Gordon Lathrop (New York: Pueblo, 1985), pp. 33–36, 77–78, 97; A.–M. Roguet, *The Liturgy of the Hours* (Collegeville, Minn.: Liturgical Press, 1971), pp. 34–35, 102–109. In *The Liturgy of the Hours in East and West* (Collegeville, Minn.: Liturgical Press, 1986), Robert Taft makes extensive reference to the liturgy and development of the vigil tradition; cf. "vigil" in the work's excellent index.

15. Christian doctrine of the resurrection of the body is rooted in wholistic Judaic faith, which perdures despite the neoplatonic influence of the emerging theology of an independent immortal soul. See A. R. van de Walle, *From Dark-*

ness to the Dawn (Mystic, Conn.: Twenty-Third, 1984), pp. 152–166, and Joseph Ratzinger, *Eschatology*, trans. Michael Waldstein, ed. Aidan Nichols (Washington, D.C.: Catholic University of America Press, 1988), pp. 67–214.

16. See Saxer, *Morts, Martyrs, Reliques*, pp. 35–119.

17. For example, the funeral crown, the *planctus* and *nenia* of the Greco-Roman wake and procession, lugubrious mourning garments in black and red (variants in violet and purple), cremation, the pagan *vale*. See Rush, *Christian Antiquity*, pp. 133–149, 163–186, 187–235, 245–256, and "The Colors of Red and Black in the Liturgy of the Dead," in *Kyriakon*, pp. 698–705; Toynbee, *Death and Burial*, pp. 39–64; Saxer, *Morts, Martyrs, Reliques*, pp. 36–53.

18. Toynbee describes torches and *candelabra* as well as incense-burners represented on a marble relief depicting a wake scene from pagan Rome of early Christian times. See Toynbee, *Death and Burial*, pp. 46–47. See also Rush, *Christian Antiquity*, pp. 221–228, for a thorough review of the antipathy but gradual acceptance of the use of torches/candles in the first four centuries A.D.

19. *Apol.* 42, 7 (CCL 1, p. 157). See, for example, Rowell, *Christian Burial*, pp. 20, 25. For an earlier summary of this material, see C. Atchley, *A History of the Use of Incense in Divine Worship*, Alcuin Collection, No. 13 (London: Longmans, Green & Co., 1909), *passim*.

20. See Saxer, *Morts, Martyrs, Reliques*, pp. 54–55.

21. Aristides, *Apology* 15, ed. J. Armitage Robinson, *The Apology of Aristides*, Texts and Studies, 1 (Cambridge: University Press, 1893; rpt. Nendeln, Liechtenstein: Kraus, 1967), pp. 49–50. See also Ntedika, *L'Evocation*, pp. 24–25.

22. Cyprian, *De Mortalitate* 1, 20–21, trans. Roy J. Deferrari, *Saint Cyprian: Treatises*, The Fathers of the Church, Vol. 36 (New York: Fathers of the Church, 1958), pp. 199, 215–216.

23. Eusebius, *The History of the Church* 7, 22, trans. G. A. Williamson (Baltimore: Penguin, 1965), pp. 305–306. Despite characteristic exaggeration, the subsequent comparison with the pagans, who are said to have abandoned their dead out

of selfish fear, reveals the author's belief in the Christian ideal.

24. Van der Meer-Mohrmann, *Atlas*, pp. 58–172.

25. Van der Meer-Mohrmann, *Atlas*, p. 71.

26. The chancel mosaic of S. Apollinare Nuovo, Ravenna, is a good example of the identical theme set in the context of the eucharist as food for eternal life. The reader is urged to compare the plates collected in Van der Meer-Mohrmann, *Atlas*, pp. 58–172. See especially p. 132.

27. Ambrose, *De Bono Mortis* 12, 57, ed. and trans. William T. Weisner, *Sancti Ambrosii De Bono Mortis*, The Catholic University of America Patristic Studies, 100 (Washington, D.C.: Catholic University of America Press, 1970), pp. 152–153.

28. Augustine, *De Civitate Dei* II, 9, trans. Gerald G. Walsh and Daniel J. Honan, *The City of God*, The Fathers of the Church, Vol. 24 (New York: Fathers of the Church, 1954), pp. 277–278:

"For the souls of the faithful departed are not divorced from Christ's kingdom which is the temporal Church. If they were, we should not be mindful of them at God's altar in the communion of the Body of Christ. . . . Why do we go to all this trouble if the faithful departed are not still Christ's members. . . ? We conclude, therefore, that even now, in time, the Church reigns with Christ both in her living and departed members. 'For to this end Christ died,' says St. Paul, 'and rose again, that he might be Lord both of the dead and of the living' (Romans 14:9)."

29. In this oration at the death of his brother Satyrus, Ambrose refers to the grief of those present as a consolation, as saving tears that wash away sins. That kind of grief looks beyond the sorrow of death and heals the pain of present sorrow with the richness of perpetual joy. *De Excessu Fratris* I, 5 (CSEL 73, p. 212).

30. In Sermon 172, 1, Augustine taught that Paul, in his Epistle to the Thessalonians, did not admonish us "not to mourn" but "not to mourn as others who have no hope." The full impact of Augustine's Latin can only be felt in the

original: *Constramur ergo nos in nostrorum mortibus necessitate amittendi, sed cum spe recipiendi. Inde angimur, hinc consolamur: inde infirmitas afficit, hinc fides reficit: inde dolet humana conditio, hinc sanat divina promissio* (*Patrologia Latina* 38, 936).

31. Ambrose, *De Obitu Theodosii* 36, ed. and trans. Mary D. Mannix, *Sancti Ambrosii Oratio de Obitu Theodosii*, The Catholic University of America Patristic Studies, 9 (Washington, D.C.: Catholic University of America Press, 1925), pp. 56, 75.

32. Ambrose, *Explanatio Psalmi*, Ps. 38:11 (CSEL 64, p. 192).

33. *De Excessu Fratris* II, 101 (CSEL 73, p. 305). See also Augustine, *De natura et origine animaé* IV, 16:24 (CSEL 60, pp. 403–404). A popular summary of the rendering of the image "bosom of Abraham" in medieval art is found in T.S.R. Boase, *Death in the Middle Ages* (New York: McGraw-Hill, 1972), pp. 26–36 (Figs. 17, 18, 21, 24). See also *The Flowering of the Middle Ages*, ed. Joan Evans (New York: McGraw-Hill, 1966), pp. 203–244.

34. *Confessiones* IX, 3:6 (CSEL 33, pp. 200–201).

35. "Prayer for one who is dead and is to be carried forth," *Euchologion*, 18, ed., F. E. Brightman, "The Sacramentary of Serapion of Thmuis," *The Journal of Theological Studies* 1 (1900), 268, 275–276; trans. John Wordsworth, *Bishop Serapion's Prayer-Book* (Hamden, Conn.: Archon, 1964; rpt. 1923 [2] revised), pp. 79–80.

36. Augustine, *Confessiones* IX, 11–12 (CSEL 33, pp. 220–223). Chrysostom, on the name "cemetery," PG 49, 393. Jerome, *Epistula* 77, 11 (CSEL 55, p. 48): *Sonabant psalmi, et aurata templorum tecta reboans in sublime alleluia quatiebat.*

37. *De cura pro mortuis gerenda*, 6–7; 22 (CSEL 41, pp. 629–633, 658). See also Ntedika, *L'Evocation*, pp. 1–45.

38. For example, Romans 14:10 and 2 Corinthians 5:10. *De cura pro mortuis gerenda*, 2 (CSEL 41, pp. 622–623); *Enchiridion* 110 (CCL 46, 108). Augustine's prayer for Monica, *Confessiones* IX, 13, 35 (CSEL 33, p. 224).

39. *De cura pro mortuis gerenda*, 6; 22 (CSEL 41, pp. 629–630, 658–659); *Enchiridion* 110 (CCL 46, pp. 108–109): *Non enim*

34

omnibus prosunt; et quare non omnibus prosunt, nisi propter differentiam vitae quam quisque gessit in corpore? Cum ergo sacrificia sive altaris quarumcumque eleemosynarum pro baptizatis defunctis omnibus offeruntur, pro valde bonis gratiarum actiones sunt; pro non valde malis propitiationes sunt; pro valade malis etiamsi nulla sunt adiumenta mortuorum; qualescumque vivorum consalationes sunt. Quibus autem prosunt, aut ad hoc prosunt ut sit plena remissio, aut certe ut tolerabilior fiat ipsa damnatio.

These words of Augustine would become very popular in medieval spirituality, as we shall see.

40. *Enchiridion* 110. See note 39 and also *De civitate Dei* XXI, 24 (CCL 48, 790): . . . *sicut etiam facta resurrectione mortuorum non deerunt, quibus post poenas, quas patiuntur spiritus mortuorum, impertiatur misericordia, ut in ignem non mittantur aeternum.*

41. Ntedika well summarizes and documents the development of Augustine's thought: *L'Evocation*, pp. 88–103. See also his bibliography and earlier articles.

42. *Aurelii Prudentii Clementis Carmina*, ed. M. P. Cunningham, CCL 126 (Turnholti: Brepols, 1966), pp. 35–50; *Liber Catherinon X: Hymnus circa Exequias Defuncti*. This work is described as "a kind of daily hymnbook, consisting of twelve sacred poems for private use," according to A. S. Walpole, *Early Latin Hymns* (Hildesheim: George Olms, 1966; Reprografischer Nachdruck der Ausgabe: Cambridge, 1922), p. 115. For the full text and English translation, see Harold Isbell, trans., *[The] Last Poets of Imperial Rome* (Baltimore: Penguin, 1971), pp. 198–203.

43. Walpole, *Hymns*, p. 140. Note also the many parallels with Horace, Ovid, Virgil, Lucretius, et al.

44. Excerpts of this hymn may be found in Rutherford, *Death*, pp. 20–22. For the full English text, see Isbell, trans., *[The] Last Poets of Imperial Rome*, pp. 198–203.

45. *Ecclesiastical Hierarchy* VII, Funeral Rites; *Patrologia Graeca* 3, 551C–584D (based on the 1634 edition by B. Cordier and including the 13th-century paraphrase by G. Pachymera). See also the English translation prepared by Thomas Camp-

bell for his 1955 dissertation (Catholic University) and subsequently published, *Dionysius the Pseudo-Areopagite: The Ecclesiastical Hierarchy* (Lanham, Md.: University Press of America, 1981), pp. 79–91.

46. See below, p. 190.

47. A classic reference work containing the texts of these canons is Carolo de Clercq, *La Législation Religieuse Franque de Clovis à Charlemange* (Louvain-Paris: Bibliothèque de L'Université-Sirey, 1936), *passim*.

48. Gregorius Papa I, *Dialogorum Liber* IV, 38–60 (Patrologia Latina 77, 389C–429A), trans. Odo J. Zimmerman, *Dialogues*, The Fathers of the Church, Vol. 39 (New York: Fathers of the Church, 1959), nn. 40–62, pp. 244–275. This translation follows Moricca, so it has a system of paragraph numbering different from the Patrologia Latina: both will be indicated in the notes. See also Ntedika, *L 'Evocation*, pp. 105–110.

49. *Dial.* IV, 55 (*Patrologia Latina* 77, 421C): . . . *res aperte claruitr quia frater qui defunctus fuerat per salutarem hostiam evasit supplicium*. See full context: *Dial.* IV, 55 (PL 77, 420A–421C), trans. Zimmerman, pp. 267–270; ed. Moricca 57).

50. The hymn *Altus prosator* comes down to us from Irish tradition as a song of praise in honor of the Blessed Trinity. Both tradition and the consensus of modern scholars of Irish history and hymnology attribute the authorship of this alphabetical hymn to St. Columba the Elder (not to be confused with his younger contemporary, Columbanus). The text of the *Altus* has been preserved in, among other sources, John H. Bernard and Robert Atkinson, eds., *The Irish Liber Hymnorum*, HBS 13–14 (London: Harrison, 1898), Vol. I, pp. 62–83; Vol. II, pp. xxvi–xxix, 23–26; 140–169. See also F. J. Kenney, *The Sources for the Early History of Ireland*, Vol. I (New York: Octagon, 1966), p. 264. Excerpts taken from Isbell, trans., *[The] Last Poets of Imperial Rome*, pp. 275–276, © Harold Isbell, 1971. Reprint by permission of Penguin Books, Ltd. For the full text and English translation, see pp. 275–277.

51. F. J. E. Raby, *A History of Christian-Latin Poetry from the Beginnings to the Close of the Middle Ages* (Oxford: Clarendon, 1973[2]), p. 134.

Chapter Two

The Order of Funerals:
Formation of a Model

Our data from the past impress upon us that care for
the deceased was an integral part of the daily Christian life from the beginning. Earlier literature and
iconography especially mirror the faith that found expression in an ever-developing Christian liturgy surrounding death and burial. It is no wonder, therefore,
that one discovers formularies for funeral liturgy
among the oldest extant manuscript witnesses to Western liturgical practice.

These earliest extant examples of funeral formularies
mark the beginning of an "order of funerals." They
were descriptions of, and guides to, "what Christians
do" at funerals, that is, the practice of the Church. At
some point around the time of Pope Gregory the Great,
Christians more and more began to set down in writing
specific aspects of their funerary practice. Sometimes
these were based on a "model funeral" from the past;
sometimes they indicated a pattern to be followed by a
cathedral chapter or were the means of teaching appropriate procedures to scattered and often uneducated
clergy. While it would be anachronistic to consider such
early manuscript witnesses of funeral liturgy normative
in any modern sense, they nevertheless reveal a great
deal about the developing Roman *ordo exsequiarum*.
They are the earliest known ancestors in the genealogy
of the 1989 *Order of Christian Funerals*.

Coincidental with the first stages of writing out rites, there existed a movement toward consolidation of practices according to the liturgical usage of the church at Rome. Thus, our first extant witnesses to a written order of funerals already mirrored both local funerary customs and what was considered authoritative Roman church practice. Moreover, monastic life, which was beginning to flourish about the same time, was already having its effect on funeral liturgy and on what was written out. Those early extant manuscript witnesses represent an amalgamation of these three sources of influence.

The basic pattern of Christian funeral care and the two principal motifs of the faith noted in Chapter One were common to all three contributing influences. Our early liturgical manuscripts point to some of the different ways in which ritual was molded on the eve of the Carolingian reform. They show how a model order of funerals eventually emerged that would guide ritual development down to the present.

These manuscript witnesses differ in shape and size. Some are simply brief collections of prayers with a rubrical title indicating their position in the funeral liturgy: This type is found as part of early Sacramentaries. Others consist only of rubrical directions and first-word indications of prayers, psalms, responses, and the like: They are found among the so-called *ordines.* Still others are more elaborate and include further rubrical details and full liturgical text. All three represent different stages of development, and by the time they are available to us in extant sources, they are already an amalgamation of liturgical usages from different times and places. Apart from several outstanding exceptions, all appeared during the eighth century and came to be widely disseminated as time went on.

The next five centuries of this history constitute a formative era for what was to become the Roman funeral liturgy. This period ended about 1250 with the appearance of an order of funerals that became, through a coincidence of history, the model for subsequent Roman funeral practice. Its influence is noticeable both in the post-Tridentine *Ritual* and in the reforms of Vatican II as seen in the present *Order of Christian Funerals*. Those 500 years from the eighth to the 13th century constitute the first stage of our survey of developing funeral rites. The other sections of this chapter will take us from the 13th century to Trent and from Trent to the present.

FUNERAL LITURGY IN FORMATION
In the ninth century, several different influences are apparent in funerary sources. Terms such as Roman, Gallican, Visigothic, and the like are broad designations for differing liturgical traditions. Taken together, they enable us to describe the most significant characteristics of the Christian funeral in Western Europe during the first phase of documented liturgical history. The period opens on the eve of the Carolingian reform. Our task is not to isolate specific traditions, such as the pure Roman liturgy of burial, for example, but to discern what Christian funeral liturgy was like. We are interested in the way specific marks of Christian faith and hope in face of death manifest themselves when, for whatever purposes, Christian funeral rituals began to be written out.

First, funerals varied greatly from place to place at that time. An urban funeral might be a solemn affair with cathedral clerics and chanters on hand, whereas in the country, funerals were necessarily much simpler. Likewise, the funeral of a bishop, civil dignitary, priest, or monk was certainly much more elaborate in general than that of a simple peasant. Each local church followed its own customary liturgical usage; no universal set of formularies existed. In fact, it is far from clear whether every deceased Christian was buried with liturgical rites at all. Subsequent Carolingian legislation placed such emphasis on the pastoral duty to see that no Christian was left to die without *viaticum*, that we can hardly expect priests to have been more available to bury the dead than to administer the sacraments before death.

Second, comparative liturgical study suggests that our earliest extant manuscript witnesses of a developing order of funerals in the West represent an amalgamation of *two* basic forms and several different content traditions. It will suffice here to review principal themes and the Christian faith they express. It is noteworthy that when these witnesses were first committed to writing, there existed a manifest unity of faith cast in a variety of traditional usages.

The simplest basic pattern is indicated in the *ordo* of the so-called Phillipps Sacramentary.[1] It consisted of the preparation of the body in the home and a funeral procession with the body to the church, where burial took place. This reflects a continuation in Christian context of the basic funerary rites of classical antiquity. Their faith and its liturgical expression made the funeral of Christians different from that of their cultural neighbors. Faith saw to the preparation of the corpse in a setting of prayer; faith expressed itself in psalms during the procession with the body; and faith rendered the church and its immediate surroundings the Christian place of burial *par excellence*.

This pattern was characterized by two principal locations of liturgical action: home and church. Here we must think of "church" as a church compound, including churchyard, cloisters, and the like—a broader architectural notion than the church edifice of today. The two liturgical services were joined by the traditional funeral procession. The church compound functioned symbolically as the heavenly Jerusalem, which the deceased drew near and entered to remain. And in the Christian community, it functioned as the place where prayer was offered for the deceased and the body laid to rest. There does not appear to have been any separate liturgy in the church apart from the service of burial, consisting of a solemn entrance, prayers for the deceased, and interment. This took place within the church compound, for example, along the wall, in the church floor, in the atrium, or along the cloister walk.[2]

This liturgical expression of Christian faith at death and burial forged a ritual bond between church and cemetery that would perdure as a theological unity between them to our own times. Even when further ritual developments effected greater geographical separation of the cemetery, funeral liturgy would embrace church building and cemetery as one entity. The simple *ordo* we just examined reflects the situation where early Christian churches had been built over the graves of martyrs, the famed *memoriae* of Christian archeology identified in Chapter One.

Typical of classical and late antiquity, those churches over cemeteries were, like the cemeteries themselves, outside the walls of cities and towns.[3] With the emancipation of Christianity and the consequent extensive building of basilicas within cities, funeral rites celebrated there would require a second procession with the corpse, from the city basilica to the cemetery, often a *memoria* chapel, outside the city. Although the ritual unity between home and church-cemetery gradually lessened and the funeral procession from the home took a back seat to the new procession from city church to extra-urban cemetery, the *theological unity* between church and cemetery remained strong in the evolving funeral rites.

41

The second basic pattern of funeral liturgy in the earliest extant manuscripts reflects this development. For purposes of description, we follow the funeral rites preserved in the Sacramentary of Rheinau.[4] This document, like the Phillipps manuscript, dates from about 800. Its funeral service is a compilation of the old Roman *ordo defunctorum* and the liturgical formulas of a so-called Gelasian Sacramentary of the eighth century. Other early manuscript witnesses also serve to verify and complete the pattern.[5]

This form shared with the Roman usage the procedures of preparation of the body in the home and burial in the church compound. Different was the practice of keeping the body of the deceased in the church for an extended vigil, a liturgical service in addition to the familiar service of prayer and burial. In this pattern the transfer of the body from the home to the church seems to have been more a transition to the liturgy in the church than an independent ritual action. The procession from the place of the vigil and funeral prayers to the place of burial within the church compound seems to have functioned as the traditional funeral procession.

In both patterns, the liturgy consists of consecutive shorter services or units which are distinguished by reason of the place where they are carried out. Both begin *in the home* or place of death and consist of liturgical rites to mark the dying person's last living moments as well as those immediately after death.[6] Then the body is *brought to the church*, during which time antiphons and psalms are sung. A prayer service follows *in the church*, where the body is buried immediately or kept until burial. Finally, the *transfer to the cemetery* (where necessary), accompanied by antiphons and psalms, and the *service at the grave* conclude the funeral. Let us now review the liturgical content of these services and processions.

The Service in the Home
This first unit, when compared to the rest of the service, stands out as the longest component. For convenience, we may divide it into the "commendation of the Christian" (the administration of *viaticum* and the *commendatio animae* before and after death) and the washing, dressing, and laying out of the corpse on a bier in preparation for transfer from the home.

It is significant that this early funeral rite did not begin with death with but with *viaticum*, the Church's sacrament for the dying Christian.[7] Here the liturgy proclaimed that the eucharist, *the* sacrament of life in Christ, was administered to the dying person as the pledge of Christian faith in Christ's promise of victory over death. Eucharistic life embraces even human death. Thus, the *ordo* directed that communion be given as soon as one sees that the sick person is approaching *exitus* or departure, for eucharistic communion will be for the dying person "a defense and a helper at the resurrection of the just, for it will raise him [or her] up."[8]

The notion of *exitus* was the central theme of the service in the home. Psalm 114, *In exitu Israel* ("When Israel came out of Egypt"), was recited at death and indicated how this key moment was understood: The deceased was indeed leaving this life, but just as the Israelites had been led out of Egypt into Canaan, he or she was entering the land of God's promise. After the administration of *viaticum* the predeath commendation consisted in readings from the Lord's Passion. One version of the *ordo* appropriately recorded Psalm 42, "As the deer longs for running waters," a litany, and a concluding prayer of commendation. In other versions of the *ordo*, Psalm 42 occurred at the transfer from the home to the church. This mobility of formulas within a basic order appeared from the beginning and points to flexibility within these ritual moments. Yet certain formulas and combinations of formulas already began to appear as constants within the larger funeral context.

Although this eucharistic emphasis was soon to shift in practice to the time of a last anointing (extreme unction) and thus leave all later funeral rituals to begin with death and the deceased, pastoral care today is recovering something of this earlier Christian emphasis on a continuity between liturgy for the dying and that for the dead. While the focus still tends to shift at death from the dying person to the family, or bereaved, it is not difficult to direct that focus to the continuity of the Christ-life for both the deceased and the living. In that way, the funeral liturgy both proclaims Christian faith and founds its consoling hope on the resurrection of Jesus.

The moment of death was immediately recognizable from the short service designed as its accompaniment. It consists in a responsory and versicle, an antiphon and psalm, and finally an oration "as contained in the Sacramentary." The formulas are still familiar to us in the *Order of Christian Funerals*, although now serving a different purpose, as we shall see.

Saints of God, come to his/her aid!
Hasten to meet him/her, angels of the Lord!

Receive his/her soul and present him/her to God the Most High.

May Christ, who called you, take you to himself;
may angels lead you to the bosom of Abraham.

(OCF, No. 174)

May the choirs of angels welcome you
and lead you to the bosom of Abraham;
and where Lazarus is poor no longer
may you find eternal rest.

(No. 176 B)

Psalm 114: When Israel came out of Egypt . . . (No. 347, 6)

The concluding oration, like the Sacramentary that preserved it, remains as yet unidentified, but its tone was surely one of commendation. Together, these formulas early formed an independent unit in this station at the home, and they would have some part in the Catholic funeral down to the present. They were well suited to the moment of death, completing the *exitus* theme of the service in the home. Images that stood out so clearly in the earlier tradition remained here in constant continuity: going to Christ, the communion of the saints, and Abraham's bosom. The same symbolism of the moment of death came to characterize other moments of the funeral as well. Psalm 114, with its Exodus theme, was the only principal formula of this short service in the home that would fall into disuse during the coming centuries. Nevertheless, its presence during the rite of final commendation at the funeral of Pope Paul VI revealed that its appropriateness had not been forgotten. It was returned to the *Ordo* 1969 and the *Order of Christian Funerals* among the alternate antiphons and psalms (No. 347, 6).

After "commendation of the soul" immediately upon death, the body was prepared for burial. While it was being washed and placed on the bier, psalms were sung, and before the deceased was carried from the home, a final prayer closed the service. This *ordo* attests the widespread cultural custom of washing the corpse before burial, with this difference: Here it was placed in the ritual framework of the Church's care for the dead. We can assume that those caring for the body and those present prayed during the service. Obviously, all this was very simple in the ordinary Christian household and far more elaborate in clerical and monastic houses, as several versions of the *ordo* reveal.

Although the liturgical formulas of the *ordo* derived more from the latter setting than from the ordinary Christian home, they do indicate the common belief expressed at that particular time. Present-day funeral liturgy, searching to recover ways in which to express the faith on such occasions as the final arranging of the body or the first viewing of the body, may find here a source of inspiration. This can be especially helpful in learning to apply and extend the models that the *Order of Christian Funerals* provides in the section Related Rites and Prayers (Nos. 98–118) as appropriate liturgical pastoral care in the time immediately following death.

Common to this kind of dual action was the chanting or recitation of antiphons or psalms. One clearly favorite antiphon noted in the early *ordo* prays: "You formed me from the earth, you clothed me with flesh; Lord, my Redeemer, raise me up on the last day." Its biblical themes (Psalm 139; Job 10:8–12, 19:25), spoken, as it were, by the deceased, rendered the physical preparation of washing and dressing the body a hymn of faith. Calling to mind God's wondrous deeds for the deceased (*anamnesis*), the Church prayed in confident trust for the fulfillment of God's promise (praise and petition).

This antiphon was joined with two favorite psalms that accompanied the action of washing, vesting, and laying out the deceased: Psalm 93, "God is king, robed in majesty," and Psalm 23, "God is my shepherd, I lack nothing." Although Psalm 93 took up the clothing theme, focusing on God's steadfastness and robe of glory, presumably awaiting the deceased, it was Psalm 23 that best extended the theme of preparation.

The twofold imagery, God as shepherd and host, and its interpretation pointing to baptism and eucharist, symbolized the reality beyond death that the deceased

Christian both had lived sacramentally and prepared for in faith and hope. Just as the deceased was once led to baptism (washing and dressing) and fortified throughout life by the eucharist (eucharistic life and finally *viaticum*), he or she is now prepared through the faith of the community to walk fearlessly through death's threatening shadows to the eschatological banquet in the Lord's house forever. On the lips of the community, every verse of this psalm of trust appropriately proclaimed paschal faith and consoling hope. It was a perfect complement to the Exodus theme of this *service in the home.*

Furthermore, from biblical times, this dual image of shepherd and king indicated the Great Day of the Lord when all who had remained faithful to God would be drawn together in one final act of restoration. This theme, at the heart of the winter feast of Dedication, was the backdrop for the account of the good shepherd in John's Gospel (Chapter 10).

From that simple liturgical action, where the symbolic language of its biblical antiphon and psalm alone expressed all that needed to be spoken, one learns that good liturgy speaks for itself—that it is transparent. This *ordo*, at the root of all future Roman funeral liturgy, can help to sensitize us to the importance of verbal restraint in present-day funeral liturgy.

The Service in the Church

A short prayer concluded the *service in the home.* When the body was ready, it was carried to the church while the singing or reciting of psalms continued. No special emphasis is given this transfer. Although antiphons and psalms were sung on the way, taking the deceased to church became part of the preparation for the vigil in the church and for the burial rites to follow. The subsequent transfer of the body from its place in the church to the site of burial (sometimes, especially in monastic communities, not far distant) had become the principal funeral procession. It is the role of the church building and the vigil there that marked the most significant Christian departure from the rites of burial in traditional culture.

By the time our earliest manuscript witnesses of the Roman *ordo* appeared, the vigil with the body had become a tradition. Nevertheless, the rites in the church remain the most perplexing of the entire *ordo*. That the funeral liturgy was undergoing continual development is abundantly clear from analysis of the manuscripts. The complexity and movement within the *service in the church* revealed in these documents are manifestations of the early stages of ritual elaboration that would one day bring the entire focus of the Catholic funeral into the church. Yet, through all that complexity, one may discover what must have characterized the earlier vigil service that preceded the burial. And that is the simple rubric, the only item common to all versions of the *ordo*, that the mourners sing "psalms and responsories (intermittently)."[9]

It is possible that this rubric is all that survives of the earlier, simple Christian vigil from a time before complicated wake services, and even the celebration of Mass, had become part of the funeral liturgy. Augustine's earlier account of celebrating eucharist at the grave of his mother before burial exemplifies a different and exceptional tradition.[10] The newer *service in the church*, already part of the extant manuscript versions of the *ordo*, evolved through confrontation with new liturgical desires, especially those of monastic life, as we shall see. According to this reading of witnesses, the deceased was simply laid out in the church and a watch was held near the body. Psalms and responses were sung intermittently until the time of burial.

The Funeral Procession

When all was ready, the body was carried in solemn procession to the grave or tomb. In some cases, as we just noted, the place of burial was located in or near the church compound itself. Here and there, subterranean cemeteries, not unlike the earlier catacombs, remained in use well into this period. The body was preceded by wax tapers and incense. Lighted tapers or candles continued earlier pagan usage, which Christians had given their own meaning. Incense at the funeral was something Christians likewise retained from earlier custom. Gradually, the use of incense as a sign of honor was applied to the deceased, undoubtedly by analogy to its use in honor of the relics of the martyrs.[11]

The singing of psalms and antiphons accompanied the procession. Three antiphon-psalm sets stand out as significant in the early funeral *ordo*. First, Psalm 25 recurred: "To you, I lift up my soul." It was again a prayer of trust that God would lead the deceased through the dangers of death to divine shelter. Nearly all its verses are especially appropriate to the funeral procession. The familiar chant *In paradisum*, already present at this point in the funeral, was noted as an antiphon with Psalm 25. Although textual scholars continue to argue whether it was of Roman origin or not, one thing is certain: This chant has been an element of the funeral procession, either as an antiphon or as an independent response, since the beginning of written funeral rites. The text as translated today reads:

May the angels lead you into paradise
may the martyrs come to welcome you
and take you to the holy city,
the new and eternal Jerusalem.

(No. 176 A)[12]

49

Both the opening clause, "May the angels lead you into paradise," and the final verse, "and take you to the holy city Jerusalem," served to make this chant appropriate for the funeral procession. For while the Christian community carried the body of a dead member to its earthly grave, the liturgy saw the community of saints and angels accompanying the deceased into the eschatological kingdom. Here, too, the optimistic hope of the earlier tradition has been preserved.

A second traditional antiphon-psalm set common to the early *ordo* combined the Hebrew processional Psalm 118, "Give thanks to the Lord, for he is good," with the Roman antiphon taken from the psalm itself. Verse 19 is the proper antiphon: "Open for me the holy gates; I will enter and praise the Lord." Using this set of funeral chants for the procession with the body, the Church embraced all the paschal imagery from the "hosannas" of a triumphal entry into the heavenly Jerusalem to the Easter acclamation, "This is the day the Lord has made." The funeral liturgy proclaimed again the Church's faith and hope in face of death. Those who shared this faith with the deceased now joined him or her in this hymn of praise and thanksgiving for the promise of victory over death in Christ.

No, I shall not die, I shall live
to recite the deeds of God;
though God has punished me often,
he has not abandoned me to Death. (Psalm 118:17–18)

This kind of funeral liturgy, beginning with the Exodus *Hallel* (Psalm 114) and ending with the last *Hallel* of Easter (Psalm 118), left no room for doubt or pessimism. Rather, a faith-filled realism permeated the funeral procession found in this early *ordo*.

One final antiphon-psalm set noted for the funeral procession deserves mention. It is Psalm 42, "Like the deer that yearns for running streams," with verse 4b of the psalm serving as antiphon, "Let them bring me to your holy mountain, to the place where you dwell." An obvious processional choice because of its sense of longing for and movement toward the "house of God," this psalm likewise expressed the reality of the confusion and fear of death. No Christian can pray Psalm 42 in the context of a funeral procession and not recognize its symbolism. The psalm's "Levite in exile," longing for the house of God, becomes the Christian, freed from the exile of sin, who goes to meet the Lord. Where there is sorrow, the psalm offers hope both for the deceased and the community:

Why are you cast down my soul,
why groan within me?
Hope in God: I will praise him still,
my savior and my God. (Psalm 42:5–6; OCF, No. 347, 3)

In closing these remarks on the funeral procession in the oldest extant *ordines*, it is pastorally important to note that the 1969 *ordo* followed by the revised *Order of Christian Funerals* restored the simple funeral procession in its Procession to the Place of Committal (Nos. 148–140, 203, 315). Among the antiphon-psalm sets proposed are the three just observed.

The Service in the Cemetery
Burial itself was also set in a liturgical context, not unlike that of the service in the home. First, there was the laying of the corpse in the grave or sarcophagus with accompanying psalms and a prayer by the priest "before covering." Psalms suggested for this moment, while the mourners have a last opportunity to look upon the body of the deceased and take their leave, include Psalm 51, "Have mercy on me, O God," the recurring Psalm 42, "Like the deer that yearns for running streams," followed by its complement Psalm 43,

51

"Defend me," and finally Psalm 132, "O Lord, remember David," with verse 14 serving as its proper antiphon: "This is my resting place forever; here I have chosen to live." Standing before the open sarcophagus or grave, the Christian community looked beyond the harsh reality of burial to the all-embracing reality of its faith. With the deceased, even now they could pray:

O rescue me, God, my helper,
and my tongue shall ring out your goodness.
O Lord, open my lips
and my mouth shall declare your praise.
                    (Psalm 51:14–15; OCF, No. 347, 4)

And as the mourners looked beyond the apparent permanence of interment to the eternal city of David, the antiphon of Psalm 132 took on special meaning at the open grave or tomb in the church compound:

For the Lord has chosen Zion;
he has desired it for his dwelling:
"This is my resting place forever,
here I have chosen to live
                    (Psalm 132: 13–14; OCF, No. 347, 15)

A familiar antiphon-psalm set also accompanies the covering. Psalm 118, "Give thanks to the Lord," with the antiphon "Open for me the gates," is a powerful statement of faith while the grave or sarcophagus is being covered. (OCF, No. 347, 8)

No mention is made in the *ordo* of any further ritual gestures. Only two prayer formulas are specifically noted at burial. One is the Frankish invitation to prayer (*praefacio sepulturae*) before covering the grave. The 1969 *Order* incorporated it as its first among recommended invitations to prayer beginning the final commendation, and the *Order of Christian Funerals* includes it first among alternates. Its revised English adaption reads:

With faith in Jesus Christ, we must reverently bury the body of our brother/sister.

Let us pray with confidence to God, in whose sight all creation lives, that he will raise up in holiness and power the mortal body of our brother/sister and command his/her soul to be numbered among the blessed.

May God grant him/her a merciful judgment, deliverance from death, and pardon of sin. May Christ the Good Shepherd carry him/her home to be at peace with the Father. May he/she rejoice for ever in the presence of the eternal King and in the company of all the saints. (No. 402, 1)

The original text of this exhortation, earlier used at the open grave or tomb, is obviously still appropriate and meaningful in today's liturgy. Pastorally, when planning funerals, both its origin and language suggest that this invitation to prayer would serve well when the final commendation and farewell is to be celebrated in the cemetery.

The simple *ordo* closed its funeral rite with a prayer of final commendation that would also characterize Roman funeral liturgy down to the present. Much like Psalm 51, it takes the sinful weakness of the deceased into the liturgy of hope and asks God's forgiveness. Simply and to the point, this prayer proclaims divine justice while never doubting God's mercy and desire to save. The English text, according to its rendering in the *Order of Christian Funerals*, reads:

To you, O Lord, we commend the soul of N., your servant;
in the sight of this world he/she is now dead;
in your sight may he/she live for ever.

Forgive whatever sins he/she committed through
human weakness
and in your goodness grant him/her everlasting peace.
We ask this through Christ our Lord.

(No. 175 B)

TOWARD A MODEL FUNERAL LITURGY

The five centuries between these first extant manuscript witnesses to funeral liturgy and the crys-
tallization of the Roman rite of burial in the 13th century saw the spread of this *ordo* across Western
Europe. Comparative study of liturgical manuscripts
shows beyond doubt that this *ordo* served as a basic
model for the developing rite of funerals. Both ritual
form and liturgical expression have their roots there.
Even where shifts in emphasis are noted, the constancy of a strong and respected model perdures.
Thus, these five centuries of gradual, spreading influence of the *ordo* tell a story of both fidelity to the
Roman tradition behind the simple rite and further
amalgamation with local Frankish practices. The earlier process of subtle amalgamation gave way during
this period to explicit adaptation. The one force most
responsible for adapting the rite of funerals and for
giving direction to its future was the medieval monastery.

Monastic influences had already had an effect on the
earliest extant witnesses of the *ordo*. No wonder, for it
was the monastic *scriptorium* that provided copies and
monks' liturgical books that preserved for posterity the
developing story of the medieval funeral. Some form
of monasticism held a predominant place in both secular and spiritual life for all those five centuries. One
recalls, for example, the new importance accorded the
Frankish monasteries during the reign of Charlemagne
and his sons and still further monastic influence under
the reform abbots of Cluny and affiliated foundations.

54

During the 11th and 12th centuries, it was the religious houses of the Augustinian canons and, to a lesser degree, the Cistercian abbeys that succeeded the Benedictine monasteries in meeting many of the religious and social needs of an expanding society. So, too, the mendicant friars, particularly the Dominicans and Franciscans, took on the new ministry demanded by the needs of the emerging cities of the 13th century. The "modern" religious family of St. Francis, in fact, became the channel most responsible for implementing contemporary liturgical adaptation.

The simple Roman *ordo* had thus been absorbed into monastic and cathedral life. Because these centers already had their own tradition of burial practices, old and new ritual patterns merged, and the result was a funeral liturgy whose normal setting was the monastery with its life-style, its church, and its cemetery. Liturgical content also underwent ritual fusion, and here, too, practice dictated how the formularies of differing traditions were to function in the emerging rite.

Some manuscript sources bear witness to the result of this evolution in its full monastic or cathedral setting; others in less elaborate circumstances. No extant sources are known, however, that explicitly preserve the far simpler practice of the village parish. Although earlier synodal decrees and similar documents state that the parish priest is expected to have a manual of celebration for such services, no such "rituals" survive from prior to the 12th century. Later ones are monastic in their elaboration.

A formulation of a newer rite found in a 9th-century manuscript, however, seems to bridge the elaborate monastic rite and what must have been parochial practice. This apparently cathedral version of Roman burial liturgy, coming from Paris (St. Denis), may have served bishop and parish priest alike as a realistic model quite adaptable to differing local needs and customs.[13] Gradually, this newly composed Carolingian funeral rite established itself on the local scene and underwent a further formative process of its own. During the two and a half centuries after 1000 A.D., it merged again with still other expressions of the earlier Roman tradition and thus influenced the redaction in the 13th century of the burial rite of the Roman curia that would dominate subsequent Roman funeral liturgy. Just as some monastic burial usages formulated in this period of development were to perdure in the rites of religious orders independent of the spreading Roman ritual, so, too, this simple Carolingian rite was destined to preserve ancient customs, some still common in modern times, in the liturgy of local churches.

Thus the monks' way of life, the role that death played in monastic spirituality, and the evermore significant place enjoyed by liturgy in the monastery—especially under the inspiration of Cluny—concurred to make the monastic funeral an elaborate liturgical event. This elaboration of the rite occasioned the introduction of new elements into the earlier funeral tradition. Some of those elements were "new" in that they represented a new use of formulas within a basic pattern. Others were entirely new additions to the structural pattern of the *ordo*, to the traditional pool of liturgical formulas, or to both.

The "New" Service in the Church
The emergence of the station in the church as the focal point of monastic funeral liturgy is the most important consequence of ritual development during this 500-year period. Yet, the dominant motif behind the development of an extended station in the church was common to the ordinary medieval funeral: supplication for the deceased. Early on, Mass offered for the dead had

become the most effective expression of such prayer. What could be more natural for the religious, whose life was centered in the monastery or convent church, than bringing deceased brothers and sisters to their church for prayer, and especially for the sacrifice of the Mass, on their behalf? By the time this practice found its way into written orders of service it was already very elaborate, and the church edifice had become the focal station of the monastic funeral.

The body was brought to the church after preparation and remained there until removed for burial. During this time, the community offered its daily Office as well as the Office of the Dead and special vigil prayers for the deceased. This wake ordinarily concluded after Mass in the morning.[14]

Because these monastic rites represented religious sensibilities of the times and had such an influence on liturgical life generally, what took place in the monastery would have had its parallel in cathedral and parochial life. Furthermore, despite variations, proper local customs, concomitant folkloristic practices, and the like, this is recorded funeral liturgy in which the church experiences and recognizes itself at prayer in face of death.

This station in the church was therefore not an isolated ritual practice but, as liturgy, stood in a living tradition—the tradition of celebrating one's passage through death to Christ that joined earlier Christian funeral liturgy with the emerging medieval rite of funerals. The element that specifically constituted the station in the church as a new ritual unit was twofold: the celebration of Mass as a specific part of Christian funeral rites before burial and the short service of suffrages at the bier after Mass. Included also was the effect this new unit had on the funeral procession.

The Funeral Mass

The key to understanding the meaning and development of the station in the church is found in the celebration of the eucharist. The Church's oldest memories of Christians caring for their dead included the celebration of the Lord's Supper. When that celebration took place and how it was understood in the funeral context are matters that vary in those earlier sources. Nevertheless, the Mass as part of the liturgy before burial was not yet, despite textual corrections in the manuscript, part of the tradition represented by the *ordo*. The new situation did include a "funeral Mass" (to use later terminology), which analysis shows must have been a new, composite formulation drawn from Masses of other contexts.[15]

The process may be best described as an attempt to incorporate a rubric about the celebration of Mass into a text that did not originally include such a rubric. The result was a new version of the *ordo*. This updated version intended to describe, among other things, an already existing and apparently widespread practice whereby the bodies of the dead were kept in the church for some time as part of the funeral and that Mass was offered for the deceased during that stay in the church. History attests that the wake in church was already customary for persons of some dignity and for clerics.[16] The inclusion of the eucharist reflects the evolving situation in which the celebration of Mass came to be considered the prayer *par excellence* to effect the forgiveness of sins and was therefore to be offered on behalf of the deceased *as part of the liturgy of burial*. Funeral liturgy itself was becoming a rite to implore God's forgiveness for the deceased. The ideal was therefore to keep the body until Mass could be celebrated. Because offering Mass had come to be reserved to a morning hour, any monk or nun dying after noon would be kept until the following morning when possible. There is no evidence to indicate that the celebration of Mass was anything other than one of the morning Masses of the monastic day.

A process of adapting existing prayer texts as well as readings and chants for Mass before burial would lead, through liturgical practice and further adaption, to proper "funeral Masses." One of those was the familiar *Requiem* Mass. Historically, it was the presence of this Mass in the 13th-century funeral liturgy of the papal court that put it in the mainstream of later Roman liturgical tradition. The *Requiem* thereby became the normative funeral Mass for adults in the Tridentine *Missale Romanum* (1570), and this characterized Roman Catholic funeral liturgy until the revised Missal of Pope Paul VI (1970).

The liturgical books of the 12th and 13th centuries likewise include signs that funeral Mass celebrated for the deceased before burial had come to be other than one of the scheduled eucharistic celebrations of the day. Rubrics began to refer to the celebration of the funeral Mass at an opportune time—meaning, of course, a morning hour. Rather than keeping watch by the body until the scheduled morning Mass, a *special* Mass became part of the funeral itself.

Both the development of specific Mass formularies for the dead, such as the *Requiem*, and the introduction of the funeral Mass as part of the funeral liturgy separate from the daily eucharist of the local church, underscored the already diminishing ecclesial sense of the Christian funeral. Late medieval funeral liturgy thus took little account either of the liturgical year or of the ecclesial community as such. All this went hand in hand with the fearful eschatology that came to characterize the medieval funeral liturgy. Time was right for innovations such as the sequence *Dies irae* and the offertory chant asking the Lord to deliver all the faithful departed from the pains of hell, from the deep pit, from the lion's mouth, and so on. Although the liturgy preserved a certain traditional balance of hope even in these chants, the "waning of the middle ages" was close at hand, and it would leave its macabre mark on the expression of faith in face of death.

In this context, it is pastorally noteworthy that the growing practice in recent years of bringing the deceased to the church for a wake service in the evening and keeping the body there overnight offers an excellent opportunity to highlight the ecclesial dimension of the revised *Order of Christian Funerals*. Furthermore, that practice logically points to the fuller ecclesial celebration whereby one of the daily parish Masses might be celebrated as the funeral Mass. Not only would the funeral liturgy thereby recover closer contact with the revised liturgical year and its Christocentric, paschal focus, but the funeral would also have a larger place in the life of the parish. Modern liturgical renewal would thus bring the Catholic funeral full circle, from an exaggerated medieval individualism that survived in the former Roman rite of burial to an invitation to partake again in the best of earlier ecclesial traditions. The faith that once brought the eucharist into the funeral liturgy itself now offers Christians, through the revised funeral liturgy, ever new eucharistic opportunities to proclaim paschal faith and eschatological hope.

Once customary, the station in the church before burial became an occasion for further elaboration, which in turn would lead to still newer elements and go on to affect the further development of written *ordines*. In the tradition of the earlier *ordo*, the rubrics simply indicate that upon arrival in the church, all pray for the deceased. When interment followed immediately, this was a brief occasion for final prayer, surely not unlike the prayers indicated in the sacramentaries.[17] Already in the earliest extant witnesses, however, expansion pointed to a longer vigil, the celebration of Mass and an Office of the Dead before interment. Younger manuscript witnesses even go on to include fully elaborated written formularies for the all-night wake services in the church.[18]

One of the first effects of this new emphasis on a station in the church was the duplication of elements within the earlier pattern of the funeral liturgy—with two notable examples. First, the station in the church acquired a conclusion that duplicated the suffrages for the dead following immediately upon death in the earlier tradition. Second, as already is apparent from the monastic influence in the oldest manuscript witnesses, the funeral processing had become two processions or transfers. The new procession to the site of burial generally took precedence as the more solemn one.

The Absolution Service

Entirely new to the earlier tradition of the simple *ordo* is the introduction of suffrages for the deceased after the celebration of Mass, before removing the body to the place of burial. This new short service, later called the *absolutio* and presently perduring as the final commendation and farewell, followed the model of the formulas assigned in the rite for the moment of death, i.e., responsories and prayers. In fact, ninth- and 10th-century sources almost without exception repeat the principal responsory of those earlier suffrages, "Saints of God," with the verse "May Christ who called you," as the first formula of the new service. Other elements vary from source to source, but a basic pattern emerges as a constant: an exhortation and/or prayer introducing one or more responsory-verse sets, each followed by a short litany and the Lord's Prayer and concluding with a closing collect. This pattern was common to the suffrages that during the same period were beginning to play a role in the monastic celebration of the hours, especially the Office of the Dead.

At the appropriate time, and when everything prescribed for the deceased had been accomplished, the monastic community and other faithful would be called together for the procession to the place of burial. A transition to this solemn, traditional moment of Christian burial was evidently found wanting. Suffrages, familiar from the opening moments of the *ordo*, were apparently the most fitting formularies at hand. Just as these suffrages placed the moment of death in a context of faith, so, too, they now sealed the celebration of eucharist and offered a transition to the solemn funeral procession.

This short service at the bier, being one of the newest elements of the funeral liturgy, was the most radical shift toward medieval fear and pessimism in face of death. First of all, whatever the intention behind its original incorporation early in the Carolingian era, it soon became the moment above all others in the funeral liturgy to ensure God's good favor and forgiveness of the deceased. The responsories of the service best illustrate the shift. Initially, in the first Carolingian witnesses to the practice, it was a simple service nearly identical to that at the moment of death. Responsories such as "Saints of God" and the Frankish formula "You knew me, Lord, before I was born" reflect the scriptural emphasis of trust. In that trust, the second clause of the latter responsory also prayed for forgiveness.[19]

It is quite a change when, in the 12th century, another tone emerged in the responsory ("Deliver me, O Lord, from eternal death") thereafter to dominate the service at the bier following the funeral Mass. A recent English version reads: "Deliver me, Lord, from everlasting death in that awful day, when the heavens and the earth shall be moved, when you will come to judge the world by fire. Dread and trembling have laid hold upon me, and I fear exceedingly because of the judgment and the wrath to come. O that day, that day of wrath, of sore distress and of all wretchedness, that great and exceeding bitter day, when you will come to judge the world by fire."[20]

Comparative studies of this responsory and its contemporary, the sequence *Dies irae*, suggest that the latter piece was composed from later trope-like verses of the responsory.[21] In any case, the popularity of both reveal how church poets, and undoubtedly the faithful as well, interpreted this liturgical moment. The emphasis is on the horrendous expectations of the last day, applied both to the living and the dead. Poetic descriptions of the last day, coupled with the theme of the worthlessness of human and worldly achievements, led to prayerful pleas that the just would be preserved from eternal damnation. Fear and insecurity dominated, as if the last day would be so terrible that even the just would run the risk of falling and be deserving of damnation.[22]

The mood was apparently such that this final service before the funeral processing served as a *memento mori* to the living while they prayed fervently to secure protection for the dead through forgiveness of sins, lest they, no longer able to help themselves, be abandoned to such horrible fate. Such emphasis on purification extended the use of incense and holy water to this service at the bier. Again, it is not until the 12th century that this addition is noted in liturgical manuscripts. The prayer of the Church for forgiveness gave the service its Latin title *absolutio*. Certain monastic practices during this period invite the interpretation that the prayer formulas of this short service implied sacramental absolution or the granting of plenary indulgences to the deceased. Scholars, however, debate whether anything more was intended than the intercession of the Church on behalf of the deceased.[23]

Nevertheless, this new mood stands out in sharp contrast to earlier, more subdued propitiatory formulas, which were clearly no longer considered an effective expression of the current mood. Yet, apparently, neither did they seem to be convertible. This indicates that the earlier spirit was not transformed or misunderstood. Quite simply, the new medieval spirituality viewed Christ's coming in judgment as a cause for fear, whereas formerly it was a source of consolation. Just as primitive Christian art expressed that hopeful mood, so—not surprisingly—the emergence of medieval frescoes and paintings of the Last Judgment may be found to coincide with liturgical pieces such as the chants *Dies irae* and "Deliver me, O Lord, from eternal death."[24]

Finally, comparative study of the absolution service throughout those first 500 years of documented ritual development reveals the *absolutio* service to be inseparably associated with the funeral Mass. Even where, for example, Mass was not celebrated before burial because the hour of the funeral liturgy was after noon, the *absolutio* remained with the Mass. If the funeral Mass was celebrated next day, the *absolutio* followed Mass just as if the body were present. This conception of the service would perdure via the Tridentine Ritual to the 20th century.

Pastorally, therefore, one notes a significant difference in the revised *Order of Christian Funerals* where the new final commendation and farewell is seen to relate directly to the deceased and the burial. Thus, even when, for whatever reason, Mass is not celebrated, the revised commendation rite is always part of the funeral liturgy. This change in emphasis follows from the totally new role the final commendation and farewell has been assigned in Catholic funeral liturgy. Emphasis is no longer primarily on absolution but on the corporate act of bidding farewell. These detailed pages on the medieval *absolutio* remind today's funeral minister where the Church has been only recently and how serious is the pastoral obligation to discern the new emphasis and its meaning for people today. It was unfortunate, for example, that one commentator covering the funeral of Pope Paul VI continued to refer to the liturgical action of this new commendation rite as "purifying the body."[25]

The Funeral Procession
One of the most important traditional units of Christian burial had been the funeral procession. Where burial in the church compound followed immediately upon a short service of prayers at the church, the procession from home to church compound was the only procession associated with burial. Whatever short prayer service took place in the church, it was part of the whole funeral and not an independent unit as it was to become in the monastery. When the body came to remain in the church for a longer time (even overnight), the procession from the home took the church, now with its long wake service, as its *terminus*. Thus, the later transfer from the church to the place of internment became the procession traditionally associated with burial—that is, the funeral procession—as we saw developing under monastic influence already in the earliest manuscript witnessses. Those examples adequately illustrate the nature of the new procession once the transposition had taken effect.

Other New Adaptations
Besides the absolution service, other elements that appeared in the expanding medieval *ordo* were the blessing of the grave, the sign of the cross, and a final prayer of absolution over the deceased.

The blessing of the tomb or grave was not part of the earlier tradition. Yet, already in the ninth century the use of holy water and incense at the site of burial was accompanied by a prayer with the title *benedictio sepulchri*. This novelty was conspicuously absent in Carolingian services. Although not familiar in that tradition and uncommon in the pontifical usage that influenced the Roman rite, this practice eventually found its way into the *Roman Ritual* of 1614 and perdures in the revised *Order of Christian Funerals* (No. 218; 405).

Similarly, the sign of the cross over the grave after burial appeared as a new element in the 10th century. Although rubrics noting this concluding gesture of blessing were rare in medieval liturgical books, they did occasionally appear. The sign of the cross was a common liturgical gesture of blessing by the High Middle Ages and undoubtedly took place often, without specific rubrics, in conjunction with certain formulas. That it became the final element in the Tridentine *Roman Ritual* of 1614 shows it enjoyed a certain popularity, at least in local traditions if not in that of the Roman curia. Closely related was another practice that was new to the earlier *ordo* but not uncommon in medieval burial rituals. This was a prayer of absolution over the deceased after burial.

Although hardly significant elements in the longer development, the sign of the cross and some sense of absolution for the deceased were nevertheless important to the popular medieval concept of burial rites. *The Song of Roland* (12th century) well attests to this. The anonymous troubadour, recounting the king's lament upon finding Roland and his army dead, described the burial as follows:

And then spake Naimon: Bid us search the field
And find our friends who fought and died for us.
That we may pray for them, and bury them.

He raised his hand. The horns of all the host
Rang loud. The Franks, dismounting, sought their
friends
And brought them to the King, and tonsured priests
Absolved and signed them with the cross of God,
And burned sweet myrrh and spices. So they laid
Their comrades in one grave, and left them there
In Spain. Alas! There was no other way.[26]

The Model Funeral Liturgy
The combined influence of the papal court and Franciscan pastoral practice in the 13th century shaped a funeral liturgy that survives as a summary model of these
five centuries of ritual development. The curial ritual
appended to the Franciscan Breviary of 1260, itself a
vade mecum of pastoral care for the friars, is a unique
window on late medieval funeral usage.[27] Recalling the
obvious adjustments that would have been necessary
in the Christian family, the friars' funeral gives us an
idea of pastoral practice in their apostolate.

As death approached, the brothers gathered around
the dying confrere to pray with him and support him
in his agony with psalms and litanies—in short, the
service later called the "commendation of the soul."
Although the rite began before death, Holy Communion as *viaticum* was no longer part of this rite; a separate order to communion of the sick now preceded the
rite for the dying. It would not be long before all these
last liturgical moments before death would also become part of a separate short rite. Certainly, in the
growing cities and widely dispersed villages and man-
ors, the priest's presence even at death itself was far
less frequent now. Yet the Franciscan model still
opened with the priest at the deathbed despite presumed earlier arrangements for *viaticum*.

At death, the same traditional suffrages were offered: the
responsory and verse, "Saints of God" and "Christ who

67

called you." A concluding prayer followed—now, however, introduced by a short list of versicles. The prayer "To you, O Lord, we commend . . ." and the above responsory illustrate that a commendation of the deceased upon death remained part of the rite of funerals.[28]

Next, the body was washed by the brothers whose charge it was to care for the dead; it was dressed for burial and laid out on a bier. The rite then indicates a selection of prayers and added versicles followed by Vespers, apparently to be prayed when the body was laid out. Thus, it appears that the actual preparation for burial in this rite no longer took place in a liturgical setting. Those prayers and psalms came rather to constitute a kind of wake service after preparation before the body was taken to church. This was another shift away from earlier customs and one that surely corresponded with changed circumstances surrounding care for the dead.

At the appointed time, the friars, chanting the familiar responsory and verse, "Saints of God" and "Christ who called you," carried the body into the church. Of the many different traditional chants marking the transfer to the church, this set is found among the earliest extant Carolingian customs (rite of St. Denis); it survived via this Franciscan rite and the *Roman Ritual* down to the 20th century. The revised *Order of Christian Funerals*, following the 1969 *Order*, includes it among alternative entrance formulas (No. 403). Nevertheless, the preference of the 1989 rite regards this set of chants as particularly appropriate to the final commendation and farewell (No. 174).

It is pastorally valuable to note the simplicity of this liturgical model, where repetition of these same chants at death, during the transfer of the deceased to church, and again after Mass, seems to echo an important facet of the faith. Almost like a mantra or litany, that simple repetition of chants embraces a treasury of faith images professing an eschatology of triumphant homecoming. Surrounded by all the saints and angels, almost arm in arm with Christ, as it were, the deceased is portrayed as welcomed by God and blessed with the comforting embrace of Abraham. One is reminded here of the homecoming of the prodigal son.

Once the body had been laid out in the church, the friars chanted Vigils (Matins) followed by short versicles for the deceased. During the concluding prayers, the priest and ministers are said to have prepared for solemn Mass if the time was opportune. In context, this implies an early morning hour. Either one of the regular daily Masses or a special early morning funeral Mass after Matins might be intended here.

In any case, after Mass, the friars gathered in a circle around the bier. The priest, standing at its head, opened the service with an invitation to prayer, and three sets of suffrages followed. Each was composed of a responsory and verse (during which the priest incensed the body), versicles, the Lord's Prayer, and a concluding prayer. Despite the multiplication of formulas, one recognizes immediately the structure that would characterize this service for the next 700 years. Even when the service became the revised final commendation of the present rite, the same basic structure was preserved. As to content, *both* the responsories already traditional to this service, such as "Saints of God," *and* the more recent composition, "Deliver me, O Lord, from eternal death," appear side by side. Whereas the latter alone would come to define the suffrages in the Tridentine rite of burial, earlier traditional responsories, such as "Saints of God," would serve as the new "song of farewell" in the 20th-century reforms.

Both in form and content, the short service after the funeral Mass in this Franciscan rite of 1260 would have an influence on the way Catholics in the 20th century take leave of their dead.

Just as the 13th-century rite expressed the faith in both old and new ways that were appropriate to late medieval Christians, so does the *Order of Christian Funerals* serve the needs of people today. In the service after the funeral Mass, for example, the new *Ordo* transforms the medieval service of suffrages to accord with the ancient Christian tradition of commendation. What once took place at death and had become lost has thus been restored to the Christian funeral in a new position.

After the final set of suffrages the friars carried the deceased to the grave, singing "May the angels lead you into paradise" and "May the choir of angels. . . ." This distance from church to grave was apparently not far in the community where this version of the rite was drafted. When all had arrived there and the antiphons were completed, the priest recited the prayer that in some other 12th-century rites bore the title "blessing of the tomb." In the 1989 order, it still serves as a "prayer over the place of committal" where it is translated as follows:

Almighty God,
you created the earth and shaped the vault of heaven;
you fixed the stars in their places.
When we were caught in the snares of death
you set us free through baptism;
in obedience to your will
our Lord Jesus Christ
broke the fetters of hell and rose to life,
bringing deliverance and resurrection
to those who are his by faith.
In your mercy look upon this grave,
so that your servant may sleep here in peace;
and on the day of judgment raise him/her up

70

to dwell with your saints in paradise.
We ask this through Christ our Lord.

(OCF, No. 405, 3)

There followed a list of six traditional funeral psalms
with antiphons, closing with the Canticle of Zechariah
and its antiphon from Lauds, "I am the resurrection."
These, the rite notes, were sung *in persona defuncti* and
apparently accompanied the actual interment. Meanwhile, in curious medieval style, the priest was directed
to recite a series of traditional funeral prayers. At the
close of this solemn burial rite, the priest blessed the
grave or tomb with holy water and said the Lord's
Prayer. After several closing prayers, including the invocation "May his/her soul and the souls of all the faithful
departed through the mercy of God rest in peace," all
returned to the church singing another responsory from
the Office of the Dead ("Remember me, O God, because
my life is like a wind; no longer shall I be seen by men").
There the priest concluded the liturgy with the commendation prayer "To you, O Lord, we commend. . . ."

The next era, leading to the *Roman Ritual* of 1614, has
little effect on the model funeral liturgy described
here. What it does reveal, however—and what makes
it worth reviewing—is how this liturgy was understood and celebrated in local churches throughout Europe. By the end of the period, many of those traditions would accompany later settlers and immigrants
to the New World and there, too, be the context
within which the Tridentine rite of burial would become the norm for funeral liturgy after the 17th century. Chapter Three will guide that final stage of our
journey into the 20th century.

NOTES

1. *Incipit de migratione animae:* Berlin, Offentliche
Wissenschaftliche Bibliothek, codex 105 (Phill. 1667), fol.

173^v–174^r. An edition of this *ordo* is available in Sicard, *La liturgie de la mort.*

2. Pre-Carolingian ecclesiastical statutes are frequently concerned with the place of interment in the church compound. Superstition concerning the burial place was apparently widespread. See Carlo de Clercq, *La Législation Réligieuse Franque de Clovis à Charlemagne* (Louvain-Paris: Bibliothèque de L'Université-Sirey, 1936).

3. See Toynbee, *Death and Burial*, pp. 48–49.

4. *Orationes super defunctis vel commendatio animae:* Zürich, Zentralbibliothek, codex Rh 30, fol. 152^v–155^r. Anton Hänggi and Alfons Schönherr, eds., *Sacramentarium Rhenaugiense,* Spicilegium Friburgense, No. 15 (Freiburg i.d. Schweiz: Universitätsverlag, 1970), pp. 273–276.

5. The other most representative manuscript sources are: *Ordo qualiter agatur in obsequium defunctorum:* Rome, Biblioteca Vaticana, codex Ottob. 312, fol. 151^v. M. Andrieu, ed., *Les Ordines romani du haut moyen âge* I, Spicilegium sacrum lovaniense 11 (Louvain: Université Catholique de Louvain, 1931), pp. 529–530.

Ordo defunctorum qualiter agatur erga defunctum a morte detento: Cologne, Dombibliothek, codex 123, fol. 80^r. G. Haenni, "Un 'ordo defunctorum' du Xe siècle," *Ephemerides Liturgicae* 73 (1959), pp. 433–434.

Qualiter erga infirmum morte detentum agatur: Paris Bibliothèque Nationale, N.B. lat. 1240, fol. 16^r–16^v. Paris manuscript studied by this author; see also Sicard, *La liturgie de la mort*, p. 18.

6. Here the Rheinau manuscript is completed by the other parallel sources.

7. See Alfred C. Rush, "The Eucharist: The Sacrament of the Dying in Christian Antiquity," *The Jurist* 34 (1974), pp. 10–35.

8. *Communio erit ei defensor et adiutor in resurrectione iustorum. Ipsa enim resuscitabit eum* (according to codex Ottob. 312).

9. *Psallant psalmos vel responsoria (per)mixt(. . .),* according to all the manuscript witnesses indicated above. See notes 1, 4, and 5.

10. See Augustine, *Confessiones*, IX, 12. Also, Damien Sicard, "The Funeral Mass" in *Reforming the Rites of Death*, ed. Johannes Wagner, Concilium 32 (New York: Paulist Press, 1968), pp. 45–52.

11. See Chapter One: The Church of the Martyrs.

12. The adjectives "new and eternal" are an addition to the original text of the older *ordines*.

13. *Incipiunt orationes agenda mortuorum:* B.N. lat. 2290, fol. 160^r–165^r. Edition with *incipits:* Edmond Martène, *De antiquis Ecclesiae ritibus* III (Antwerp: J. B. de La Bry, 1736–1738), pp. 385–386.

14. See for example *Regularis Concordia*, ed. T. Symons (London: Nelson & Sons, 1953), p. 65, and *Decreta Lanfranci*, ed. David Knowles, *The Monastic Constitutions of Lanfranc*, (London: Nelson & Sons, 1951), pp. 127–129.

15. See Sicard, "The Funeral Mass," *passim*.

16. See Rush, *Christian Antiquity*, pp. 154–162, 170–186.

17. For example, *orationes antequam ad sepulcrum deferatur* or *orationes ad sepulcrum, priusquam sepeliatur* (according to Vat. Reg. 316), i.e., "prayers before the deceased is carried to the tomb" or "prayers at the tomb before the deceased is buried."

18. For example, the ninth-century funeral manual found in the Vatican Ms. Pal. Lat. 550, fol. 2^r–24^v, presents "decades" of psalms to be recited during the long wake.

19. The full text, as preserved in the *Order of Christian Funerals*, reads:

You knew me, Lord, before I was born. You shaped me into your image and likeness. R/ I breathe forth my spirit to you, my Creator.

Merciful Lord, I tremble before you: I am ashamed of the things I have done; R/ do not condemn me when you come in judgment. (OCF, No. 403, 3)

20. *Saint Andrew Bible Missal* (Bruges: Biblica, 1962), p. 1152.

21. Clemens Dreves and Guido Blume, *Analecta Hymnica Medii Aevi* 49 (Leipzig, 1906; repr. New York–London: Johnson Reprint Corp., 1961), pp. 369–389.

22. Dreves–Blume, *Analecta* 49, pp. 377–378. For a different view, see Josef Szöverffy, *Die Annalen der Lateinischen Hymnendich-tung: Ein Handbuch* II (Berlin: E. Schmidt Verlag, 1965), pp. 220–224, where the author argues in favor of a good balance in the sequence *Dies irae* between hope and fear, anticipation and tension, and refers to it as ultimately a "chant d'esperance."

23. See for example, Pierre-Marie Gy, "Le Nouveau Rituel Romain des Funérailles," *La Maison-Dieu* 101 (1970), p. 25 and his note 22.

24. For a thorough review of this period, see the collection of essays in Herman Braet and Werner Verbeke, eds., *Death in the Middle Ages* (Leuven: Leuven University Press, 1983). Note in particular Rolf Sprandel, "Alter und Todesfurcht nach der spätmittelalterlichen Bibelexegese," pp. 107–116, and Claude Thiry, "De la Mort Marâtre à la Mort Vaincue: Attitudes devant la Mort dans la déploration funèbre française," pp. 239–257.

25. See below, p. 190, and *ordo Exsequiarum*, no. 10.

26. Reprinted with permission of Macmillan Publishing Co., Inc. from *The Song of Roland*, translated by Frederick B. Luquiens. Copyright 1952 by Macmillan Publishing Co., Inc.

27. Stephan J. P. van Dijk, *Sources of the Modern Roman Liturgy. The Ordinals of Haymo of Faversham and related documents (1243–1307)* II (Leiden: Brill, 1963), pp. 385–397.

28. See OCF, Nos. 174 and 175 B.

Chapter Three

The Order of Funerals:
The Model Becomes Norm

During the nearly four centuries between the initial influence of the Franciscan-curial model (1260) and the
Rituale of 1614, life in Europe became far too complex
to permit generalizations about funeral practice. This
was the era of the "waning of the Middle Ages," the
Black Death, and the Dance of Death. Most of the
funerary customs usually identified with it (prayers
against sudden death, elaborate cemeteries and sepul-
chral monuments, and the like) were expressions of
popular piety surrounding the liturgy.[1] Nevertheless,
the funeral liturgy itself was not entirely static.

Existing diocesan and Roman formularies were apparently respected as models that local churches adapted
according to specific needs. These mostly exhibited a
trend toward simplification of the station in the church
for the ordinary funeral and an elaboration of graveside rites. Unfortunately, these adaptations are scarcely
indicated in extant ritual books. Even where the need
for new parochial manuals was met, the funeral liturgy incorporated into them followed earlier standard
models with minor variations.[2] Adaptations of the
model formularies seem to have been a matter of local
tradition, and it was apparently not considered necessary to write them out, even where the ordinarily pro-
hibitive cost of recopying ritual manuscripts could be
afforded.

For our purposes, the best approach to this diverse history, of which little direct liturgical documentation has survived, is to compare earlier patterns of ritual development with the large body of liturgical data that becomes available after 1500. With the invention of printing, many dioceses were able to reproduce ritual books that had worn out through centuries of pastoral use. Some of these "manuals," as many were called, reproduced old diocesan funeral liturgies; others, especially in the immediate context of Tridentine reform legislation, took the opportunity provided by printing to update their rites in light of current pastoral practice and conciliar decrees. Such updating at the time new books were produced was common throughout liturgical history. Printing added considerable efficiency to the process. As in the past, the result remained a witness both to ideal rites *and* to the incorporation of changes that were already part of current practice. Together, ideal and actual use constituted the diocesan model. Thus, diocesan rituals from the early 16th century mirror for us both earlier and contemporary funeral usage.

Still another kind of ritual book appeared for the first time during the early 16th century. This was a general pastoral manual not intended for any one diocese or region. Its purpose was the pastoral education of the clergy. This kind of ritual was didactic in approach, seeking to teach the ideal Roman liturgy. One of these works stands out as a valuable witness for our purposes, the *Sacerdotale Romanum* edited by the Dominican Albertus Castellani in 1523.[3] This project enjoyed the explicit approval of Pope Leo X, who died, however, shortly before it appeared in print. Its popularity and influence is attested by its 16 editions during the 16th century alone.

The final special witness to this era of ritual life is a unique, encyclopedic work produced by Julius Cardinal Sanctorius during the last quarter of the 16th century. This *Rituale Sacramentorum Romanum*,[4] originally intended to be the Ritual of the Council of Trent, was judged too impractical for pastoral use. Nevertheless, it is exceedingly valuable to the researcher, for its funeral liturgy brings together the many sources, both old and recent, that the scholarly Cardinal considered representative of the Roman tradition. His guiding principle that the best of the past is the ideal for the present produced a distinct kind of ritual encyclopedia that would have been impossible prior to the advent of scientific historical scholarship in the 16th century.

Whereas the earlier diocesan manuals provided pastoral guides to existing local funeral usages, both the general manuals and the Sanctorius *Rituale* were written in a didactic and normative tone reflecting the spirit of reform that led the Council of Trent to order uniform liturgical books for the entire Roman Catholic Church.

The liturgical scene around 1500 was far more diverse than this brief sketch suggests. Funeral liturgy often revealed even greater diversity and vitality than sacramental liturgies. Together with reform principles and normative liturgical manuals, it was ultimately the familiar, living liturgical practice that determined the final character of the funeral rite incorporated in the *Roman Ritual* of 1614. We note, therefore, the importance among our witnesses of: first, the general manual; second, the Sanctorius *Rituale*; and finally, ritual books reflecting the burial practice of churches whose usages also served as models for the editorial commission of the *Roman Ritual* of 1614. It will be for the final section of this chapter to review briefly the Rite of Burial in that *Ritual* and the role it played in Roman liturgical practice in the subsequent 350 years before Vatican II.

The Rite of Burial in the General Manuals
Our witness to the new general manuals appearing in
the 16th century is the *Sacerdotale Romanum* edited by
Castellani in 1523. A first noteworthy difference between this and earlier extant books is that it presents a
ritual with separate rites for the burial of clergy and of
lay adults.

There is no doubt that the ordinary parochial funeral
in the Middle Ages was simpler than that of the clergy
and religious as celebrated in cathedrals and monasteries. But the *Sacerdotale Romanum* contains a new
feature—the juxtaposition of rites for clergy and lay
burial. A practice that had been taken for granted was
now set down in writing. Yet, the order of burial for
laity was nothing other than an abridged version of
the clerical order.

The rites of burial presented in Castellani's manual are
models to be followed for proper liturgical celebration
according to the Roman tradition. The solemn clerical
rite of burial that Castellani incorporated as his ideal
followed minutely the prototype of the medieval rite
in the Franciscan *Breviary* of 1260. In other words, the
order Castellani presented as the ideal for contemporary burial practice is nothing other than the clerical
funeral liturgy that the Franciscans adapted from the
13th-century *Pontifical* of the papal curia.

Not only did Castellani find this 13th-century order
predominant among his sources, but he recognized in
it the prototype of the rite of burial for clergy in his
day. What better rite to follow as a clerical model? Furthermore, its venerable Roman tradition and direct
roots in the papal curia gave it an aura of authority
that was influential indeed during the troubled 1520s.

The situation of the lay funeral was different. Contemporary experience of the Roman tradition in parochial
funerals varied greatly, often even from parish to par-

ish. In formulating his burial rite for lay persons, Castellani clearly allowed himself to be guided by certain existing simplified burial orders, especially with respect to the basic form and liturgical content. There is, nonetheless, an obvious direct dependence of Castellani's rite of burial for laity on his ideal Roman model for the burial of clerics.

This order differed markedly from the longer clerical version in two moments of the rite. Both were liturgically significant: the *absolutio* before removing the body from the church for burial and the chanting of psalms and antiphons during the interment rites.

At the absolution, where the pontifical model presented the traditional threefold suffrages, the simpler rite showed two. Given the history of the development of these suffrages, this appears to reveal an earlier simplicity. An even simpler form of the *absolutio* characterized the diocesan orders of burial for lay persons, as we shall see. Increasing the number of suffrages was a medieval way of adding greater solemnity to the funeral, especially of a bishop, pope, or other dignitary, a practice that continued into modern times.[5]

Similarly, during the cemetery service before burial, the funeral order for clerics in the *Sacerdotale Romanum* preserved the chanting of a series of antiphons and psalms *in persona defuncti* (as if the deceased himself were offering the prayer). These are recognizable from medieval rituals as traditional chants at burial, where there was a wide choice of psalms and antiphons. All these antiphons and chants, except one set, disappeared from Castellani's simplified lay order, and even that one became the last of the processional chants, possibly as the community reached the grave.

The nature of these two changes appears to be one of simplification by means of systematic abridgment. Following his authoritative 13th-century model, Castellani seemingly formed the burial order for laity by removing from his model two traditionally self-contained segments: the middle set of suffrages and the psalms before burial. Put in another way, those elements that in his experience and/or research had showed themselves to be specifically proper to the burial order were retained; the solemn "extras" were eliminated.

In the absolution service, two sets of responsories, "Saints of God" and "Deliver me, O Lord, from eternal death," had become constant elements. They show how the liturgy absorbed the new piety of dread while preserving the hope implied in the heavenly welcome awaiting the deceased. That the middle set was the one omitted apparently had nothing at all to do with its content. Compared with the other two suffrages, this set could be excised without seriously altering the contemporary expression of funeral piety. Yet this logical excision removed more than just a given set of liturgical texts. It eliminated in the new model for lay Christians precisely one of those moments in the service where local traditions had preserved a variety of expression. A comparative study of sources reveals that, while the first and third set of suffrages became more or less fixed and proper, the middle set remained variable, showing different responsories and collects representative of Christian burial tradition and faith.

Castellani apparently judged the chanting of the canticle *Benedictus* with its antiphon, "I am the resurrection," to be an essential element in the cemetery service, for it was the only set of chants he retained there. We can assume that chanting the full set of traditional psalms and antiphons, followed by the canticle set, happened infrequently in medieval parochial practice. Nevertheless, other *rituals* did preserve these venerable burial psalms and antiphons so that one or more was bound to have been chosen on occasion.

Castellani's choice of the canticle *Benedictus* no doubt rested on his experience with other current usages. But by preserving *only* this fixed chant set, Castellani's model limited the traditional options in a new, deliberate way. The result also separated the canticle set "I am the resurrection"–*Benedictus* from its original context of Psalms 148–150. What was itself a remnant of a morning Office once included with the traditional burial psalms had now been reduced to the canticle and antiphon alone. Not only had ancient psalms thus been removed from the cemetery service for laity, but the new element itself was to lead a life of its own. Already in the *Sacerdotale Romanum*, this canticle and antiphon functioned differently in the rite for clerics from their role in the new rite for laity. Soon they would become a proper Roman chant for the funeral procession.

Thus, while attempting to form his authoritative 13th-century model into a new burial order for lay people, Castellani employed a principle whereby elements that he judged representative and constant were identified as essential and necessary. But when only "constant" elements are retained to the exclusion of variants, often every bit as "necessary," a traditional means to a variable expression of faith is cut off as well. What is "constant" then becomes rigidly fixed and normative.

What is most distinctly different here is not the ritual development itself. The process whereby priority comes to be accorded certain liturgical elements while others are removed to the background or disappear entirely is commonplace and familiar to liturgical study. Rather, in this situation, a reformulation seems to have been imposed from outside the normal pattern of ritual development. In the more normal situation, reformulation of rites served to bring liturgical books into line with already changed practice, and was far less radical. Liturgy is not as much a matter of logic as Castellani's work implied. Ordinarily, reformulation involves changing emphasis, and custom on the local scene determines practice. In such a natural process, changes like those noted in the *Sacerdotale Romanum* do occur, but only after indications of emphasis in earlier ritual books show that the practice in question has, in fact, fallen into disuse. As our comparison with contemporary diocesan manuals will show, that was not the case with either variant suffrages at the absolution service or with the traditional psalms at burial.

Castellani's was a praiseworthy effort to reduce liturgical chaos in the early 16th century and to educate the clergy in the proper celebration of Roman liturgy. Nevertheless, by constructing this abridged version of the Roman rite of burial for parochial use, he set precedent for reform that would contribute to an impoverished, rigid liturgy of Christian burial in the years to come. From then on the burial liturgy itself rather than any influence from conciliar decrees and papal bulls, would be responsible for the rigidity of the burial rite.

The Rite of Burial in the Sanctorius Ritual
In addition to the published edition of the *Rituale* of Cardinal Sanctorius, the Vatican Library preserves the annotated manuscript from which the final edition was produced.[6] Sanctorius there explains his ritual reforms and notes the sources that support his reasoning. In the funeral liturgy, he followed the 13th-century models and Castellani almost *verbatim*. His notes justify that choice as most in accord with the ancient and current Roman usage.

It was only by way of exception that Sanctorius incorporated a simpler rite for the burial of lay persons.

He explains that this is a novelty in the long Roman tradition where, in contrast to other liturgical usages, no distinctions are made in the funeral of clerics, religious, or lay Christians. Thus he urges pastors to celebrate the complete funeral liturgy, including the full Office of the Dead, for all deceased. Only truly bona fide custom (200 years or older) or very serious pastoral reasons, such as multiple funerals, are considered sufficient to justify the shorter rite. For use in those cases, Sanctorius followed Castellani's rite for the burial of laity as the most opportune. Unfortunately for us, he does not comment on the structure of the lay rite or on its actual use. The intended implication seems to be that it was rarely found in practice.

Both Sanctorius' strong protests and the constant presence of Castellani's rite in subsequent ritual books, however, indicate that the shorter rite was used quite frequently in pastoral practice. Despite the worthy Roman liturgical tradition of not distinguishing between persons in the liturgy of their funerals, in practice, that liturgy itself had outgrown the tradition and become too complex for general use. The simple version of funeral liturgy was here to stay. However, it would take the reforms of Vatican II and Paul VI to return to the Roman simplicity of celebrating the same funeral liturgy for all the baptized. The funeral of Pope Paul VI was itself the best exemplification of Sanctorius' principle of liturgical equity in the liturgy of Christian burial.

Meanwhile, from the 16th century to the present, the funeral liturgy for lay Christians according to Roman ritual books would bear the marks of Castellani and the influence of Sanctorius. Fortunately, the editorial committee for the *Roman Ritual* of 1614 consisted of pastors as well as scholars and followed the influence of existing diocesan practice as much as the didactic norms of Castellani and Sanctorius. Thus, it is to this third group of sources for the *Roman Ritual* that we now turn.

The Rite of Burial in Diocesan Rituals

Another kind of ritual, prepared for use in a specific diocese or province and authorized by the local ordinary, reflects both the variety of local liturgical usages that are reminiscent of the Middle Ages and the desire for local reform. This is not the place to provide an exhaustive study of these manuals, nor is any such intended. We are interested, rather, in a cross-section of documented information concerning diocesan rites of burial. A study of such manuals for some 25 dioceses across 16th-century Europe reveals a wide variety of expression within the traditionally familiar pattern. Some observe ritual types (or families) that stand in a direct ancestral line with earlier medieval tradition. Others reflect "modern" trends such as those in the *Sacerdotale Romanum*. We concentrate our attention on the former group, those preserving a type of parochial burial rite not yet influenced by an ideal Roman model such as Castellani's.

Witnesses of this type give an impression of the variety of traditional liturgical expression that was preserved in contemporary diocesan rites of burial. Assuming that such manuals, often recently updated, intended to express the faith of the contemporary Roman Catholic Church, one may examine the variety of expression preserved in them as an indication of that faith. In other words, these burial orders preserve for us genuine expressions of faith, which the ideal Roman rite of burial (according to Castellani and successors) relegated to the library shelf. Let us examine in some detail the two ritual moments whose transformation in ritual books we have been following.

The Absolution Service

At first glance, one is struck by the predominant place held in most of these burial orders by the responsories "Saints of God" and "Deliver me, O Lord, from eternal death" at the absolution in the church. Without a doubt, these two responsories had become an integral part of Christian burial during the Middle Ages. Together, they summarized the two major emphases of medieval prayer for the dead: an earlier Christian hope that the deceased will be received by God (Subvenite) and the subsequent fear of judgment and damnation (Libera me). That was the 13th-century "solution" Castellani preserved. Diocesan manuals, neither following the Roman-Franciscan model nor influenced by Castellani's reformulation, reflected different approaches.

The most striking is the one noted in some 16th-century French manuals that preserved intact an earlier absolution service dating to the Carolingian model of ninth-century Paris (St. Denis).[7] In these rituals, the earlier type of suffrages revealed a realistic Christian hope as their dominant motif. In addition to the responsory "Saints of God," one finds the richly scriptural responsory "You knew me, Lord, before I was born" (OCF, No. 403, 3). Its accompanying verse was a confession of human sinfulness and a prayer not to be condemned, thus reflecting an earlier Christian realism regarding judgment where trust in God's mercy was the prevailing tone rather than fear of hell.

These manuals support the assumption that a simple form of the absolution service had been preserved in parochial rituals. Moreover, they kept alive the spirit and balance of the Christian tradition incorporated in the St. Denis model, a tradition closer to Roman origins than that preserved in the later Roman model of the 13th century.

The responsory "Deliver me, O Lord" and the fearful faith it expressed had won the day. In fact, there are indications in some diocesan manuals that even the almost universally traditional practice of chanting the responsory "Saints of God" at the absolution could be supplanted.

That most hopeful of chants, praying for a safe passage through death and reception in eternity by Christ himself, unconditionally trusted God's mercy and forgiveness. For the still medieval Christian of the 16th century, fear colored such a trust, and anxious prayer for an almost unhoped-for mercy seemed far more urgent. Castellani's absolution service thus remains a reflection of traditional faith and late medieval religious sensibility. Although his model rite of burial limited the formulas of expression in the absolution, it preserved a sense of the traditional balance. Nevertheless, the shift in emphasis is apparent. For we encounter burial orders where not only the responsory "Saints of God" disappears altogether from these suffrages but where its counterpart, "Deliver me, O Lord," becomes the one and only responsory.[8] It is clear that the transition to the absolution service that would be included in the *Roman Ritual* of 1614 has already taken place. Further simplification would finally reduce the expression of faith at the absolution to the responsory "Deliver me, O Lord" alone.

Interment Services
The model Roman rite of burial for laity formulated by Castellani presented a cemetery service that was little more than an outline of liturgical actions, chants, and prayers proper to burial. The liturgical action consisted of a procession with the body to the place of burial, followed by interment and a final rite of sprinkling with holy water. The chant pieces, "May the angels lead you" and the Canticle of Zechariah with the anti-

phon "I am the resurrection" are indicated to accompany the first action while a short service, including the Lord's Prayer, some short versicles, and a prayer, filled out the rite of sprinkling.

Among diocesan manuals that continue the same Roman tradition as Castellani, some are seen to have preserved only the longer rite of burial (Castellani's rite for clerics, probably abbreviated in practice) while others printed an actual shorter version. The latter are of greater direct interest for our purposes, for they indicate how the simpler rites functioned in past oral usage.

The *Ritual* of the diocese Toulouse (1514, and possibly unchanged since the 1476 edition) provides an even earlier example of a shorter Roman interment service. This cemetery service recorded a practice which had preserved some very ancient liturgical elements, for example, Psalm 114, "When Israel came out of Egypt," as processional chant with the traditional antiphon *In paradisum*. Here too, as in Castellani's order, the traditional list of burial antiphons and psalms no longer played any role at all. The three morning psalms (148–150) with the antiphon "Let everything that has breath praise the Lord . . ." were included here among the processional chants. Upon arrival at the site of burial, after a blessing of the grave and an alternate antiphon with the canticle *Benedictus*, there was also the antiphon "I am the resurrection."

The redactor of this diocesan rite could take for granted that local custom determined when interment took place. We can assume that burial preceded the rite of final blessing and thus seems to have occurred during the chanting of this New Testament canticle with its antiphon.

In this Toulouse *Ritual*, we witness a shorter interment service that is older than Castellani's model. It appears therefore that precedents existed for the liturgical content of Castellani's abbreviated cemetery service. What remains interesting, however is the difference of pastoral manner between the two approaches to the same liturgy. Some later 16th-century manuals[9] also indicate that the antiphon "I am the resurrection" and canticle *Benedictus* accompanied burial itself. Taken together, these diocesan manuals reveal, however, tenuously, the living context within which the reform of Castellani and Sanctorius ought to be observed. Moreover, they clearly point to the pastoral tradition that the funeral liturgy of 1614 would stabilize for the universal Roman Catholic Church.

Some longer diocesan rituals faithfully preserve the tradition of psalms at burial, again dating from the ninth-century Carolingian model of St. Denis.[10] One Paris version corresponds almost totally to its ninth-century prototype. Its one additional rubric pertains to the custom whereby the priest threw some earth onto the casket while the antiphon-psalm set "Of earth you formed me" and Psalm 139 were chanted. This practice may be observed first in the monastic service of the 12th century where ritually covering the grave at burial in the earth became the parallel usage to closing the sarcophagus or tomb that was familiar in earlier medieval practice. This gesture was very popular indeed. Many diocesan rituals after Trent continued it and thus offer a good example of how post-Tridentine books continued to preserve in practice significant local liturgical customs after 1614.

Finally, one of the most influential diocesan pastoral rituals to exemplify this ongoing process is the famous *Pastorale* of Mechelen or Malines (Belgium). Its first three editions (1589, 1598, and 1607) contributed much to pastoral renewal throughout northern Europe in the decades between the council and the promulgation of the *Roman Ritual* in 1614. And this work has been identified as one of the sources of pastoral directives used by the editorial committee that produced that *Ritual*.

The cemetery service proper to the Mechelen diocese illustrates how Christian faith gave meaning to the essentially cultural action of laying to rest and leave-taking. Its widespread use outside Mechelen shows that this funeral liturgy was also popular elsewhere. A brief sketch can assist funeral ministers today both to appreciate similar funeral customs among certain ethnic groups and to recognize the potential for liturgical action at interment. Contrast, for example, the all-too-common antiseptic procedures of the modern cemetery that sometimes bespeak little faith or hope, with the down-to-earth truth of this diocesan rite.

The chants *In paradisum* and *Chorus angelorum* accompanied the funeral procession. Upon arrival at the grave, the body was laid to rest and sprinkled with holy water as the presider proclaimed: "Today, may your resting place be in peace and your dwelling in holy Sion. Through Christ our Lord. Amen." Taking the processional cross the priest signed the grave three times: "I sign this body with the sign of the holy cross so that on the day of judgment it may rise and possess everlasting life. Through Jesus Christ our Lord. Amen."

Then followed the older custom noted above of throwing earth onto the casket with the words adapted from Psalm 139 and Job 10 and 19; "Of earth you formed him (her); you wove him (her) with bones and sinews, O Lord: raise him (her) up on the last day. Through Jesus Christ our Lord. Amen." A short litany, versicles, and prayers followed. Finally, the grave was sprinkled again as the celebrant said: "May God shower you with dew from heaven in the name of the Father and of the Son and of the Holy Spirit. Amen." Where this rite is observed today, relatives and friends often sprinkle the grave or throw a handful of earth or a flower onto the casket as they pass by one final time before leaving—a sign of the constancy with which tradition perdures in contemporary liturgical usage.

Before closing this brief review of funeral *liturgica* before Trent, it is worth noting that toward the end of the Middle Ages, liturgical manuscripts began to reveal additional formularies entitled "for the burial of children." The origins of celebrating a separate funeral liturgy for baptized children remain shrouded in medieval history. In the 13th century, it seems, the same funeral liturgy was still observed for adults and children. St. Thomas Aquinas provides an indication that this was general practice, for he uses such liturgical usage to argue that baptized children pertain to the unity of the mystical body of Christ.[11]

Funeral Liturgy for Children
When these formularies for the burial of children first appear in our witnesses, children's funerals still had the same shape as adults' but a content of their own. A rite for the burial of children was familiar to Castellani and Sanctorius from, among other sources, a 15th-century manuscript ritual from Capua and the general *Libellus catechumenorum* (Brescia, 1511). These represented two distinct liturgies, and it was the Capua version, apparently more representatively Roman, that survived. With very slight variants, that service for children appeared in Castellani's *Sacerdotale Romanum* (and other later general manuals), the Sanctorius *Ritual*, a wide variety of 16th-century diocesan manuals, and finally in the *Roman Ritual* of 1614.

This funeral rite itself was thoroughly scriptural, except for the prayer formulas. These exemplified the tendency of the times toward theologizing in the liturgy. The predominant tone was one of joy and thanksgiving. Despite St. Thomas' explanation that the funeral Mass for baptized children was a consolation to the living, the absence of any reference to the pain of the bereaved at such an untimely death surprises the modern reader. Clearly, late medieval attitudes toward death and bereavement were different from ours.

The antiphons, psalms, and canticles accommodated biblical texts about children to the funeral setting. For example, Psalm 113, "You servants [Vulgate: children] of God, praise, praise the name of the Lord," set the opening tone. Psalm 24, "To God belong the earth and all it holds," dwelt on the innocence of the deceased child. In procession to the cemetery, all chanted Psalm 148, "Let the heavens praise the Lord," using verse 12 as antiphon, "Young men and girls, old people and children, too—let them praise the name of the Lord. . ."

The prayers, on the other hand, proclaimed theologically the absolute dependence of all, even children, on the infinite goodness of God. They taught the effects of baptism and reminded the living of their commitments. Few of the surviving prayers represent the theological balance with which St. Thomas Aquinas had described the celebration of Mass for deceased children. Emphasizing, of course, that Mass for baptized children was never celebrated for the remission of sin nor for the increase of grace (a debated position), St. Thomas taught that such celebrations consoled the living, proclaimed the mystery of redemption (because children, too, through no merit of their own, received eternal salvation), and demonstrated that they belonged to the mystical body of Christ.[12] These pastoral theological explanations apply beautifully to the spirit of funeral renewal after Vatican II. In the 16th century, they were still too overshadowed by late medieval preoccupations with the dread of death (hell) to find complete fruition even in the funeral liturgy for children.

Pastoral instructions published with the various rites reveal that the question of Mass for baptized infants and children who died before the age of reason remained a serious issue. All insisted that *Mass for the Dead* was not to be celebrated for them because they had never committed sin—a clear commentary on how the funeral Mass was understood. Sanctorius hesitatingly allowed that such a Mass could be celebrated *on the occasion* of their funeral but *for* their *deceased* adult relatives or others. Most other sources recommended one of the votive Masses in honor of the Trinity, the Holy Spirit, or the Angels. Occasionally, a suggestion appeared favoring the Mass of the day, especially if it was a feast, including a commemoration of the dead child. Among the diocesan manuals studied, only one incorporates a special set of Mass formularies for the funeral of children, and even that disappeared in the next edition of the book.[13] Editions of the *Roman Ritual* of 1614 were silent about Mass on those occasions, but the practice of choosing one of the votive Masses became the custom, particularly the Mass of the Angels. From this would follow the reference to deceased infants as "little angels before the face of God" and the designation of their special part of the cemetery by infant cherubs.

A very different matter indeed was the funeral of children who died without baptism. Across the entire spectrum of witnesses to funeral liturgy for children before Trent, priests and faithful were explicitly forbidden to mark the burial of the unbaptized with any Christian ceremony whatsoever. Such children were to be buried in a plot outside the cemetery and often in the evening. The liturgy of the Church offered neither prayer for them nor consolation to their parents. The most frequently cited authority for this harsh but logically consistent attitude was a canon of the second Council of Braga (ca. 560) that forbade both the celebration of Mass and the chanting of psalms for "catechumens who died without the redemption of baptism."[14] They were compared with suicides by the Braga Council.

Despite the matter-of-fact tone of our sources, the faithful undoubtedly experienced this to be painfully severe. Reactions led to abuses. Sanctorius commented, for example, on the practice by some ignorant priests and laity of burying such unfortunate infants under the eaves of churches in the superstitious hope that rainwater running off the roof would "baptize" them.

Although the *Roman Ritual* of 1614 did not explicitly prohibit funeral liturgy for nonbaptized children, the custom of burial without rites continued well into the 20th century. As infant deaths became fewer and fewer, the loss of a child caused even greater pain, and Christian parents felt ever more deeply the silence and seeming rejection on the part of their church. The revised *Order of Christian Funerals* would offer their 20th-century counterparts new hope at such a tragedy. In the meantime, however, reform movements after Trent attempted to soften the blow by revising the language of the prohibition. Yet only a revised theology and renewal of liturgy could affect the kind of change embodied in the 1969 *Ordo*.

FUNERAL LITURGY FROM THE ROMAN RITUAL (1614) TO THE ORDER OF FUNERALS (1969)
The history of funeral liturgy up to this final turning point has shown that the so-called Tridentine rite of burial was no stranger when it appeared in the early 17th century. Nor will it be a surprise, by this stage of our survey, that funeral liturgy would continue to develop locally in much the same way as it always had.

One major difference, however, was the normative character that the Roman liturgical books were given by order of the Council of Trent and by the popes who promulgated them. Although Pope Paul V allowed greater freedom in his promulgation of the *Roman Ritual* of 1614, there is no question that it was regarded as normative in practice. The postconciliar years—the period of the Counter-Reformation—was an age in need of norms. The more such an attitude came to be coupled with the growing centralization of ecclesiastical jurisdiction in the papal curia, the more the *Roman Ritual* became in fact a normative manual. Its official interpreter was the recently founded Congregation of Rites.

The apparent hope of Pope Paul V for a "peaceful coexistence"[15] between authorized diocesan rituals and the *Roman Ritual* could not prevent the decline of the former in the face of the subtle forces aligned against them, i.e., the authority of Rome and the prestige Roman norms enjoyed among clergy and people. Although the *Ritual* of 1614 itself professed to respect other genuinely revered traditions, its tone was unmistakably normative, and contemporaries understood that it was meant to be the norm for the Roman Catholic Church. Even the titles of those diocesan books that continued to maintain genuine local traditions spoke of "accommodation to the *Roman Ritual*." For example, later editions of the familiar manual of Mechelen bore the title *Pastorale Rituali Romano Accommodatum*.

This was thus a normative age with two consequences for funeral liturgy. Not only did the rite of burial in the *Roman Ritual* become the norm, but local rites were made to conform to that norm, with the result that liturgy was becoming a matter of correctly executing appropriate rites. Consequently, funeral liturgy became more and more divorced from the human experience of death and from the pastoral care for the dying and the bereaved. It became more a reliquary of late medieval Christianity than a proclamation of a living paschal faith in everlasting life through Jesus, dead and risen, that can give real hope to the bereaved in the Christian community.

This is not to say that such faith did not exist. Faith was indeed alive, but it concentrated its attention on the lot of the deceased in purgatory, mirrored in the funeral rites, and expressed its vitality more in popular devotions than in the liturgy. Novenas and pious practices such as visits to the Blessed Sacrament and the rosary, as well as an emphasis on indulgences gained "for the poor souls" meant more to the faithful than the funeral liturgy. In this context, even the Mass was "applied" for the release of souls from purgatory. By this point in ritual history, "saying Mass" had come, by way of later medieval piety, to mean performing the ritual of the order of Mass correctly so that the fruits of Calvary could be applied to the living and the dead. In the same way, funeral liturgy, including the funeral Mass, came to be performed for the repose of the soul of the deceased.

When such rubricism began to predominate in ecclesial life, it was fortunate that those responsible for drafting the rite of burial for the *Roman Ritual* of 1614 had for their consultation a dozen or more pastoral sources such as the *Pastorale* of Mechelen and that they preserved a sense of the longer funerary tradition as documented and popularized by such pastoral scholars as Castellani and Sanctorius. Above all, we should be grateful for the drafters' willingness to rely more on the pastoral practice of living liturgy than on their personal theological propensities.

However dominant its emphasis on the fearful lot of the deceased, the post-Tridentine rite of burial sufficiently enshrined the tradition to preserve an essential balance between confident hope and realistic prayer for forgiveness. How that rite and its "balance" was experienced varied a great deal from the 17th to the 20th century. One can imagine the effect of the many influences during those formative times of modern history, such as the late Baroque period, the rise and spread of Protestantism, missionary expansion to the Orient and the Americas, the age of reason, political revolutions and independence, Neo-Gallicanism, Jansenism, Romanticism, two world wars, and so on. After reviewing the rite, which itself remained virtually unchanged during all those changing times, we shall comment briefly on its world context.

The Funeral Liturgy in the Roman Ritual of 1614
The *exsequiarum ordo*[16] opened with the parish priest and ministers going to meet the body at the home of the deceased. There the body was sprinkled with holy water, and Psalm 130, "Out of the depths I cry to you, O Lord," was recited. Although this psalm of trust in God's mercy preserved a tone of Christian hope through many centuries of funeral liturgy, later medieval spirituality concentrated on the image of the opening words: "Out of the depths." The proper antiphon (verse 3), "If you, O Lord, mark iniquities, Lord, who can stand?" indicates the attitude with which the psalm was prayed. This was quite a shift from the earlier spirituality that suggested the antiphon *In paradisum* with Psalm 130.

When the body was brought out of the house, the priest intoned in a serious tone (*gravi voce*) the processional antiphon, "They will rejoice in the Lord (the bones that you have crushed)" with Psalm 51, "Have mercy on me, O God. . . ." Here again, the antiphon (Psalm 51: 8) carried the promise of rejoicing and yet dwelt on the negative, rendering this once hope-filled psalm a somber penitential plea in the funeral liturgy. The common earlier antiphon used with Psalm 51 during this transfer read: "Lord, grant that the soul you have taken up from its body may rejoice with your saints in glory. . . ." This antiphon was reinstated in the 1969 *Ordo*, where the English version adapted the body-soul language as well as the meaning of the last phrase to read: "Lord, may our brother (sister), whom you have called to yourself, find happiness in the glory of your saints" (ROF, No. 149). In the more concise style of the *Order of Christian Funerals*, the antiphon reads: "Caught up with Christ, rejoice with the saints in glory" (No. 347, 4).

This rite of transfer was identical to local usage in the diocese of Brescia, whose pastoral manual served as one of the sources of the *Roman Ritual*.[17] This is a good example of how local liturgical usage found its way into the universal practice of the post-Tridentine Church. Moreover, it was understandable that the 1612 editorial committee would have looked to a diocesan ritual for the liturgy of this transfer. Neither general manuals, such as that of Albertus Castellani, nor the Roman pontifical versions represented current practice in this matter. Among the committee's respected diocesan sources, the Ritual of Brescia presented a practical pastoral solution to the transfer that was at once sufficiently Roman in its tradition and enjoyed the authority of Brescia's reform-minded Bishop Bollanus. Whatever else contributed to their choice, such considerations surely played a role.

In addition to Psalm 51, other psalms are indicated for occasions when the distance between home and church was long. Upon arrival at the church door, the antiphon was repeated in full. Then, with the entrance of the body into the church, the service continued along the lines set forth in most contemporary manuals. In cases that involved long distances, it is evident that the transfer from the home was already a lay responsibility. The parish priest would meet the procession at the entrance to the town or sometimes at the churchyard.[18]

When the body entered the church, the post-Tridentine rite, following the widespread practice of the time, presented the responsory "Saints of God" with its appropriate verse. Traditional directives for arranging the body in the church and for chanting the Office of the Dead followed. After the *Benedictus* of Lauds, with its antiphon, "I am the resurrection," a short service of versicles and a prayer of absolution closed the Hours. During Lauds, however, the priest was directed to prepare for the solemn celebration of Mass, if the hour was opportune.

Late editions of the *Roman Ritual* would make an alternative provision. Even in the 1614 edition, the presumption seems to be that the body remain in the church until Mass could be celebrated next day. This was quite explicit elsewhere, for example, in the Salisbury (Sarum) *Manuale Sacerdotum* of 1610,[19] with its "ancient Catholic tradition," and in the practice of the *Pastorale* of Mechelen, a neighbor to Douai, where the English Catholic exiles printed the Sarum text of 1610. The Mass to be celebrated was that of the recently published *Missale Romanum* (1570), i.e., the *Requiem*. After Mass, the priest and ministers were directed to gather at the bier. The rubrics here are explicitly clear, undoubtedly the work of a rubrical stylist. The absolution service that followed revealed an attempt to be, again, both pastoral and Roman.

Taking the reform even beyond abbreviations of Castellani, the editorial committee followed an absolution service that was already in use elsewhere, for example, in the diocese of Verona.[20] As indicated above, pastoral practice seems to have preserved only one set of suffrages, i.e., a prayer, the responsory "Deliver me, O Lord, from eternal death" with its verses, followed by versicles, the Lord's Prayer, and a closing prayer. The opening, no longer an invitation to prayer, but since the 13th century a prayer formula, read:

"Do not enter into judgment with your servant, O Lord, for in your sight no man shall be justified, except that you grant him remission of all his sins. Do not, therefore, permit, we beseech you, your sentence of judgment to weigh heavily upon him, for his true petition of Christian faith commends him to you. But by the help of your grace, may he deserve to escape the judgment of vengeance, he who while he lived was sealed with the sign of the Blessed Trinity: who lives and reigns forever. Amen."

This typically Mozarabic text, which became commonplace in the Roman funeral liturgy, exemplifies how Catholic faith was preserved in medieval prayer while the emphasis revealed the preoccupations of contemporary piety. There is little wonder that the present Roman *Ordo* did not choose to retain this prayer. But in the context of 1614, when many aspects of late medieval spirituality still prevailed, it set the tone well for the responsory to follow, "Deliver me, O Lord, from eternal death." During the singing of this responsory, incense and holy water were prepared, and afterward, while the Lord's Prayer was said (silently, except for intonation and closing), the priest incensed and sprinkled the deceased. Versicles followed, and the closing prayer of the absolution was read:

"O God, whose nature it is to be merciful and to pardon, humbly we beseech you for the sake of the soul of your servant, (name), which today you ordered to depart this world. Do not deliver it into the hands of the enemy nor forget it at the end [of time], but order it to be taken by the holy angels and brought to the fatherland of paradise, so that because it hoped and believed in you, [this soul] may not suffer the pains of hell but possess everlasting joy. Through Christ our Lord. Amen."

This literal translation preserves the emphasis of the original Latin on the prayer's concern with the lot of the separated soul as well as its view of God as judge. While faith in the just God who is *merciful* has indeed been preserved, the prayer speaks most to the merciful God who demands *justice*.

The final note of this absolution prayer looked ahead to the antiphon indicated for the recessional with the body, the very traditional processional chant "May the angels lead you into paradise." Here the companion chant, "May the choir of angels," was joined with *In paradisum* to form one recessional piece, a musical anomaly because they had been sung traditionally in two different chant modes, the seventh and eighth, respectively. Apparently, as the 1613 manuscript reveals, the text of the rite of 1614 was drafted without considering the musical quality of these (or any) chants.

Because the antiphons *In paradisum* and *Chorus angelorum* had for centuries followed each other as alternate processional chants, it is likely that in practice they had been sung together, possibly as one chant. There is a hint of evidence for this in the Franciscan *Breviary* of 1260, where they appear written as one. Nevertheless, the committee's most direct sources, such as Castellani and Sanctorius, as well as the diocesan rituals of Brescia, Mechelen, and Verona, referred to them as distinct *antiphonae*. Whether the Tridentine editors were regularizing custom in writing or setting a new course, the result was that these two traditional chants, *In paradisum* and *Chorus angelorum*, were treated as one *antiphona* by Roman funeral liturgy for the next 350 years.

It is apparent from the shift of emphasis in later editions of the *Roman Ritual* that these chants became more and more part of the service in church and less of processional antiphons. In 1614, the direction was to omit the responsory *In paradisum* when the body was not taken directly to the grave, just as the blessing of the grave was omitted when it had already been blessed. Later editions revealed, however, that in such cases the combined antiphon was to be sung all the time *in eodem loco* (in the same place). Thus, the *processional* antiphon *In paradisum-Chorus angelorum* of the earlier tradition would become inseparable from Catholic funeral liturgy *in the church*.

The 20th-century drafters of the 1969 *Ordo* followed this practice by placing it in a similar interim position as recessional chant (OF, No. 50), even where the funeral procession as such no longer survives. In this way, the chant would accompany at least the initial movement with the body toward its last resting place, corresponding to the original theme "May the angels lead you into paradise." Happily, the *Order of Christian Funerals* (1989) has eliminated the interim recessional by restoring the funeral procession and the *In paradisum-Chorus angelorum* chants to their traditional place in the *ordo* (No. 176).

The *Roman Ritual* of 1614, like its model sources, did not conceive of a long distance from church to grave. Burial in church or adjacent churchyard was still the implied practice. Upon arrival, after singing or reciting the processional chants, the grave was blessed (if necessary) using the following prayer that the 1989 *Order* also preserves among alternate texts in an adapted English translation:

O God,
by whose mercy the faithful departed find rest,
bless this grave,
and send your holy angel to watch over it.

As we bury here the body of our brother/sister,
deliver his/her soul from every bond of sin,
that he/she may rejoice in you with your saints for
ever.

We ask this through Christ our Lord.

(No. 405, 2)

Compared with the different local traditions that had
developed and lasted as Christian graveside rituals,
such as the one from Mechelen reviewed above, the
Tridentine funeral liturgy was stark. In this, it was
even more austere than the earlier traditional Roman
cemetery service with its psalms during interment, covering, and the like. Reform influence such as that of
Castellani was probably more responsible for this than
Roman austerity.

When it was time for burial, the priest was to sprinkle
the body and the grave with holy water and to incense them. Without further mention of interment or
other disposition, the *Roman Ritual* next presented the
New Testament canticle *Benedictus*, with its antiphon,
"I am the resurrection." Practice differed as to
whether burial took place before, during, or after this
canticle. Even where churches preserved local customs
of throwing earth or covering, signing with the cross,
etc., some inserted these before and some after the assigned *Benedictus*. However appropriate to the final
cemetery action this johannine antiphon might have
been, the *Roman Ritual* remained vague about its specific function. Some of the arbitrariness of Castellani's
short rite remained here. This is noteworthy when
compared with the explicit, almost exaggerated detail
of the absolution rubrics. Such differences point up
the rite's priorities.

The familiar funerary versicles and the Lord's Prayer
were a preparation for the final prayer that the editors
of 1613 found to be a popular closing prayer in their

102

sources (e.g., Verona, 1536). They prescribed it as conclusion to the cemetery service, and the present rite retains it (in an adapted English version) in the same position.

God of holiness and power,
accept our prayers on behalf of your servant N.;
do not count his/her deeds against him/her,
for in his/her heart he/she desired to do your will.
As his/her faith united him/her to your people on earth,
so may your mercy join him/her to the angels in heaven.

We ask this through Christ our Lord. (No. 222, A)

For more than a thousand years this prayer has preserved the theological balance of Catholic funeral liturgy: faith, church, community of saints, divine mercy and forgiveness, and a joyful life everlasting. This is realistic liturgy founded on paschal faith. It neither denies human weakness and sin nor exaggerates fear of a vengeful God; it neither denies the paschal mystery nor exaggerates resurrection without death.

After this prayer, the rite of 1614 provided an antiphon-psalm set to be recited while returning to the church (or sacristy). Although this was more than likely a clerical directive, it stood in a long tradition of maintaining a prayerful unity from beginning to end of the funeral liturgy.

Finally, two corrections in the 1613 manuscript of the cemetery service deserve attention. One is the addition of a rubric connected to the Lord's Prayer, indicating that the priest was to sprinkle the body with holy water. This obvious duplication in short succession, clearly by analogy to the absolution service, alerts the observer to the starkness and lack of tradition in this recently abbreviated Roman interment liturgy.

The second and more significant is the editorially added rubric that emphasized the independent liturgical role acquired by the New Testament canticle and antiphon *Benedictus-Ego sum resurrectio* (with accompanying versicles and prayer). The rubric specified that these were never to be omitted (*quod numquam omittitur*). Thus, when the body was not to be taken to burial, the chant *In paradisum-Chorus angelorum* was to be omitted and the canticle and antiphon *Ego sum resurrectio-Benedictus*, together with versicles, responses, and oration, would be sung or recited in the church.

This reflects the reformist tendency of Castellani and others. In the *Roman Ritual* of 1614, certain formularies, chants, and gestures were edited to constitute the rite of burial. When they were carried out according to the rubrics, whether or not in correspondence to their meaning (for example, processional chant, burial formulary, or the like), that was still considered funeral liturgy. The "rubrical funeral" of the *Roman Ritual* would become, in the years ahead, more a context of personal expression, both devotional piety and secular pomp reflecting the moods of the times, than vital liturgical expression of faith in the paschal mystery. When it no longer mattered whether liturgy really meant what it said or did (as praying over an empty catafalque), then other practices emerged to express the piety—and sometimes the superstition—of the clergy and faithful. When liturgy is divorced from life, devotional practices and folklore tend to replace it altogether rather than co-exist with it in natural symbiosis of religious expression.

Funeral Liturgy After Trent
To glean a faint idea of liturgical life at the time when the *Roman Ritual* was published, we might imagine ourselves with one foot in the late Middle Ages and

the other in the emerging "modern" era. In some
ways, the 20th-century experience of "future shock" is
similar. Liturgically, basic form and content changed
very little after Trent. In fact, the council's liturgical
goal was to preserve and protect that form and content against Protestant opposition to Catholic liturgical
forms. Funeral liturgy was an explicit target of Reformation eschatology. As the form and content of funeral liturgy remained virtually unchanged, the context within which that liturgy was performed changed
with the cultural patterns of a world that was developing economically, technologically, and internationally.
The ethnic web of European cultures expanded both
East and West. Through all that, the Tridentine rite of
burial remained a clerical liturgy whereby parish
priests in old Europe as well as missionaries to Japan
and the Americas laid their dead to rest while the
faithful stood by and watched.[21]

Piety after Trent has been characterized as didactic,
pragmatic, and aliturgical.[22] Some of the concerns we
meet in the pastoral manuals on funeral liturgy confirm this general judgment. Considerable emphasis,
for example, was put on explaining to parish priests
the rites and practices of the liturgy so that they might
teach their people its meaning. This was especially apparent in churches that were surrounded by Protestant
communities with their teaching against public liturgy
on behalf of the dead.[23]

Popular piety outside the liturgy also taught its lesson.
Tolling church bells at the time of a funeral, for example, not only honored the deceased and called all to
pray for the dead but was a recurring reminder of
faith in the immortality of the soul. So-called death
planks carved with skulls and symbols of death were
frequent reminders of death in villages and at country-
side crossroads. Inscriptions on cemetery gates taught
the passerby: "What you are now, so once was I; what

I am now, soon you will be." Even the funeral liturgy itself served as a *memento mori*, and prayer for the deceased was not entirely untainted by concern for one's own death and the expectation of like suffrages for oneself.

One widespread exception to accommodation to and gradual adoption of the *Roman Ritual* after Trent stands out in the "neo-Gallican" dioceses of France. During the 17th and 18th centuries, they created rituals that contained thorough pastoral directives pertaining both to funerary care and theology and to new liturgical rites. Although many of these differed from earlier diocesan traditions *and* from the *Roman Ritual*, they stood in continuity with the longer tradition generally.

The best example of such a book was the influential and widely used ritual of the diocese of Alet (1667). More interesting than the funeral liturgy it presents is its companion, *Instructions of the Ritual*.[24] Arranged in question-and-answer form, this pastoral manual explained Catholic liturgy and the faith it expressed in easily understandable language. With regard to the funeral, it took up questions of the tradition (Why does the priest go to meet the deceased? Why do Christians burn candles at funerals?) as well as issues of concern even today (Why offer Mass for the dead? Why do prayers imply that the deceased is still going to meet God when he or she has already died?). Throughout the 15 pages devoted to the funeral, a concern for a biblical emphasis and a reserve about unchristian pomp is notable. In the late 20th century, this pastoral approach to the liturgy would be appreciated. In the wake of Trent, however, it appeared but one national barrier to the new uniform ecclesiology.

The explicit didacticism of liturgy during the later Enlightenment built upon these tendencies and sought to

106

channel their potential to achieve even greater results for the betterment of society. Typical of this approach was a proposal for a new ritual in the diocese of Constance (1806). It was intended as a guide to better pastoral use of the *Roman Ritual*. Its section on funeral liturgy was laced with vernacular hymns, prayers, and a closing exhortation. One rubric insisted on the use of the vernacular for the words "Remember man, you are dust." The rest was in Latin. The priest's final exhortation at the cemetery exemplified the "edification theology" of the Catholic Enlightenment in German lands. Aware of the grief that is present at funerals, the text spoke of how death makes one think of the needs of this world and teaches truth, virtue, and devotion. Reflection on death was not to sadden the Christian but to strengthen courage and to give consolation and relief under the weight of the burdens of life.[25]

The funeral after Trent was generally characterized more by pastoral attention on the part of the clergy—whatever their theologies at different times—than by inner liturgical reform. Where pastoral care touched the liturgy, it was often as an appendage to the *Roman Ritual*. For example, model words of consolation and encouragement in the vernacular are appended at the conclusion to the rite of burial in many diocesan books. In the same way, an insert with formularies for centuries-old local usages—at the cemetery, for example—are bound in their proper place but clearly as a supplement to the universal *Ritual*.

Together with authoritative Roman commentaries such as that by Hieronymus Baruffaldo (1735),[26] local books, such as the French and German manuals just mentioned, illustrated the way in which Catholic funeral liturgy between the 16th and the mid-20th century was experienced. Immigrant churches abroad were no different, except that ethnic traditions, even at funerals, soon gave way entirely to the universal *Roman Ritual*, especially under the influence of romanticism and ultramontanism during the 19th century. As the 20th century progressed, ethnic customs died out quite naturally when they were in fact no longer authentic expressions of third- and fourth-generation descendents of earlier immigrants.

Despite all the pastoral emphasis surrounding it, the Catholic funeral remained something the Church performed *for* the deceased. Similarly, it was not funeral liturgy as such that responded to the emergence in the 20th century of the modern burial customs. As recently as 1952, for example, one commentary superbly continued the pastoral effort to place the Tridentine rite of burial in its best light.[27] Yet the rite itself read as if almost nothing had changed since 1614 and before.

In practice, however, the *Roman Ritual* was accommodating itself to growing cities, remote cemeteries, the new prominence of the funeral home, embalming, and the like. The *English ritual* of 1964 marked the end of a process already well under way in the first edition of the *Ritual* of 1614, whereby rites surrounding the funeral Mass became "telescoped" in the church. In the United States, for example, funeral liturgy in 1964 ordinarily began at the entrance to the church. Similarly, due to distance, weather, and other inconveniences, it likewise frequently absorbed into the closing rite of absolution the *Canticle of Zechariah* and its antiphon, "I am the resurrection," from the cemetery service. In this telescoped 20th-century version, the *Ego sum* and *Benedictus* are added to the *In Paradisum-Chorus* chants, which in the 1614 edition were to be omitted on such occasions.

That same year, 1964, exactly 350 years after the promulgation of the *Roman Ritual*, marked the beginning of a process of liturgical renewal promulgated by Vatican Council II the previous December. The following chapters will study the first quarter century of that renewal as it has transformed the liturgy of the Christian funeral. After this long journey through funerary and ritual development one will understand that the revised *Ordo exsequiarum* and its 1989 English rendering in the *Order of Christian Funerals* are themselves but a beginning of renewal of Roman Catholic funeral liturgy, according to Vatican II. They offer us a vastly restored proclamation of faith and constitute the current stage in a process that we have followed from its origins.

NOTES

1. See Philippe Ariès, *The Hour of Our Death* (New York: Knopf, 1981).

2. See for example K. Ottosen, N. K. Rasmussen, and C. Thodberg, eds., *The Manuals from Notmark* (Gl. kgl. Saml. 3453, 80/14th c. on vellum), Bibliotheca Liturgica Danica, Series Latina, I (Copenhagen: G.E.C. Gad, 1970), pp. 97–108, and A. Franz, "Zur Geschichte der gedruckten Passauer Ritualien," *Theologischpraktische Monats-Schrift* 9 (1899), pp. 75–85, 180–185, and 288–299 (including comparison of the 15th c. Ritual of Passau).

3. *Liber Sacerdotalis* (Venetiis: M. Sessam-P. de Rauanis Socios, 1523), capita 21:31.

4. *Rituale Sacramentorum Romanum Gregorii Papae XIII Pont. Max. iussu editum* (Rome, 1584). See Bruno Löwenberg, *Das Rituale des Kardinals Julius Antonius Sanctorius. Ein Beitrag zur Entstehungsgeschichte des Rituale Romanum* (Diss. 1937, Teildruk, Munich: Druk der Salesianischen Offizin., 1937).

5. The funeral of Pope Paul VI in 1978 sealed the end of that era and demonstrated dramatically how great can be the solemnity of noble simplicity.

6. Vat. lat. ms. 6116. The author wishes to express his gratitude to the Rev. Damien Sicard, who introduced him to this

manuscript and generously shared his microfilm copy of it until it was possible to consult the work itself in the Vatican Library.

7. B. N. lat. ms. 2290. Edition with *incipits:* E. Martène, *De antiquis Ecclesiae ritibus,* III (Antwerp, 1736), pp. 385–386. Among these are Rituals of the churches of Meaux (ed. 1546), Paris (ed. 1552), and Rouen (ed. 1587).

8. Already in 1536, a manual of the diocese of Verona presents the following absolution service:
Oratio: *Non intres . . .*
Resp.: *Libera me, Domine, de morte . . .*
VV.: *Tremens . . . , Dies illa . . . , Requiem . . . Kyrie . . . Pater . . .*
Oratio: *Deus cui omnia/indulgendo. per*

9. For example, those of Yper (ed. 1576), Bordeaux (ed. 1588), and Madrid (ed. 1595).

10. These include, among others, the *Institutio Catholica* of Paris (ed. 1552) and the *manuals* of Meaux (ed. 1546) and Rouen (ed. 1587).

11. Maria Fabianus Moos, O.P., ed., *S. Thomae Aquinatis Scriptum Super Sententiis Magistri Petri Lombardi,* Tome IV, super Lib. IV, d.12, q.2, art.1, 2m. (Paris: P. Lethielleux, 1947), p. 526. The full text reads:

Ad secundum dicendum quod pro pueris baptizatis Missarum solemnia celebratur, non quia eis juventur quantum ad remissionem alicujus culpae vel quantum ad augmentum gloriae, sed propter alias rationes: tum propter solatium vivorum; tum ad ostendendum parvulos ad unitatem corporis mystici pertinere, dum idem modus exequiarum servatur in ipsis et in aliis; tum ad commendandum redemptionis mysterium quod in hoc sacramento commemoratur, per quod parvuli sine proprio merito salutem consequuntur aeternam.

12. See St. Thomas' explanation above and also, among others, the *ritual* of Reims (ed. 1621): *Missa celebratur, pro parvulis baptisatis, non quidem ad remissionem culpae, nec ad augmentum gloriae, sed ad solatium vivorum, et ad commendandum redemptionis nostrae mysterium, ad gratiarum actiones pro eis et ad ostendendum quod pertinent ad corpus christi mysticum.*

13. See the Cambrai manuals of 1562, 1606, and 1622.

14. *Item placuit, ut catechumenis sine redemptione baptismi defunctis, simili modo, neque oblationis commemoratio neque psallendi impendatur officum: nam et hoc per ignorantiam usurpatum est.* See Giovanni Domenico Mansi, ed. *Sacrorum conciliorum nova et amplissima collectio*, IX (Paris: H. Welter, 1900–1927), pp. 779–780. (Although referred to as the "first" Council of Braga in our rituals and by Isidore and the earlier Jesuit collection in Paris, the council in question has been shown to be in fact the second Council of Braga. See Mansi, IX, p. 779, 1.)

15. Term used in this context by Balthasar Fischer, "Das *Rituale Romanum* (1614–1964): Die Schicksale eines liturgischen Buches," *Trierer Theologische Zeitschrift* 73 (1964), pp. 257–271.

16. The following brief description is based on the final manuscript version of the *Rituale* (1613) that belonged to the Barnabite priest J. A. Gabutius (member of the editorial commission) and used with the kind permission of Professor Dr. Balthasar Fischer, Liturgisches Institut, Trier.

17. *Rituale Sacramentorum* authorized by D. Bollanus, Bishop of Brescia, 1675. This ritual served as a model for both Sanctorius and the Tridentine commission of editors.

18. For example, *Rituale Sacramentorum* of Geneva issued by authority of Bishop Francis de Sales (Lyons: J. Charvet, 1614).

19. A. J. Collins, ed., *Manuale as usum percelebris ecclesiae Sarisburienis, Henry Bradshaw Society* 91 (1958), ms. p. 296.

20. *Liber catechumenorum*, Verona, 1536.

21. See, for example, the Japanese ritual, *Manuale ad Sacramenta Ecclesiae Ministranda*, D. Ludovici Cerquerira Japonensis Episcopi opera ad usum sui cleri ordinatum cum approbatione et facultate (Nangasaquii: Collegio Japonico Societatis Jesu, 1605) and the ritual of Peru, *Rituale seu Manuale Peruanum*, L. J. de Ore (Naples, 1607).

22. Aloys Schrott, "Die Trienter Reform im Spiegel der nachfolgenden Andachtsliteratur," in G. Schreiber, ed., *Das Weltkonzil von Trient*, I (Freiburg: Herder, 1951), pp. 349–350.

23. For example, the *Rituale Sacramentorum* of Bishop Francis de Sales (Lyons: J. Charvet, 1614). See also, Rowell, *Christian Burial*, pp. 74–98.

24. *Les Instructiones du Rituel du diocese d'Alet* (Paris: A. Des Hayes, 1719).

25. *Entwurf eines neuen Rituals von einer Gesellschaft katholischer Geistlichen des Bistums Constanz* (Tübingen: J. F. Heerbrandt, 1806).

26. Hieronymus Baruffaldo, *Ad Rituale Romanum Commentaria* (Augsburg: J. C. Bencards, 1735).

27. Philip T. Weller, *The Roman Ritual*, II (Milwaukee: Bruce, 1952), pp. v–xviii, 2–37.

The Reformed
Order of Christian Funerals

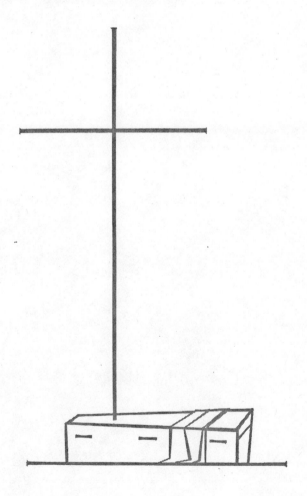

Chapter Four

The Order in General

On August 15, 1969, the Sacred Congregation for Divine Worship published for the universal Roman Catholic Church the official Latin version of the *Ordo Exsequiarum*.[1] This publication marked the end of the most extensive authorized program of guided liturgical experimentation up to that time in the post-Vatican II revision of the liturgical books. It likewise heralded the imminent appearance of the first indigenous funeral rites for the English-speaking world reflecting the results of international contributions to the work of revision. Thus, study of the Catholic funeral today embraces both the Latin model (typical edition) and the culturally adapted editions of regional churches. In English-speaking countries—for example, Canada or Great Britain—funeral liturgy differs in cultural detail from practice in the United States. Yet all these are versions of the Roman *Ordo Exsequiarum*, revised and culturally adapted over the years.[2]

To distinguish the various ritual books that bear witness to this development, this present work uses the title *Order of Funerals* (1969) as the standard translation of the Latin typical edition *Ordo Exsequiarum*, while the *Rite of Funerals* (1970) designates the provisional rite used in the United States between 1970 and 1989. The *Order of Christian Funerals* (1989) is the title given the definitive edition, which has been approved by the national episcopal conferences for use in English-speaking countries, including the United States, and confirmed by the Holy See.[3] This chapter is primarily concerned with understanding the General Introduction of the *Order of Christian Funerals* and its relationship to the Introduction (*Praenotanda*) of the *Order of Funerals* and the *Rite of Funerals*. Chapter Five comments specifically on the funeral liturgy itself in the *Order of Christian Funerals*.

The Introduction to the 1969 *Ordo* serves as the foundation for all proper national or regional rituals and is the key to understanding rituals prepared for use in the English-speaking world. The Introduction, together with the official letter promulgating the 1969 *Ordo*, is printed in each national ritual. An English rendering of its current version (September 12, 1983, reflecting the revised *Code of Canon Law*) has been included as an appendix to the *Order of Christian Funerals*.

The funeral liturgy thus born and described in the Introduction to the *Ordo* will grow and develop, taking on a living character of its own. It is far more than a mere set of rubrics for disposing of a corpse; it has become a truly human Christian symbolic language allowing death and the grief of loss a rightful voice in the faith community. As we turn to the Catholic funeral in its present form, all these ritual aspects will be an inseparable part of our considerations.

THE ORDER/RITE OF FUNERALS (1969/1970)
Ordo exsequiarum recalls the archaic word "obsequies," suggesting that "funeral" includes more than a simple rite of leave-taking. When Americans speak of "going to a funeral," they usually mean attending a farewell service of some kind, either in a place of worship or a funeral home. Sometimes this service includes accompanying the body of the deceased to a cemetery or crematorium, with a closing ritual of leave-taking.

The Roman Catholic *Order of Funerals* embraces a broader understanding of "obsequies" that includes all the rituals surrounding human death, from the time of death itself to the final leave-taking with accompanying expressions of (Christian) consolation. Although the *Order* itself closes with rites at the committal, contemporary Catholic pastoral care extends beyond the funeral to include commemoration within each eucharistic prayer, certain ethnic practices (*novenas*), monthly and annual memorials, All Souls Day, services of remembrance in Catholic cemeteries, and the like.

This Catholic usage is not surprising when one considers the place funeral liturgy holds in the Christian tradition. In Chapter Two we saw, for example, how even the moment of death itself was once considered part of the liturgy for the dead and how the funeral procession (*funus*) was the central action of the obsequies, from which we inherited our current term "funeral." Thus the *Order of Funerals* provides basic patterns for funeral liturgy that pertain to all aspects of attention to the dead among Catholics. In this way the *Ordo* and its vernacular adaptations continue the thread of Christian funerary tradition, inviting churches everywhere to provide a liturgically adequate cultural expression of that tradition for their people.

Three Models for the Universal Church
After international consultation, the subcommittee preparing the *Order of Funerals* presented three models or patterns (*typi*) of funeral rites representing Catholic practice throughout the world. Professor Pierre-Marie Gy, a major contributor to the revision, described these three models: "According to the first model, viz., that of the traditional *Roman Ritual*, . . . the principal liturgical action of the funeral takes place in the church. According to a second model, quite wide-

spread in German-speaking countries—at least in the cities—the body of the deceased is not taken to the church but directly to the cemetery where the principal liturgical action is held. Finally, there exists a third model according to which the principal action takes place in the home of the deceased, either because of the distance from the church or cemetery or because of local traditions; such is the case in certain regions of Africa".[4] As Gy states, the subcommittee believed that these different models for the funeral would meet real needs deriving from legitimate customs.

The First Model
The typical American Catholic funeral before 1971 was already an adapted version of the Roman *Rite for the Burial of Adults;* it followed basically the same three-stage pattern, with the principal liturgical action centered in the church. Already, the station in the home (*in domo*) of the deceased had shifted to the funeral home, with the result that the domestic liturgical opening of the funeral was gradually telescoped into the liturgy at the church. It became customary for the liturgy in the church to begin with a meeting of the body at the entrance.[5] Mass, followed by the absolution service, constituted the essential funeral liturgy, which had remained virtually unchanged since the 1614 *Rituale Romanum.* Gradually, the service at the cemetery was becoming quite independent of the preceding rites, a farewell by the family and close friends, with a parish priest officiating when possible. Pastoral adaptations of the traditional *Rite for Burial* had already abandoned the processions between stations because of problems inherent in modern urban life and traffic.

Consultation by the Commission for the Implementation of the Constitution on the Liturgy revealed that similar adaptations of the funeral liturgy were taking

118

place worldwide. For example, the process of urbanization favors Model II, but where Model I perdures, urbanization has contributed to the elimination of processions with the body and even of the stations in the home of the deceased and the cemetery. Taking such developments into consideration, the *Order of Funerals* set out to facilitate a truly Christian celebration of funerals not only where mostly rural conditions still prevail but also under the changed conditions of urban life and ministry.

Although the *Ordo* accepts these changes as a cultural given and recognizes the adaptation that the form of the funeral has undergone in various countries, the spiritual value and consolation of these liturgical moments before and after the station in the church are not to be denied. The Introduction explicitly states that in the absence of a priest or deacon, the faithful themselves must be urged to recite those customary prayers and psalms. Even where circumstances have virtually eliminated stations in the (funeral) home and cemetery, the *Ordo* strived to preserve their spiritual and pastoral value. Only when this is impossible, should one omit these stations entirely.

The Second and Third Models
Models II and III of the *Ordo* are noted briefly. The second model has only two stations: in the cemetery chapel and at the grave. However, the pastoral reader is reminded that the celebration of the eucharist in this model is to take place either before or after the funeral without the body present (OF, No. 59). Model II is most common among German-speaking peoples, where it has long been the custom, or even the law of the land, not to bring the corpse into the church.

Less likely in First World practice is Model III, where the principal funeral liturgy is celebrated in the home of the deceased (OF, No. 78). Nevertheless, it teaches pastoral liturgical principles of value, illustrating, for example, that celebrating Christian faith at death and the disposition of the dead is a living tradition, capable of adapting to many different needs. The *Ordo* remains a means, as the circumstances of Model III so well demonstrate; it is not an end in itself.

National Rituals
Closing these general remarks on the three models, the *Order of Funerals* summarizes the procedure for preparing particular rituals in harmony with the Roman typical edition. Because of the great variety of funeral customs worldwide, national conferences of bishops were accorded extensive freedom in arranging versions of the *Ordo* according to their own pastoral needs. Guidelines for that process are spelled out in OF, Nos. 21–22.

Some national conferences, such as those of the bishops of Canada and Ireland, chose for their edition of the *Ordo* the one model that was customary in the region.[6] Although a single model may indeed be the ordinary usage, familiarity with the other models and their rationale opens new possibilities of pastoral awareness.[7]

In the United States, the Secretariat for the Liturgy of the National Conference of Catholic Bishops confronted a situation not unlike that faced by the *consilium* for the universal Roman Catholic Church and chose a similar solution: an edition of the *Ordo* that established a threefold model to serve all local pastoral needs. The *Rite of Funerals* (1970) differed from the Roman typical edition by establishing Model I as the general American practice but including optional adaptations that corresponded to already existing usages among American Catholics. This choice was made in strict adherence to Roman directives, with American adaptations included throughout the body of the text.

In effect, the United States bishops' edition presented the American version of Model I, including options for prayers, readings, chants, and the like, as the usual practice; the other two models follow as options. That book, which posed many editorial problems, has not been easy to use pastorally. Nevertheless, the American editors deserve credit for tackling the problem of presenting all the potential of the 1969 *Ordo*, a fortuitous turn of events in view of the diverse ethnic expressions now requiring pastoral attention among African American, Hispanic and Asian Catholics in the United States. Almost two decades of experience rendered the 1989 *Order of Christian Funerals* a more satisfactory pastoral manual and collection of funeral rites.

THE ORDER OF CHRISTIAN FUNERALS: THE GENERAL INTRODUCTION

The Vatican typical edition of the *Ordo* opens with the Introductory Notes (*praenotanda*), which can be termed an "instruction on the liturgy of funerals." Those few pages are, practically speaking, every bit as important as the ritual patterns and texts that constitute the rest of the work. This pastoral instruction summarizes contemporary Catholic teaching about death, about the death-resurrection mystery, and about giving this faith ritual expression in the world today, so that a clear understanding will prevent the rite from being reduced to mere ritualism. ICEL observed the requirements of Rome by presenting the Introductory Notes in a comprehensive pastorally oriented translation. The editions of the *Ordo* prepared for France (1972) and Germany (1973) are earlier examples of national adaptation.[8]

The following pages offer some comments on the General Introduction to the *Order of Christian Funerals*, which will also reflect on the ritual itself. To facilitate serious study of both the typical edition and the current English edition, the paragraph headings of this chapter are the same as the headings of the General Introduction to the *Order of Christian Funerals*. Cross-references are made to the 1969 Introduction (as revised and printed in the new ICEL edition, Appendix). Where necessary for clarification, reference numbers to OCF (*Order of Christian Funerals*) or OF (*Order of Funerals*) will precede paragraph numbers.

THE CATHOLIC FUNERAL

The General Introduction (Nos. 1–7) opens by stating what is specifically Christian about the Roman Catholic funeral. Essentially, the Church celebrates in the Christian funeral the paschal mystery of Christ, as graphically indicated in the very opening words of the 1969 Introduction, *"Paschale Christi mysterium."*

Paschal Mystery

The liturgical movement of this century has profoundly emphasized the paschal mystery of Christ as the center of Christian life. With great wisdom, the *Constitution on the Sacred Liturgy* (No. 81) established the paschal character of Christian death as the principle of reforming Catholic funeral rites. The Church confesses in faith and practice that Christian life is born of the paschal mystery and proclaims the message and the meaning of the death and resurrection of Jesus. It is through living out in practice its faith in the paschal mystery that the church bears witness to the Kingdom of God, both present and to come.

The fact of death is the greatest human threat to faith in the paschal mystery. There is nothing in death that even hints at the viability of such a paschal faith. Yet the Church, facing human death, proclaims life founded on the death and resurrection of Jesus Christ. For this reason, the Christian funeral is, above all, a celebration of the paschal mystery, a profession of faith in the hope of sharing Jesus' own resurrection to the fullness of life in God.

Sacramental Life and Eschatology

Death for a Christian is inseparable from the faith context of the paschal mystery. The death of a Christian is not an isolated, though significant, event that ends a person's life; it is, rather, a moment that touches every other moment of life by virtue of the Christian's incorporation into the risen, living Christ. Sacramental incorporation into the paschal mystery of life transformed by Jesus' death and resurrection begins with Christian initiation and is continued each time eucharist is celebrated, the liturgy *par excellence* of the paschal mystery. Indeed, every sacramental sign of the Christian life proclaims the paschal mystery.

Thus the Roman Catholic funeral proclaims in word and sacrament that the life in Christ of the paschal mystery does not end with human death but extends into the eternal present of God's Kingdom beyond death. This is the kerygmatic truth that the Introduction to the *Order of Funerals* asserts in the opening sentence: "It is the paschal mystery of Christ that the Church confidently celebrates in the funerals of its children, for those who through baptism have been incorporated into the body of Christ dead and risen [will] pass with him through death to life—their souls purified and taken into heaven with the saints; their bodies meanwhile awaiting the blessed hope of Christ's coming and the resurrection of the dead" (OF, No. 1).[9] This statement of faith, combining the language both of theological reflection and biblical imagery, expresses unequivocally the characteristic mark of a Christian funeral.[10]

This fundamental insight of faith is the major influence that christianizes all other funeral concerns. Accordingly, the Christian funeral becomes an act of thanksgiving for the deceased's life in Christ, as well as an occasion of prayer for the dead person. This is what determines the preference for *Alleluia* over *Dies Irae*. This is what enables the Christian funeral to be a source of true consolation to the bereaved, for not only this death with all its personal sorrow but the whole past and future life of the deceased have been given meaning through the gift of Jesus' risen life. This is death touched by the paschal mystery of Christ, a mystery that does not remove any of the human sting but is yet a mystery that allows Christians to call even the funeral an occasion of celebration in praise of God.

"Paschal mystery" and "everlasting life" are not merely images that lend a Christian flavor to the coping rituals and grief therapy of people who happen to call themselves Christians. These are images that proclaim the very bedrock of the Christian faith. One may hope that Christians will acknowledge that the therapeutic value of their funeral rites rests on this faith in Jesus dead and risen. With its opening paragraphs, the Introduction invites Catholics to experience their faith in a new and vibrant way, akin to the experience of the earliest Christians.

Spiritual Help and the Consolation of Hope
Roman Catholic funeral liturgy articulates in ritual form the Christian faith at the center of the life-death experience, affirming that both the living and the dead are bonded in the paschal mystery of Christ. The eucharist takes first place in this celebration, accompanied by prayers and petitions. Eucharist and prayer serve together to console the living here on earth and provide spiritual help to the dead who have gone before us. Neither the *Order of Funerals* nor the current ritual intends to define theologically the effects of eu-

charist and prayers/petitions for the dead. Nor does either intend these Masses and prayers for the deceased to be divorced from the consolation of hope for the living.[11]

Mass for the Dead
"The Church, therefore, offers the eucharistic sacrifice of Christ's Passover for the dead. . . . " With these words, the 1969 Introduction (No. 1) states clearly that the relationship between the death of a Christian and the paschal mystery of Jesus' death and resurrection establishes the rationale for the Catholic practice of celebrating the eucharist when a Christian dies. Indeed, the eucharist is the liturgy *par excellence* of the paschal mystery[12] and of the Christian funeral. The preceding chapters have shown how this same faith and practice are rooted in early, specifically Christian responses to death, and contemporary usage continues the long tradition of celebrating eucharist in the context of the funeral liturgy and on certain established anniversaries. Whereas all Christians profess the relationship of their own death and personal salvation to the paschal mystery of Jesus' death and resurrection, liturgical celebration of this belief, especially in eucharist, has been characteristically Catholic.[13] Through ecumenical liturgical understanding, many Reformation churches now also include the celebration of the Lord's Supper as an option in their funeral service books.[14]

Prayers for the Dead
Prayers and petitions for the dead bring spiritual help to them, according to the Roman Catholic tradition that the living can aid the faithful dead who stand in need of atonement. The exact nature of this "spiritual help" is not easy to define, yet the expectation of faith is that God, through the atoning work of Christ, accepts the prayers and devotions offered by the living

on behalf of the dead in atonement for the evil effects of the deceased person's sins.

This distinction between "eucharistic celebration" and "prayers" is liturgical; no distinction in effectiveness is intended. The *Order of Funerals* presents the eucharist as *the* sacramental celebration of life in Christ in the face of death. Included in this proclamation of the paschal mystery on behalf of the deceased are other prayers and petitions for God to accept the devotion of the Church, that the deceased may enjoy the fulfillment of the paschal mystery celebrated in the eucharist.

Consolation of Hope
The celebration of the eucharist and prayers for the dead bring a special consolation to the living, "the consolation of hope" or "consoling hope" (Nos. 4 and 7). A further specifically Christian note is struck, which the Introduction sets in a distinctively Catholic context. Faith in the life in Christ, through which the faithful share the risen Christ's victory over death, has always been a source of consolation to the bereaved Christian. This is not the consolation of the skeptic, who regards death as consoling because it frees one from the prison of the body or the misery of life; nor is it the empty, platitudinous consolation of mere religious sentiment. Consoling hope (*spei solacium*) is founded on the certainty of Christian faith in the eschatological promise of Jesus. This hope neither stands alone nor makes a sudden appearance at a funeral. This is the hope Christians proclaim and celebrate in every eucharist, the divine pledge of everlasting life. This is the hope affirmed by Catholics in every commemoration of the dead at mass and in every profession of the creed: "I believe in the Communion of Saints, the forgiveness of sins, the resurrection of the dead, and the life of the world to come."

126

This age-long hope is at the very heart of Christianity. It is a "consoling hope" to the bereaved not because it takes away or lessens the pain of loss but because it enables the believer to look upon death with all its pain in the grace-filled light of Jesus' saving death and victorious resurrection. It is a consoling hope because it gives the bereaved the conviction that despite death, there is life—a risen life that perfects every individual in an eschatological kingdom where, somehow, even the body now dead will also be transformed.

Whatever is meant by this biblical image of the resurrection of the body, it, too, speaks of consoling hope to the bereaved. However grief-laden the thought of bodily decomposition, the believer can look beyond the grave to God, where even this ultimate experience of human finitude receives meaning. This is not "cheap hope," for it is a proclamation too absurd for anyone but a true believer in Jesus dead and risen to even dream. The "resurrection of the dead" is a source of consoling hope because it states unequivocally Jesus' pledge of everlasting life for those of faith who live the Christian life. It gives courage, confidence, and security. All of these flow together in Tertullian's classic profession of resurrection faith: *"Resurrectio mortuorum fiducia christianorum"* (*De Resurrectione Mortuorum*, 1).

MINISTRY AND PARTICIPATION

Community
The General Introduction now turns in great detail to the context within which alone Catholic funerals can have their full meaning: the Christian community. The *Order of Christian Funerals* (Nos. 9–13) goes beyond the 1960 *Ordo* (Nos. 16–20) in explaining the essential quality of the funeral liturgy according to contemporary expectations. All who belong to the People of God have

127

a responsibility to the dead determined by their role within the Christian community. The ecclesial community shares a concern for the funeral liturgy, each member contributing to the celebration and offering consolation to the bereaved. This expectation is a challenge to laity and priests alike.

For the Christian, the interval between death and burial is a time when the reality of death and faith in eternal life coincide, a time when faith becomes inseparably entwined with personal suffering. It is a time of special need, when the human psyche seeks solace in the cultural customs of grief and consolation. Catholic funeral liturgy grew out of the experience of Christian people through the centuries, providing a context of faith in which to begin the process of coping and adapting to a new life situation caused by the loss of the deceased.

Human sciences, such as sociology and psychology, agree that grief and suffering need the kind of resolution that is offered by Christian faith and the Catholic funeral liturgy.[15] For example, just as grief therapists describe the need for social support during this time, the *Ordo* acknowledges the importance of the Christian community. This implies that liturgy should be celebrated at times when it is convenient for people to attend.

Equally important is the genuineness of community. Without the effort to build a community of genuine support, "going to a funeral" often may be merely an outward, hypocritical gesture. The ritual presupposes such a community and serves as an opportunity for a renewal of ecclesial life. The *Order of Christian Funerals* embodies this presupposition in its General Introduction and ensuing rites: "The Church calls each member of Christ's body—priest, deacon, lay person—to participate in the ministry of consolation: to care for the dying, to pray for the dead, to comfort those who mourn" (No. 8).

Coming together during this interval for prayer and fellowship with the bereaved bespeaks a quality of support that they can count on in the lonely weeks and months ahead. The *Ordo*, complementing social psychology, emphasizes Christian community, especially as expressed in the liturgical assembly. The *Order of Funerals* clearly expresses the need, recognized by psychologists, to actualize loss and express sorrow by providing the context of faith that nurtures this grieving process. "Christian hope faces the reality of death and the anguish of grief but trusts confidently that the power of sin and death has been vanquished by the risen Lord" (No. 8).

Liturgical Ministers
Christian community is the ecclesial context in which liturgical ministers exercise their offices and ministry. Recognizing the ecclesiology of shared liturgical leadership in the Catholic funeral, the *Order of Christian Funerals* (No. 14) first addresses the "presiding minister." It is clear that the role of the ordained pastor as presiding minister is paramount: "Priests, as teachers of faith and ministers of comfort, preside at the funeral rites, especially the Mass; the celebration of the funeral liturgy is especially entrusted to pastors and associate pastors" (No. 14). In the context of Christian community, rather than being an isolated figure who performs church rituals, the pastor serves an essential Christian need of the bereaved and the community.

As teacher of faith, he himself will have wrestled prayerfully with the enigma of death and the paschal mystery, so that he may better open the Scriptures and Catholic tradition to those he touches personally and to those who share in his homily and his interpretation of the liturgical rites. In the role as minister of

consolation, the priest's own faith in Jesus dead and
risen and hope in the fullness of baptismal life beyond
death are the most powerful tools of ministry at that
moment. Where words are superfluous, the priestly
presence and that of the helping Church are all that
may be required.

Under the title "The Function of the Priest," the *Order
of Funerals* summarizes the priest's duties of preparing
and planning the funeral (Nos. 23–25). His responsibility and freedom are emphasized, and general guidelines specify relevant points in the *Ordo* that should
command his attention. This funeral ministry is
placed, appropriately, in a total pastoral context. Those
few concise lines devoted to the specific responsibili-
ties of the priest leave no doubt about the awesome
importance of his ministry to the dead and the bereaved. Viewing the funeral from before death
through follow-up pastoral visits, one finds there are
few other pastoral opportunities its equal.

One of these duties is to highlight the importance of
faith in the Catholic funeral. In addition to spiritually
preparing the bereaved for the funeral liturgy, a duty
of the priest and other ministers is "to raise the hope
of those present and to build up their faith in the paschal mystery and the resurrection of the dead" (OF,
No. 17). This requires a sense of balance, so that while
focusing attention on commendation of the deceased,
the liturgy likewise includes the living by supporting
their faith and hope in full sensitivity to their grief.

With this appreciation of the blend of paschal faith
and the consolation of hope sensitive to grief and
mourning, we now look more closely at this pastoral
sensitivity to grief in both the *Ordo* and the *Order of
Christian Funerals*. It is unfortunate when presiders at
funeral liturgies confuse paschal joy with joviality,
whereby the secular mood of denying death influences

130

liturgical expression of a faith that takes death seriously. Christians rejoice in faith because a dead person enters a new form of union with God, a subtle part of the mystery of death. Christian joy, which accepts death in faith, cannot deny grief. Like other people, Christians grieve not because of what they believe has happened to the deceased but because they have lost a loved one. Injustice is done to the bereaved when the *Ordo*, which offers so much by way of Christian support and hope, is misused as an attempt, however unconsciously, to cover up grief and the reality of death with saccharine eulogies, canned music, and sentimental rhetoric. In the face of such misguided interpretation, we need reminding of the importance of devoting time to prayerful and faith-filled study of Christian eschatology implicit in the *Order of Christian Funerals*. By deepening their own paschal faith and accepting their own mortality, presiders at funeral liturgy must realize the duty to attend to the spiritual needs of the faithful while respecting the reality of loss and bereavement.

Having acknowledged the specific duties of the priest, and especially pastors and associate pastors, the General Introduction continues with an equally compelling argument: "When no priest is available, deacons as ministers of the word, of the altar, and of charity, preside at funeral rites. When no priest or deacon is available for the vigil and related rites or the rite of committal, a layperson presides" (No. 14).

What is the ecclesial rationale for this firm commitment to the presence of the ministerial church in the face of death? Death itself, we should remember, holds an important place in the mystery of Christian life; the death of any one Christian is a communal, ecclesial affair. It places demands on the entire community, requiring the Church's immediate attention to the needs of the deceased and the living. The responsibility to see that those pastoral needs are met belongs first to the office of the ordained minister: bishop, priest, and deacon. The pastor, because of his office in relationship to the Catholic community, is primarily responsible for ensuring that the Christian deceased and bereaved enjoy the full ministry of the Church in the funeral liturgy. He is the first responsible minister of that liturgy; current canon law, reflected in the *Ordo*, extends to the deacon the "ordinary" ministry of presiding at the funeral, except for the funeral mass.[16]

The same pastoral principle, responding to the spiritual needs of the faithful as fully as possible, extends liturgical funeral ministry to the laity in the absence of a priest or deacon. For the fullest possible exercise of this ministry, the *Ordo* urges local bishops, priests, and deacons to involve lay ministers in this work. Because the Christian funeral is an ecclesial duty of spiritual benefit to the deceased and bereaved, pastoral necessity calls forth lay ministers to exercise this liturgical ministry in the absence of the priest or deacon. This is an "extraordinary," or special, funeral ministry, flowing from the authority of either the local Ordinary or from liturgical law itself, the *Ordo*. Being "extraordinary" does not imply that lay ministry is "exceptional" (No. 14). Lay presiders at occasional services, such as the funeral or part of the funeral rites (including giving an instruction on the reading according to No. 27), are increasing in numbers, and they are far from being the "exception" in the ordinary experience of their churches.[17]

Having established the principle of lay presiding at the vigil and related rites or the rite of committal in the absence of an ordained minister, the General Introduction proceeds to discuss shared ministry—when both ordained and lay ministers are present (No. 15). At first glance, this paragraph on "other liturgical ministers" may seem commonplace, especially in parishes where lay people customarily serve as readers, musicians, ushers, pallbearers, and special ministers of the eucharist in the celebration of the funeral rites. Yet, these visible ministries in parish funerals are an explicit and memorable expression of the presence and meaning of church for both the immediately bereaved and the assembly as a whole. Thus, they serve an ecclesiological function beyond the immediate liturgical duties they perform. Furthermore, research among bereaved Catholics has confirmed the comfort and support that the presense of such lay ministers from the parish community has provided relatives and friends in their experience of the "consolation of the faith." Similarly, when family members of the deceased are not inhibited because of grief or other reasons, their participation in these various ministries has been reported as helpful to them and their families as natural, normal ways to participate in the initial stages of their own bereavement. Thus, the *Order* rightly encourages pastors and other priests, and by extension all who are responsible for funeral and bereavement ministry, to "instill in these ministers an appreciation of how much the reverent exercise of their ministries contributes to the celebration of the funeral rites" (No. 15) and, one may add, to the impact of those ritual moments on the lives of the bereaved and the parish community alike.

MINISTRY FOR THE MOURNERS AND THE DECEASED
No Catholic should face the death of a loved one without the prayer of the Church for the deceased or the funeral celebration of paschal faith and the consolation of Christian hope for the living. Once again, this prayer (*lex orandi*) affirms the importance for faith (*lex credendi*) of the full Catholic funeral. Nevertheless, in practice, the bereaved and other mourners are not sufficiently prepared to lead the assembly in prayer; even when they are, as in the case of readers, eucharistic

ministers, and certain members of prayer groups, the situation is frequently too emotional for them to exercise this ministry. Much pastoral catechesis remains to be done; the charismatic renewal can contribute much in this area of lay group prayer. In short, we are made aware of the need to train lay bereavement ministers.

Here again, we see post-Vatican II renewal is inviting us "to be somewhere we have never been before." Consider this scenario: A parish priest or deacon, accompanied by a trained lay minister, visits the family. These two ministers will probably not be strangers to the family, certainly not if the deceased has suffered a prolonged illness. A deacon, offering a ministry of service, may have been even more directly involved with the family than the pastor. While arrangements are being made for the funeral liturgy, the ordained minister explains to the family the role of the lay minister, whose service as a leader of prayer at special moments in the funeral home and cemetery is then offered. These same ministers, if possible, should also assist the priest at the funeral liturgy in the church, especially at the eucharist and the final commendation. Their presence extends the thread of continuity throughout the full liturgy of the funeral. This kind of shared ministry throughout the funeral is the best long-term preparation by the parish, including the deacon and lay ministers, for the times when the deacon or laity alone care for the entire funeral.

Is such a scenario unrealistic? Not at all where Catholics today continue to pursue the priorities of renewal. Sharing the ministry of funerals with deacons and lay ministers, especially ministers of bereavement and music, is not merely a new patch on an old wineskin. It is already proving to be a new approach by which the liturgy of paschal faith and hopeful consolation can be fully celebrated.

The 1969 Introduction closes this overview of shared responsibility for funeral ministry with a direct quotation of the *Constitution on the Sacred Liturgy*, No. 32: "Apart from the marks of distinction arising from a person's liturgical function or holy orders and those honors due to civil authorities according to liturgical law, no special honors are to be paid in the celebration of a funeral to any private persons or classes of persons" (OF, No. 20). In the liturgy, and certainly in death, all persons are equal before God. Those responsible for the liturgy of funerals are advised by the Council itself that the days when funerals were ranked according to prestige and stipends belong to the past. Any hint of distinctions, other than office within the Church, are inappropriate, and even some of these deserve monitoring. Gospel simplicity lends the Christian funeral its most noble beauty, a gospel simplicity that is the same for all.

Family and Friends
"In planning and carrying out the funeral rites, the pastor and all other ministers should keep in mind the life of the deceased and the circumstances of death. They should also take into consideration the spiritual and psychological needs of the family and friends of the deceased to express grief and their sense of loss, to accept the reality of death, and to comfort one another" (No. 16). The minister's attitude toward the deceased and his or her family and friends must always be expressed in terms of faith, with pastoral sensitivity. This does not mean that any and every wish of the bereaved must be carried out—the "anything you want" attitude. Feelings and fashionable customs are not meant to dictate the proclamation of faith in our funeral liturgy, but they may provide the setting in which the funeral message is celebrated, as touchstones of receptivity. The General Introduction, while

135

describing an appropriate pastoral sensitivity, alerts the minister to avoid the traps of all-too-frequent situations, of which the following are two extremes.

Catholics sometimes complain that such and such a funeral was "canned, resurrectionist pietism," completely out of touch with the reality of the bereaved family. Or they may complain of a funeral that was overly concerned with the emotional and religious state of the family, afraid to celebrate the very faith they wanted to affirm. This *caveat* offered by the General Introduction pertains to practice as well as to personal feelings and reminds us that the funeral liturgy is as important "for the assembled Church" as it is "for the bereaved."

Most intimately related to the deceased are, of course, the parents, spouse, close friends, and relatives: those we term "the bereaved." They minister to the dead and are themselves ministered to by the community. The ministry of the bereaved consists mostly in preparing a last farewell, in calling family and friends together for leave-taking.

Here, the funeral plays an important role for Catholics. It is anomalous that most time and effort devoted to the funeral barely has anything to do with spiritual matters. Most bereaved come to the liturgy in the church spiritually unprepared, with a deep sigh of relief that "it is almost over." They desire most simply to sit back and rest peacefully, drinking in the consolation of their faith, while the priest does what the Church requires for Christian burial. Of course, their participation in the liturgy is above all an active silence, of listening and being touched. Whatever their grief allows them to sing or say or hear is sufficient; others of us perform those ministries both for them and the deceased. Yet even they have a ministry of preparing the funeral, not only for themselves but for their family and friends—a ministry that cannot ignore the climactic moments of the Catholic funeral that occur liturgically between the moment of death and the time of burial. It is the ministry of the priest and those who care for funerals (parish lay ministers, funeral directors, and cemetery personnel) to support and encourage the bereaved in their ministry of preparation.

This approach to preparing funerals is gaining ground, thanks to some long-term parish catechesis by pastors and lay ministers. Seeing it happen little by little, over and over again, cannot but convince all of its value. The era of the "pornography of death" is now past.[18] People are willing to talk about death and dying. With the right counsel, many will become more involved in pre-planning funerals in the period before death, especially in the area of liturgy. Spiritually and psychologically, such an approach is good grief therapy as long as it does not itself become either death-denying through exaggeration or limiting through narrow exclusivism. The funeral liturgy plays this important role of bonding the reality of death with life itself, embracing the entire area of caring for the dead and the bereaved (No. 17).[19]

Deceased
Catholics would do well to discern how much of the typical modern funeral really deserves the full Christian respect and acceptance it seems to enjoy. Does it offer the quality of faith that Christians expect in their celebration of the paschal mystery? This is no criticism of American funeral-service professionals, particularly those who adhere to the directives on clergy/church relations prepared by the National Funeral Directors Association in its *Resource Manual*.[20] It is, however, a challenge to contemporary Catholics wherever the American-style funeral, with its emphasis on lifelike appearance, slumber rooms, ostentatious floral arrange-

ments, and the like, is becoming a marketable commodity.

Wide experience with modern funeral directors indicates that they are essentially businesspeople who desire to serve and to satisfy their clients. One may well ask, "What might Catholics request of the funeral-service industry in order to celebrate more authentically the paschal faith and proclaim the spirit of the gospel." Demand, quite simply, paschal faith and the spirit of the gospel.

Paschal faith proclaims risen life through death. This implies an acceptance of the death that has occurred, something that also concerns the grief therapist, funeral-service professionals, and the cemeterian. Denial of death, encouraged by whatever means, is unacceptable to Christian funerary care as well as to sound psychology. Obviously, this, too, is an area where great pastoral sensitivity is needed. What may be death-denying for one person or family (for example, viewing the body "restored to a lifelike appearance") may be a clear acceptance of death in the case of others. The same can be said for the closed-casket funeral or immediate disposition of the body followed by the funeral liturgy. Pastorally, the minister must be alert to just about any combination of possibilities.

Part of proclaiming paschal faith is to assist people in this process of accepting death, and for Catholics today, the *Order of Christian Funerals* is the indispensable guide. Except for sudden, unexpected death, the process of acceptance does not ordinarily begin with death. The relationship between pastoral care for the sick and the dying and funeral ministry is obvious, yet still not widely enough acknowledged at the level of practice.[21] Where a minister comes to the funeral having been present in faith with the deceased and the bereaved during the time of dying, there is a better

138

chance that such a funeral will proclaim a paschal faith. Cooperation between the parish team and funeral counselors, a service not uncommon in funeral homes, could help Catholic families better integrate the needs of their life and faith at this critical time.

The spirit of the gospel suggests Christian priorities that reputable funeral directors would honor if requested. Certain values stand out in particular: community, prayerfulness, and simplicity. Funeral-home arrangements differ considerably from region to region, but most facilities do remain generally flexible and multipurpose. There is little that should inhibit viewing arrangements, which serve to support the bereaved and foster times of prayer. Christian community requires an arrangement of casket and chairs that best suits the gathering of people as an assembly of faith and prayer. Christian simplicity demands rooms and furnishings that serve their purpose in good taste without drawing attention to themselves. The stereotypical viewing parlors and mortuary chapels do not correspond to these values; such stereotyping has emerged in response to different priorities, which Christians cannot help but question.[22] Where the plush interior of a funeral parlor does more to distract than to aid the purpose for gathering, it is in effect a conspiracy to mask the reality of death. Christians can demand the kind of space that both is discrete and serves the recognition of death. Where this cannot be provided, the Catholic community should not hesitate to avoid such funeral parlors and encourage celebration of the entire funeral liturgy in the parish church itself.

There are likewise extravagances in the application of the cosmetic art that do not serve the Christian's purpose. A good mortician can use the same "code of beauty" to accommodate both the simplicity of death and reverent viewing.

This issue of cosmetic art raises the question of embalming. Christians wishing to provide the opportunity for family and friends to view the deceased as they pay their respects and pray together are, practically speaking, obliged to choose embalming. Parish ministry teams owe it to their people to be knowledgeable about the embalming requirements of their state and alternatives to embalming, such as preservation by refrigeration until burial.[23] Furthermore, embalming, and cosmetic restoration of the body are not one and the same thing. Because the embalmed corpse without makeup is not customary in the experience of most Americans, some cosmetic work is recommended. Many morticians recommend it even for a closed-casket funeral, if only to ease the brief moment when family members or personal friends come to view or identify the body.

Nevertheless, the family (or the deceased before death) has the prerogative as a consumer to arrange whatever embalming and cosmetic services are desired. Cosmetic restoration remains a matter of further choice and also deserves monitoring on the basis of Christian values. In short, any cosmetic work ought to contribute to the proclamation of paschal faith and the spirit of the gospel rather than be guided merely by the principle of restoring the body to lifelike appearances. For the Christian, the funeral proclaims life through death and not through the appearance of life. The *Order of Christian Funerals* summarizes this point succinctly: "In countries or regions where an undertaker, and not the family or community, carries out the preparation and transfer of the body, the pastor and other ministers are to ensure that the undertakers appreciate the values and beliefs of the Christian community" (No. 20).

"Since in baptism the body was marked with the seal of the Trinity and became the Temple of the Holy

Spirit, Christians respect and honor the bodies of the dead and the places where they rest. Any customs associated with the preparation of the body of the deceased should always be marked with dignity and reverence and never with the despair of those who have no hope" (No. 19).

The General Introduction notes the importance Christians place on showing respect and honor to the body of the deceased. Whether the body is available for viewing or the casket is closed during reception times for family and friends, the same point is made: this dead body is important. One can hardly show Christian honor to the body of a deceased loved one without beginning at least to face the reality of what has happened, the reality of loss. Because the General Introduction assumes that when cremation is chosen, it follows the funeral liturgy, nothing more is asserted here than the provision for cremation itself. We will take up the matter of the *Ordo* and cremation in Chapter Six.[24]

During this time between death and burial, recommended prayer services should embrace themes, prayers, psalms, and other scriptural texts that make the reality of loss very actual indeed. Psalms, especially, give the bereaved, in the midst of a supportive community, an opportunity to articulate some deeply human expressions of loss, sorrow, and grief. They also convey very real sentiments of hope and trust in God, as affirmed in the *Order of Christian Funerals* (Nos. 25–26) and treated more thoroughly in our commentary in Chapter Five.

For the bereaved to take part in these services, however passively, is one means of acknowledging the fact that the deceased is gone. Through such a ritualized statement, the harsh reality of loss is gathered into prayer; it puts on the lips of the bereaved words that cannot be avoided, admitting the emotion flowing from the loss. What begins in liturgy often overflows into conversations with others and into personal expressions of sorrow.

This faith perspective, this special expression of sorrow and hope, is the Christian way of taking leave of the dead and facing the loss. Human needs and Christian faith flow as a unified life experience. In face of death, the faith does not have its own separate grief therapy; but it brings to the grieving process the values of life in Christ. While the *Order of Christian Funerals* respects the customs and choices of the bereaved with regard to laying out the deceased and expressing condolences, it also urges gospel simplicity, which only Christian discretion can ensure. Honor and respect are due to the deceased because this body was so recently alive, as temple of the Holy Spirit, with God's own life-giving grace. The faithful Christian whose body lies in death now lives life victorious over death, in whatever state of fulfillment. The person awaits only the future perfection of that life in Christ which this inert body, in some way, holds in expectation. Yet the same mystery that requires honor and respect for the dead also repudiates pomp and empty display.

The custom of paying the body final respect ("last respects") has value, although funeral directors speak of the increasing numbers who request immediate disposition with no funeral services of any kind. The custom has a further value for Christians as an expression of faith in Jesus' promise of risen life. This is an unfathomable mystery, yet Christians believe that the whole person, spirit and flesh, has been destined for the fullness of life with God. Whatever, in the language of faith, the mystery of the resurrection of the body will ultimately mean, Christians show their faith in that mystery by special symbolic respect for the bodily remains during this interval between death and burial and after final disposition. In this context, special attention is needed in the pastoral care of the deceased and the bereaved when cremation has been selected. Likewise, the Catholic cemetery remains a traditional place of postfuneral memorialization for Catholics (No. 19).

Exaggeration or extremes, whether through lack of respect (such as immediate, disrespectful disposal) or absolute preservation of the corpse (as if natural decomposition negates the mystery of final resurrection) are as much out of line with Christian belief as are those extravagant scenarios of displaying the corpse in the manner of *The Loved One*.[25]

LITURGICAL ELEMENTS
With characteristic sensitivity to the symbolic nature of liturgy, the General Introduction begins this section on the specific funeral rites of the *Order of Christian Funerals* with a reminder that "liturgical celebration involves the whole person" and "requires attentiveness to all that affects the senses" (No. 21) of both mourners and other participants in the liturgy.

Those introductory remarks are more important than the casual reader might assume, for it is becoming clear from multidisciplinary research that by engaging the imagination of participants, religious rites constitute a significant factor in bereavement therapy.[26] Paragraph 21 continues with consequent directives, affecting all funeral ministers (ordained or lay), funeral directors, and cemetery personnel.

"The readings and prayers, psalms and songs, should be proclaimed or sung with understanding, conviction, and reverence. Music for the assembly should be truly expressive of the texts and at the same time simple and easily sung. The ritual gestures, processions, and postures should express and foster an attitude of reverent reflectiveness in those taking part in the funeral rites. The funeral rites should be celebrated in an atmosphere of simple beauty, in a setting that encourages participation. Liturgical signs and symbols affirming Christian belief and hope in the paschal mystery are abundant in the celebration of the funeral rites, but their undue multiplication or repetition should be avoided. Care must be taken that the choice and use of signs and symbols are in accord with the culture of the people" (No. 21).

THE WORD OF GOD

Readings
The *Order of Funerals* showed clearly how the biblical emphasis guided the entire process of liturgical renewal. Readings from Holy Scripture play a primary role in the *Order of Christian Funerals*. "The readings proclaim to the assembly the paschal mystery, teach remembrance of the dead, convey the hope of being gathered together again in God's kingdom, and encourage the witness of Christian life" (No. 22). The biblical readings are to be emphasized precisely because they open up to those assembled the God-given source of the paschal faith and consoling hope that makes the funeral Christian. Note the broad ecclesial context assumed here. The entire assembly receives the proclamation of God's word, not just the bereaved. Presuming the presence of biblical readings in the funeral liturgy, the purpose of paragraphs 22–29 is to encourage their proper emphasis.

A different question concerns the appropriateness of readings other than biblical. Whereas the 1969 Introduction did not address this issue, the *Order of Christian Funerals* states clearly: "In the celebration of *the liturgy of the word at the funeral liturgy*, the biblical readings *may not be replaced* by nonbiblical readings. But

144

during *prayer services* with the family, nonbiblical readings may be used *in addition to* readings from Scripture" (No. 23, emphases added). This follows the guidelines in the *Lectionary* and the General Instruction on the *Roman Missal*. It clarifies that there are sufficient opportunities during the times of visitation or wake, as well as at the cemetery or place of disposition, when those other-than-biblical pieces may appropriately be read to honor or pay tribute to the deceased.

Furthermore, a reference or very brief piece that was a "favorite" of the deceased might also be included in the homily, elaborating on the biblical faith as proclaimed by the readings. To replace Scripture with any other reading, regardless of its quality, is to rob the Catholic funeral of an essential access to faith through God's word. The pastoral task required by the ritual is to bring this death into touch with the word of God. Any other "word" that can help do that, although a welcome aid, should never become a substitute.

Psalmody
The *Order of Funerals* invokes the prayer of the psalms "as an expression of grief and a sure source of trust" (OF, No. 12). The General Introduction continues its emphasis on the place of Scripture in the Catholic funeral by treating the psalms next in order of importance (OCF, Nos. 25–26).

The psalms are the inspired prayers of God's people, both individually and collectively. For the Christian, psalms are ecclesial and christological prayers, two important factors for their use in the funeral.

Throughout the long Christian tradition of funeral liturgy, there can be no doubt about the importance of the psalms and their primary liturgical role in the contemporary Catholic funeral. The primacy of the psalms among funeral chants stems from the belief that inspired prayer, by its nature, is the expression and the nourishment of faith. Psalms open to the bereaved Christian a means of uttering in prayer every movement of the soul faced with death, from the deepest anger to the most confident trust. Likewise, the psalms paint in vivid biblical imagery the meaning of the sacramental actions through which the Christian community takes leave of its own. The psalms and their antiphons (especially those in the first person) put on the lips of the community the deceased's own prayers of praise and intercession. As such, they are the accompaniment *par excellence* of every liturgical action surrounding the funeral; they guide the bereaved community meaningfully, step by step, from the very time death approaches, through burial, and into future times of commemoration.[27]

Special attention was paid the funeral psalms in the revision of the funeral liturgy during the 1980s. The *Order of Christian Funerals* attaches great importance to an adequate catechesis about their meaningful use. Since psalms are so important to the celebration of the Catholic funeral, genuine renewal of the liturgy, up to now only barely begun, will ultimately succeed or fail by the way people make the psalms their own prayers of grief and hope.

The General Introduction takes for granted that the psalms are poetic pieces to be sung. Since Vatican II, much research has been conducted into the liturgical use of the *Psalter* with regard to biblical exegesis and musical forms. Parish song books have already done much to encourage the chanting of Sunday responsorial psalms, and more adventurous musical settings of psalm texts are appearing with greater frequency.

When funeral psalms are not sung (for whatever reason), an appropriate style of recitation ought to be

146

adopted—one that respects the faith content and literary form of the psalm. With very few exceptions, the psalms should never be regarded as mere readings. Blending the voice of a solo cantor or reader with an instrumental background achieves a more desirable, poetic recitation. When songs other than psalms are chosen because of "pastoral considerations," the 1969 Introduction (No. 12) directs that "these should reflect a 'warm and living love for sacred scripture' (*Sacrosanctum Concilium*, No. 24) and a liturgical spirit." This spirit is best discerned through prayerful study of the funeral psalms themselves and through a historical study of the biblical cultic origins of these texts.[28] The quest for liturgically sound hymns and songs for use at funerals has led many parishes to a new appreciation of the psalms. It is not surprising that they next found ways to allow those psalms their rightful, musical place in the funeral.

Homily
"A brief homily based on the readings is always given after the gospel reading at the funeral liturgy and may also be given after the readings at the vigil service; but there is never to be a eulogy" (Nos. 27 and 141). The Latin of the typical edition reads *"brevis habeatur homilia,"* which the *Order of Christian Funerals* interprets as stating a pastoral norm. A funeral without a homily would thus be the exception.

The homily is not a eulogy to honor the deceased. We gather to remember one whose achievements have touched us "for the good." We gather because we believe he or she is alive and with God. We are not merely looking to the past and honoring our dead; we are hearing words that speak of life—life changed and not ended. The homily is addressed to us, the living, to keep alive our faith. Why are we here on earth? How shall God's kingdom come among us? What is there about life that denies its own death? What sense can we make of an empty tomb? And who are we, this communion of saints past, present, and yet to come, who gather lest we forget a memory of any empty tomb and a risen Lord? Dying takes on an entirely new perspective when it is understood as a community experience. A community has a long memory; it can never forget what has been promised and demonstrated in its history. In the face of death, life becomes aware of its full meaning.

The homilist at the funeral liturgy is counseled by the *Ordo* to avoid the kind of banal remarks that could apply to any death, but rather to take into account the authenticity of faith that marked the life and death of the deceased. Relating the death of a given deceased person to the saving death and resurrection of Jesus will certainly take his or her life into account. The Christian funeral proclaims reconciliation and salvation through the paschal mystery. Yet how often the funeral appears to be more like the canonization of the deceased than a proclamation of God's saving grace through Jesus. While the homilist would have no reason to dwell on the sinfulness of the deceased, human frailty deserves to be acknowledged alongside outstanding virtue.

Preparing a funeral homily has to be one of the most difficult tasks of any preacher. Together with some recent articles on pastoral approach, sensitivity, use of Scripture, and the like,[29] the *Order of Christian Funerals* itself provides the best description of the funeral homily. "Attentive to the grief of those present, the homilist should dwell on God's compassionate love and on the paschal mystery of the Lord, as proclaimed in the Scripture readings. The homilist should also help the members of the assembly to understand that the mystery of God's love and the mystery of Jesus' victorious death and resurrection were present in the

148

life and death of the deceased and that these mysteries are active in their own lives as well. Through the
homily, members of the family and community should
receive consolation and strength to face the death of
one of their members with a hope nourished by the
saving word of God" (No. 27). The importance of this
nourishment requires that in the absence of an ordained minister, "laypersons who preside at the funeral rites give an instruction on readings" (No. 27).

Prayers and Intercessions
The prayers of the funeral liturgy both declare in faith
and petition in hope that the faithful dead enjoy happiness with God. Although these prayers express the
same faith as is revealed in the readings and made
one's own in the homily and psalms, they serve a liturgically different purpose. In the prayers, people articulate in a contemporary way this heritage of faith. In
the mid-1960s, the drafters of the *Ordo* had to face
many questions in this regard. The translation of
prayer formulae likewise remained the single most sensitive issue through the entire process of revision, national episcopal approval, and the Holy See's confirmation of the 1989 *Ordo*. The journey that their English
translations and new compositions endured during
two decades was tedious and not without compromise. Grateful to those who labored under such frus-
trating circumstances, liturgical ministers in pastoral
care will use the prayers of the *Order of Christian Funerals* critically and guide English-speaking *praxis* into the
next stage of inculturation.

The intention with which prayers were composed or
restored in the 1969 typical edition is ably summarized
in the commentary of Fr. Pierre-Marie Gy.[30] According
to Gy, these prayers were to express, in a manner accessible to our contemporaries, the significance of the
funeral liturgy: a demonstration of the Church's faith

in human destiny, respect due a deceased person, and prayer for salvation. With regard to faith, it was fitting that the prayers express better and more amply the relation of Christian death to the paschal mystery; this has been done abundantly. It was equally desirable that prayer for the deceased, asking that he or she be purified of personal sins (prayer in which the substance of Catholic tradition about purgatory is implied), should be disengaged from certain allusions to a mythical journey undertaken by the soul after death. From time to time, the criticism is heard, in the name of biblical anthropology, that the Roman prayers for the dead place undue emphasis on those images as well as on prayer for the soul of the deceased. Certainly, it is neither necessary nor desirable that every prayer contain the entirety of Christian eschatology, but it is fitting that funeral prayers, taken as a whole, proclaim clearly that each individual human being will be called to bodily resurrection and, except in the case of infants, will be in need of reconciliation to enter the fullness of relationship with God.

The first of these truths is part of the New Testament heritage of faith. The second, not supported with any clarity by the New Testament, is found in the prayer of the Church from antiquity. Yet, all truths are not of equal import; nor does this exclude research into new ways of expressing the deposit of faith in the liturgy.

Formerly, Roman Catholic funeral liturgy prayed for the deceased, not for the living in their grief. In the 16th century, the reformers generally adopted an opposite position: the living should pray for themselves, since to pray for the dead does not conform to the gospel. In the light of the liturgical heritage of the Reformation and the religious circumstances of the funeral, it was appropriate to include prayers both of entreaty for the bereaved and in thanksgiving for what love of God had achieved in the life of the deceased. These are welcome additions that in no way detract from the importance of prayer for the deceased required by the Catholic faith. In some cases, Anglican tradition provided a source of inspiration, even models for editing texts that conform to the genius of the *Roman Ritual*, always less sober and less austere than the *Missal*.[31]

The editors of the *Ordo* of 1969 conclude their reflections by pointing out one special difficulty with funeral services. Prescinding from the particular character of the mass and the rite of final commendation, funeral services do not require a thematic progression, and their prayers are very often interchangeable, as encouraged by the *Order of Christian Funerals*. "From a variety of prayers provided, the minister in consultation with the family should carefully select texts that truly capture the unspoken prayers and hopes of the assembly and also respond to the needs of the mourners" (No. 28). Particular attention should always be paid to the choice of presidential prayers at the beginning of the funeral rites, acknowledging the faith of the assembly gathered for the funeral.[32]

The liturgy of the word traditionally concludes with the general intercessions or prayer of the faithful. Prayers are made on behalf of the catechumens and the baptized alike, living and dead. In the intercessions, we continue to use another ancient form of prayer, the litany. A litany is a short, urgent way of prayer, with petitions stated by a cantor, or prayer leader, and repetitive response made by the assembly. We ask for God's blessing and favor "that we may live." We also pray for God to be present here now: with the dead person, with the mourners and with ourselves. This prayer of the faithful is the prayer of the whole community, living and dead. We don't merely pray for the dead; we pray *with* them.

The General Introduction alerts the minister to the importance of the prayers of intercession enabling the assembly to make its own the commitment of the Church in accompanying the deceased and the bereaved with prayerful support. Here, again, the ecclesiology of the *Order of Christian Funerals* embraces the bereaved by taking their present grief seriously, at the same time giving them an opportunity to recognize that they are not alone in carrying the cross of death. Even in their moment of greatest pain, they find themselves praying for others who suffer, including the world's poor (No. 29).

Music
Music in the Catholic funeral is a long-established tradition. In Anglo-Saxon churches, this has taken the form of listening passively to a choir or soloist or simply an organist. Liturgical renewal aims to translate this passivity into active participation, with music assuming a rightful place as an integral part of funeral liturgy. The *Order of Christian Funerals* is explicit in regarding music as one of the constitutive liturgical elements of the funeral rites.

"Music is integral to the funeral rites. It allows the community to express convictions and feelings that words alone may fail to convey. It has the power to console and uplift the mourners and to strengthen the unity of the assembly in faith and love. The texts of the songs chosen for a particular celebration should express the paschal mystery of the Lord's suffering, death, and triumph over death and should be related to the readings from Scripture" (No. 30). Some examples of how western Catholicism today is fulfilling this mandate of the *Order of Christian Funerals* will be treated in Chapter Six.

The *Order of Christian Funerals* itself offers general guidelines for practical application by alerting parish ministers that the sectional commentaries preceding each of the funeral rites suggest places where music is appropriate, and encourages the development and expansion of the parish's repertory for use at funerals (No. 32).[33] The importance of song within the celebration must be seen as a priority, and time and effort must be taken by pastor and faithful alike to achieve that goal. The *Order of Christian Funerals* points the way, and recently published hymnals continue to make the growing repertory of funeral music widely accessible.[34]

Silence and Symbols
Ritual silence and the symbols of the funeral liturgy are taken up in detail in their specific settings in the *Order of Christian Funerals*.[35] Nevertheless, it is worthwhile to affirm here the pastoral importance of becoming familiar with all the symbols described in the General Introduction (Nos. 35–39). These *verba visibilia*, or acted signs, play an indispensable role in the process of engaging the religious imagination of the bereaved and the larger community of the Church gathered for the funeral. It is becoming increasingly clear that the body itself of the deceased is one of the primary symbols of the funeral liturgy. In addition to the specific ritual symbols identified by the *Order of Christian Funerals*, we should become pastorally attentive to how those symbols relate to the focal symbol of the body in the coffin.[36]

NOTES

1. *Rituale Romanum* ex decreto sacrosancti oecumenici Concilii Vaticani II instauratum auctoritate Pauli PP VI promulgatum, *Ordo Exsequiarum* (Rome: Typis Polyglottis Vaticanis, 1969).

2. Already in November 1970, the U.S. Bishops' Committee on the Liturgy had received the approval of the Holy See for

the complete list of adaptations that have since come to characterize Catholic funeral liturgy in the United States. All who took part in the various stages of developing, testing, and evaluating the so-called "experimental funeral rite" recognized in this version the fruit of some five years of work. Not a few American liturgists expected that more of this work would have appeared in the typical edition as well, but the Congregation for Divine Worship opted for a more universal model. Dioceses such as Atlanta, Chicago, Green Bay, and St. Louis were pioneers among those designated to work on the pastoral revision of the rite. It was above all the adaptation of the Roman rite prepared by the Commission on the Sacred Liturgy in the Archdiocese of Chicago between 1966 and 1970 that became the American model. Those parts that now correspond most to Catholic funerary customs in the United States bear the distinctive marks of Chicago's experimental Rite of Christian Burial. [Commission on the Sacred Liturgy, *The Rite of Christian Burial* (Chicago: Archdiocese of Chicago, 1968)].

By the summer of 1971, published editions of the new Roman Rite of Funerals for use by Catholics in the United States appeared. On November 1—only two years after the Vatican's typical edition—Catholic churches across the United States began to appropriate the Rite of Funerals. [*The Roman Ritual* revised by decree of the Second Vatican Ecumenical Council and published by authority of Pope Paul VI, *Rite of Funerals:* Study Edition (Washington, D.C.: United States Catholic Conference, 1971). Editions by other publishers are listed in *BCL Newsletter* 7/6 (1971), s.v. Funeral Rite—Official Books.] For a pastoral review of its early impact, see Frederick R. McManus, "The Reformed Funeral Rite," *American Ecclesiastical Review* 116 (1972), pp. 45–59, 124–139.

3. *Order of Christian Funerals.* Approved for use in the dioceses of the United States of America by the National Conference of Catholic Bishops and confirmed by the Apostolic See. Published by authority of the Committee on the Liturgy, National Conference of Catholic Bishops, for liturgical use by three American publishing houses: Catholic Book Publishing Co.; Liturgical Training Publications; and Liturgical Press.

4. Pierre-Marie Gy, "Le Nouveau Rituel Romain des Funérailles," *La Masion-Dieu* 101 (1970), 20–21. An English translation of this entire article, "The Liturgy of Death. The Funeral Rite of the New Roman Ritual," is available in *The Way Supplement* 11 (Fall 1970), pp. 59–75.

5. See *Rite of Funerals* (1970) for the "Introductory Note" to Chapter II for use in the United States.

6. See, for example, *Christian Burial* (Mount St. Anne's Liturgy Center: Killenard, Portarlington [Ireland], 1975) and National Office for Liturgy, *Catholic Funeral Rite* (Ottawa: Canadian Catholic Conference, 1973).

7. The rich variety of ritual practice in the *Order of Christian Funerals* (1989) illustrates the fruit of this approach.

8. Centre Nationale de Pastorale Liturgique, *La Célébration des Obsèques* I (Paris: Desclée-Mame, 1972), pp. 7–14; *Die Kirchliche Begräbnisfeier in den katholischen Bistümern des deutschen Sprachgebietes,* hrsg. im Auftrag der Bischofskonferenzen Deutsch-lands, Österreichs und der Schweiz und des Bischofs von Luxemburg (Einsiedelin-Köln-Freiburg-Basel-Regensburg-Wien-Salzburg-Linz, 1973), pp. 11–20.

9. This translation renders the Latin as literally as possible to demonstrate the rhetorical effect of its opening with the words "paschale Christi mysterium." The English rendering of the 1983 emended edition of the OF Introduction reads as follows: "At the funerals of its children the Church confidently celebrates Christ's paschal mystery. Its intention is that those who by baptism were made one body with the dead and risen Christ may with him pass from death to life. In soul they are to be cleansed and taken up into heaven with the saints and elect; in body they await the blessed hope of Christ's coming and the resurrection of the dead." OCF, Appendix, p. 381.

10. This is not the place to discuss the precise theological meaning of traditional eschatological images such as incorporation into Christ dead and risen, passage through death to life, purification of souls, assumption into heaven with the saints, the parousia, or bodily resurrection. We take these as

the Introduction itself intends, viz., as an assertion of faith in the paschal mystery and all its consequences for the faithful.

A good contemporary summary of such theological reflection may be found in: Michael Schamus, *Dogma VI: Justification and the Last Things* (Kansas City-London: Sheed & Ward, 1977); A. R. van de Walle, *From Darkness to the Dawn. How Belief in the Afterlife Affects Living* (Mystic, Conn.: Twenty-Third Publications, 1984); and Joseph Ratzinger, *Eschatology* (Washington, D.C.: Catholic University of America Press, 1988). For consideration of how this biblical faith serves as a corrective of unrealistic funeral liturgy, see John P. Meier, "Catholic Funerals in the Light of Scripture, *Worship* 48 (1974), pp. 206–216, and Lawrence Boadt, "The Scriptures on Death and Dying and the New Funeral Rite" in Anthony F. Sherman, ed., *Rites of Death and Dying* (Collegeville, Minn.: Liturgical Press, 1988), pp. 7–29.

11. See the *General Instruction of the Roman Missal* (*GIRM*). No. 135, where the very same text is used when referring to the Mass only.

12. See *GIRM*, Nos. 1–4.

13. The Latin version reads: *offerre*. Although the ICEL (1970) rendering of *offerre pro* by "celebrate for" was quite understandable, the 1983 revised translation reads "offer for" (OCF, Appendix, p. 381). This distinction ought to be kept in mind as one studies contemporary American attitudes toward Mass and prayers *for the dead*. Appendix II explores the way many contemporary western Catholics understand "offering the eucharist for the dead" (*offerre . . . pro defunctis*).

14. For example, the revised American Episcopal *Book of Common Prayer* (1977) has restored the practice, which had not entirely disappeared from the preserve of Anglican tradition despite offical *Prayer Book* editions after 1552. See also the *Lutheran Book of Worship* (1978). For a thorough survey of Reformation and post-reformation rites and contemporary revisions, see Rowell, *Christian Burial*, 74–98 and 102–110; Bruno Bürki, *Im Herrn entschlafen* (Heidelberg: Quelle & Meyer, 1969), pp. 238–241 and 265–270; and James White, *Introduc-*

tion to Christian Worship (Nashville: Abingdon, 1980), pp. 267–271.

15. For greater detail, see Rutherford-Kandelman, *Religious Ritual*, and Rutherford, "Funeral Liturgy," with accompanying bibliographies. See also Rutherford, *Pastoral Care, passim*.

16. *Lumen Gentium*, No. 29, in Austin Flannery, ed., *Vatican Council II. The Conciliar and Post-Conciliar Documents* (Northport, N.Y.: Costello, 1975), p. 387; *Motu proprio Sacrum diaconatus ordinem*, No. 22, 5, in *The Pope Speaks* 12 (1967), pp. 237–243. See also Reiner Kaczynski, *Enchiridion Documentorum Instaurationis Liturgicae* I (Rome: Marietti, 1976), pp. 352–353. For the deacon with diocesan appointment this is "ordinary" ministry in the traditional Catholic sense of the term. Neither the absence of a priest nor designation by the local ordinary for specific funerals is necessary to validly exercise this ministry. The deacon exercises it by virtue of his ordination to service (*ad ministerium*) and his pastoral appointment. It is understood, however, that he is replacing the parish priest who carries the primary responsibility but who, for legitimate reasons, is hindered from being present.

17. See Kathleen Hughes, *Lay Presiding: The Art of Leading Prayer* (Washington, D.C.: Pastoral Press, 1988).

18. See Geoffrey Gorer, "The Pornography of Death," in Geoffrey Gorer, *Death, Grief and Mourning in Contemporary Britain* (New York: Doubleday, 1965; London: Cresset Press, 1965), *passim*.

19. See the excellent planning guide, Peter Gilmour, ed., *Now and at the Hour of Our Death* (Chicago, Ill.: Liturgy Training Publications, 1989).

20. Howard Raether, ed, *The NFDA Resource Manual* (Milwaukee: NFDA Learning Resource Center, 1988).

21. See *Order of Funerals* (1969), No. 25,1, and *Pastoral Care of the Sick: Rites of Anointing and Viaticum* (1983), Nos. 26–30, as well as Charles Gusmer, *And You Visited Me: Sacramental Ministry to the Sick and the Dying* (New York: Pueblo, 1984).

22. In the western United States, the practice of shielding the immediately bereaved from those who gather for

funeral-parlor services is being questioned more and more by practicing Catholics who wish to be one with the community for the liturgy of vigil and other serives. Neither minister nor funeral director should assume that separation is the preferred expectation of the bereaved.

23. Most American states do not require embalming unless the body is to be shipped by common carrier (if the condition of the body permits) or the cause of death was by virulent or dangerous disease, usually according to State statutes. The State Board of Health and Hygiene (or analogous title) should be consulted for specific regulations in each state. Diocesan cemetery directors are also a good resource for information about embalming and other specific requirements.

24. See below, pp. 324–328 and the more detailed treatment in a forthcoming booklet by this author and the Liturgical Press (tentative title: Honoring the Dead: Catholics and Cremation).

25. Evelyn Waugh, *The Loved One* (Boston: Little, Brown & Co., 1948). See the same author's nonfictional account of his visit to Forest Lawn in *Life* 23 (1947), pp. 73–83.

26. See Rutherford-Kandelman, *Religious Ritual*, pp. 38–47, and Rutherford, "Funeral Liturgy," pp. 83–100.

27. See Sparkes-Rutherford, "Lament," and Lawrence Boadt, "The Scriptures on Death and Dying and the New Funeral Rite," in Anthony F. Sherman, ed., *Rites of Death and Dying* (Collegeville, Minn.: Liturgical Press, 1988), pp. 20–25.

28. This is the basic tenet of Sigmund Mowinckel in *The Psalms and Israel's Worship* (Nashville: Abingdon, 1962; Oxford: Blackwell, 1962.)

29. See for example: Reginald H. Fuller, "Lectionary for Funerals," *Worship* 56 (1982), pp. 36–63; Richard Dillon, "The Unavoidable Discomforts of Preaching about Death," *Worship* 57 (1983), pp. 486–496; and Robert Krieg, "The Funeral Homily: The Theological View," *Worship* 58 (1984), pp. 222–239.

30. P-M. Gy, "Le Nouveau Rituel," pp. 15–33.

31. *Book of Common Prayer, Scottish Book of Common Order, The Liturgy of South India.* For an excellent summary of the Anglican position, see also T. Lloyd, *Anglican Worship Today* (London: Collins, 1980), pp. 206–227, the chapter on "Funeral Services."

32. Here concludes the summary of P-M. Gy's review.

33. For specific examples of such directives, see OCF, Nos. 68, 135–136, 139–140, 144, 147, 149, 157, 181, 214, 242, 270, 274, and the like.

34. The American edition of the *Order* by the Liturgical Press (Collegeville, Minn.) supports this renewal by including a Music Supplement, pp. 387–473.

35. Please consult the index for cross-referencing between specific rites and their symbols.

36. See Mary Dombeck, "Death Rituals and Life Values: The American Way," in Anthony F. Sherman, ed., *Rites of Death and Dying* (Collegeville, Minn.: Liturgical Press, 1988), pp. 59–62.

Chapter Five

The Order in Specific

The *Order of Christian Funerals* (Nos. 44 and 48) expresses clearly its desire that these funeral rites serve as models for appropriate pastoral practice in every situation of death in the parish community. Far from establishing a ritual rigidity to be imposed on every funeral, the General Introduction offers this collection of rites as the embodiment of the authentic Catholic tradition. Following the best of parish practice, the pastoral theology of the *Order of Christian Funerals* recognizes that the task of preparing the liturgy for any funeral will begin with the life and death of the deceased. Only then can "the book" provide appropriate models and patterns to shape the celebration. "The *Order of Christian Funerals* makes provision for the minister, in consultation with the family, to choose those rites and texts best suited to the situation: those that most closely apply to the needs of the mourners, the circumstances of the death, and the customs of the local Christian community" (No. 43).

One approach to successful pastoral use of the funeral rites is to regard the ritual moments as three movements in a symphony giving liturgical expression to the aspects of death: between death and the central funeral liturgy; the central funeral liturgy itself; and after the funeral liturgy, including committal and postfuneral memorialization. The *Order of Christian Fu-*

nerals includes models for each of these three moments and offers sound pastoral, theological guidelines for each of these model rites. "The minister and family may be assisted in the choice of a rite or rites by the reflections preceding each rite or group of rites" (No. 43).

Vigil and Related Rites and Prayers
(Nos. 51–127, 243–263, and 348–396) "This section . . . includes rites that may be celebrated between the time of death and the funeral liturgy or, should there be no funeral liturgy, before the rite of committal" (No. 45). Although the term "vigil" in the *Order of Christian Funerals* designates a particular liturgical rite of "vigil for the deceased," we can best serve the needs of the faithful at such a critical moment in their lives by regarding the whole span of time surrounding death and committal as a liminal time of "vigil."

The General Introduction accurately describes this first ritual moment of the funerals of Christians. "The time immediately following death is often one of bewilderment and may involve shock or heartrending grief for the family and close friends" (No. 52). How do we understand such a time of "vigil" in the light of tradition?

Nightwatch Vigils
We recall, first of all, how the Church was born out of a vigil around an empty tomb, nourished by the most basic belief of Christianity: Christ is risen and will soon return. To this day, Christians are a nightwatch people who gather to keep alive their hope in the return of the risen Lord, an assembly of believers for whom the memory of an empty tomb is a rich one. Lest we forget this essential truth of our faith, we remind each other time and again in the liturgy that Christ has died, is risen, and will come again. Jesus is

161

Lord forever, and Christian life knows no end. In this hope, the young apostolic church gathered to keep vigil—and we still do so to this day.

Theological emphases have changed over the centuries. We no longer live with that same sense of urgent expectation of the early church, that the risen Lord will return any day. As a consequence, the concept of vigil has also lost its urgency, its excitement, its sense of anticipation. Indeed, we celebrate only one vigil a year, the Easter vigil. Christmas and Pentecost show little trace of their original nightwatch celebration, and in contrast to those earlier Christians, we rarely meet to keep vigil on the memorial of death of some martyr, saint, or local personage. Vigils, other than Easter, mean little to us. Yet, we still identify with those early Christians as a pilgrim people, even though we may not share their patience—or impatience—about precisely when the Lord will return to claim all who have remained faithful to him.

Little wonder that Christian antiquity gave special emphasis to keeping vigil at the death of a member of the community, on certain days after death, and on the anniversary (*dies natalis*) of the person's birth into heaven. As we saw in Chapter One, the custom of keeping vigil had become so important that shrines, churches, and basilicas were built on the exact sites where burial had taken place, particularly of a martyr or bishop of the local community, in whose memory pilgrims gathered each year. We have seen how the Christian vigil in the context of funeral liturgy has played a unique part in the origin of the religious cemetery and the building of our first churches.

In the *Order of Christian Funerals*, the Church claims "vigil" as a prayerful, active experience. Keeping watch begins before the person has died; we gather at the bedside of a dying person to pray together with

162

the family. The revised rites, *Pastoral Care of the Sick* (with Viaticum and its prayers for use at the bedside in the dying moments of the adult Christian) and the *Order of Christian Funerals* enjoy a continuity of ministry. The Church celebrates the sacraments of the sick (Anointing) and of the dying (Viaticum) as a sign that God is our strength and hope; that Jesus' death and resurrection gives us hope; and that the Church is a caring, supportive community.

The revised *Order of Christian Funerals* acknowledges this continuity in the Vigil and Related Rites and Prayers for adults when introducing this first of three principal ritual moments in the funeral of Christians (No. 52). It then emphasizes the Church's supportive ministry of gently accompanying the mourners in their initial adjustment, cognizant of their need to express the sorrow of bereavement and to enjoy the treasure of consolation their faith holds for them. In this aspect of vigil or wake, the assembly shows its love for the deceased by how it cares for his or her family and closest friends suffering loss. Furthermore, it suggests how this occasion in itself can evangelize the Church, especially as an occasion of reconciliation (No. 53).

The Vigil and Related Rites and Prayers are opportunities for liturgical prayer that may be celebrated during this time between death and the funeral liturgy or committal. They enable the specifically Christian expressions of faith and hope to find an appropriate place in the funeral. This is an important pastoral emphasis, specifying the guiding principle of faith and its liturgical expression for everything that follows. Funeral rites provide the accepted Catholic form; they suggest those scriptural passages and prayers that help to make a funeral Christian. But it is the bereaved themselves, with the help of the funeral minister and the support of the community, who make any funeral a truly Christian proclamation of paschal faith

163

and prayer for the deceased. The *Ordo* cannot do that for us; it can only show the way.

The 1969 Introduction acknowledges the role of local custom in determining the significant moments for keeping vigil. "Depending on local custom, such special moments include the vigil at the home of the deceased, the laying out of the body, and the carrying of the body to the place of burial. They should be marked by the gathering of family and friends and, if possible, of the whole community to receive in the liturgy of the word, the consolation of hope and to offer together the eucharistic sacrifice, and to pay last respects to the deceased by a final farewell" (OF, No. 3). Neither the *Order of Funerals* itself nor local law canonizes these times. Family customs, unexpected circumstances (such as travel difficulties), work schedules, and the like must be considered when discerning these "significant moments."

What is "local custom"? In the United States, for example, during the past 50 years, the funeral home has almost entirely replaced the family home as the place of the "wake." Yet the notion of "wake" or spending time with the corpse, remains a customary part of the American funeral. Analysts of changing funeral customs include the "visitation or wake" among those that should continue.[1] This kind of wake provides a temporal context during which the proposed vigil and some of the related rites and prayers might take place.

Prayer during this interval of the wake has long been the custom in the United States. Generally speaking, Americans have inherited from their ethnic churches the practice of praying the rosary at wakes, a practice that was eventually carried over from the home wake to the funeral home. With the telescoping of extended periods of time in the home, appropriately punctuated by praying the rosary, into shorter periods of formal

164

visitation at the funeral home, the rosary took on a different role. It became identified as the formal Catholic prayer for wakes.

The *Ordo*, following the spirit of liturgical renewal, returns to the earlier nightwatch tradition and restores a scriptural service, modeled after the ancient vigil, as the principal liturgical action during this time of wake (Nos. 54–97; see also the Office for the Dead, Nos. 348–395).

The *Order of Funerals* does not discourage popular devotional prayer during the wake. Rather, it follows the principle of the *Constitution on the Liturgy* (No. 13), which encourages the integration of devotional and liturgical prayer in Catholic life. Although the General Introduction does not mention the rosary, this is not to imply that the rosary is no longer fitting as a popular devotion during the wake. In fact, recent efforts have been made to render the rosary even more fitting to the occasion by drawing the prayerful attention of the participants to the paschal mystery, for example, by reading short passages from Scripture between the decades and by reflecting on the relationship of the mysteries to the mystery of death.[2]

The *Ordo* encourages and offers models for liturgical prayer during this "nightwatch" time of vigil, by opening to the community a centuries-old treasure of Christian worship. In this way, it shapes the Catholic source from which devotions such as the rosary have their proper place and take on their fullest meaning. We have seen how both faithful people and funeral ministers are growing to appreciate more deeply the value of ecclesial community and to understand what it means in the funeral liturgy to worship as Church. More and more, the rosary is becoming the special devotional prayer of parish groups that gather to honor a deceased member, while the vigil for the deceased is recognized as the principal corporate act of celebration of the parish during the time of the wake.[3] Because of its importance, the vigil holds the first place in the *Order's* title for this time between death and the funeral liturgy and will be taken up first here.

The Vigil for the Deceased
"The vigil is the principal celebration of the Christian community during the time before the funeral liturgy (or, should there be no funeral liturgy, before the rite of committal). It may take the form of a liturgy of the word or of some form of the office for the dead" (No. 45). The model for the liturgy of the word is in two forms: vigil for the deceased, where the body is already present (Nos. 69–81) and vigil for the deceased with reception at the church (Nos. 82–97). The first form of vigil may be celebrated at the home, funeral parlor, or church, and is to be adapted to the place and circumstances. "The second service is used when the vigil is celebrated in the church and the body is to be received at that time" (No. 45).

Pastorally, it is worth emphasizing the adaptability of these model vigil rites. For example, when the vigil liturgy is celebrated in the church, it is to be scheduled "at a time well before the funeral liturgy, so that the funeral liturgy will not be lengthy and the liturgy of the word repetitious."[4] Similarly, "if the reception of the body at the church is celebrated apart from the vigil or the funeral liturgy, the 'Vigil for the Deceased with Reception at the Church' may be used and simplified" (No. 55).

To many American Catholics, the 1969 *Ordo*'s reference to "vigil at the home of the deceased" probably sounds archaic. It may seem like a medieval anachronism or perhaps reminiscent of old-time Irish wakes, stories about how great-grandmother had been laid out and "waked" in her own living room. This prac-

166

tice of "waking" the dead at home is still quite common outside the United States, and some parishes have reintroduced the home vigil, generally without the body present, as a time when the family and closest friends might remember and celebrate the deceased. It has proven to be one more way of spending important "quality" time together during the interval between death and the funeral liturgy. In some cases, especially where the bereaved are elderly or confined to their homes, the pastoral option to celebrate Mass in the home of the deceased is an appropriate climax to such a vigil.[5]

In the vigil, the liturgy of the word consists of several familiar parts. There are introductory rites of greeting, gathering song, invitation to prayer, and opening prayer that precede the celebration of the word itself: reading, psalm of response, gospel, and homily. General intercessions follow with an invitation to prayer, an intercessory litany for the assembly, the family, and the deceased, completed by the Lord's Prayer, a final prayer, and concluding rites of blessing and song. When celebrated with reception of the body at the church, a special rite of introduction replaces this rite with a greeting, a sprinkling of the coffin with holy water, the placing of the pall, an entrance procession with song, placing of Christian symbols where appropriate, an invitation to prayer, and the opening prayer.

While death is a time of intense personal grief, the liturgical celebration of death is not private; it is communal. Covenant with God is communal, and our worship reflects this. The vigil liturgy of the dead is more than collective personalism; it is the birthright of the assembly to celebrate communally the death of one of its members. Sometimes the assembly is denied the right of liturgical celebration by the wishes of individual family members about music, active participation, and the like. Death is a mystical moment in the life of the assembly, and the whole parish is entitled to celebrate its faith and hope on that occasion.

When we meet to celebrate the risen Lord among us in vigil, the most fitting form of response is song. We do not "celebrate" resurrection in silence. Words by themselves are insufficient. The assembly is enriched and grows in faith when it gathers publicly to celebrate in song and scripture the vigil liturgy of one of its deceased members. The *Order of Christian Funerals* leaves no doubt about this norm: "Music is integral to any vigil, especially the vigil for the deceased. In the difficult circumstances following death, well-chosen music can touch the mourners and others present at levels of human need that words alone often fail to reach. Such music can enliven the faith of the community gathered to support the family and to affirm hope in the resurrection."

"Whenever possible, an instrumentalist and a cantor or leader of song should assist the assembly's full participation in the singing."

"In the choice of music for the vigil, preference should be given to the singing of the opening song and the responsorial psalm. The litany, the Lord's Prayer, and a closing song may also be sung" (No. 68).

Office for the Dead (Nos. 348–396)
The Office of the Dead forms Part IV of the *Order of Christian Funerals* and consists of an introduction (Nos. 348–372), an order of Morning Prayer (Nos. 373–384), an order of Evening Prayer (Nos. 385–395), and a collection of five Additional Hymns (No. 396). This section of the *Ordo* is new to parochial practice in modern times. The 1969 *Ordo Exsequiarum* and the 1970 *Rite of Funerals* were developed within a Church no longer familiar with parochial prayer of the liturgical hours. In this context, the *Order of Christian Funerals* is seen to

reflect the desire of the Roman Catholic Church to encourage the whole liturgical assembly to pray the Divine Office not only as a vigil for the deceased but also as a liturgy of remembrance after the funeral has taken place. Together with the Mass, the Office is a public prayer that engages the whole Church in communion, both living and deceased. In both liturgical activities, we offer unending prayer and praise.

In the introduction to Part IV, the vigil for the deceased is associated with the celebration of some form of Morning or Evening Prayer (No. 348). It reflects on the community assembled to praise God (No. 349) and then compares the differing natures of Morning and Evening Prayer (Nos. 350–351).[6] The structures of these two liturgical hours are outlined (Nos. 352–367), with explanations and practical suggestions about the use of the resources provided. Finally, the section on ministry and participation (Nos. 368–372) discusses the importance of catechesis in encouraging the use of the liturgical hours and explores a variety of ways to enhance the celebration of these hours. (Appendix III presents a more thorough commentary on Morning and Evening Prayer in view of their pastoral place in the funeral liturgy.)

Vigil for a Deceased Child

In the vigil liturgy for adults, the assembly celebrates its own faith in the risen Lord, prays for God's continued healing presence, supports the bereaved, and commends the deceased to God's loving care. The vigil for a deceased child differs slightly. The order of service is similar in structure, but a special introduction sets out the differences (Nos. 234–242). "Children" are defined as "infants and young children, including those of early school age." There is more flexibility to adapt the rite to suit the occasion, with more appropriate texts specifically adapted to the needs of the family suffering such a tragic loss. Although the liturgy is intended for the whole assembly, the grief is likely to be contained within the family and groups of the child's playmates, family friends, and professional associates within the assembly. The Church worships God as author of life, commends the child to God's love, and prays for the consolation of the immediate family.

The *Order of Christian Funerals* (Nos. 240–242) has sensitively incorporated the fruit of much labor in current bereavement studies on the death of a child in relation to parents, siblings, and peers. Parish ministers are encouraged to follow the *Order's* lead by preparing themselves thoroughly for this special bereavement ministry.[7]

Following the revised Code of Canon Law (Can. 1183, 2), the emended version of the General Introduction to the *Ordo* has incorporated ecclesial praxis and provides for the funeral liturgy to be celebrated for unbaptized children whose parents intended them to be baptized (OF, No. 14 bis). By commending them to God's love, the Church prays that the bereaved may be consoled by Jesus' affirmation that the Kingdom belongs to these little children (Matthew 19:14).[8] The *Order of Christian Funerals* is careful to include an explanatory note to guide pastoral practice in this delicate matter and change of discipline. "In the general catechesis of the faithful, pastors and other ministers should explain that the celebration of the funeral rites for children who die before baptism is not intended to weaken the Church's teaching on the necessity of baptism" (No. 237, note 1). The long Catholic tradition of infant baptism, grounded in the faith of the parents and sponsors, and current liturgical law with regard to catechumens provide adequate foundation for successful catechesis in this matter. Rather than doubt the necessity of baptism, most Catholics find this new attitude quite in accord with Church teaching.

Particular consideration is to be given to any sisters, brothers, friends, classmates, or special relationships of the deceased child. The selection of music, prayers, and forms of the service should be prepared with these people in mind. Children may likewise participate in special ways, "as readers, acolytes, or musicians, or assist in the reading of the general intercessions and in the procession with gifts" (No. 242). The *Directory for Masses with Children* includes other adaptations that may be appropriate as well and ought to be consulted.

Adaptation to embrace intense parental grief and to encourage participation by other children is urged. Here, as above, the *Order of Christian Funerals* is providing direction and a model. One should note especially the need to simplify or shorten elements of the model vigil, while "other elements or symbols that have special meaning for those taking part may be incorporated into the celebration" (No. 246). Variations in text are given for baptized and unbaptized children, and the proposed readings speak about God's love.

In this section on vigils, the *Order of Christian Funerals* has maintained a good balance between liturgical authenticity and pastoral requirements. The liturgical aspect shows a genuine attempt to discover the roots of funeral practices in Western Christendom dating from the earliest times. The restoration of vigil as an integral part of the Catholic funeral is long overdue, and the models proposed are not strange to today's church. The liturgy of the word has become a familiar form of worship, and the liturgy of the hours is gradually becoming a more regular feature in the life of many parishes. The occasion of gathering for liturgy (public worship) in addition to devotion (collective piety) is one that should now be promoted with as much pastoral energy as can be mustered. We are not making new traditions but rediscovering some of the

171

most basic pastoral practices of our liturgical life.[9]
Moreover, the *Ordo* links the liturgical celebration of
the death of a Christian, child or adult, with life itself.
The celebrating assembly is simultaneously a supportive community. We gather to honor our dead through
worship precisely because we have shared the pain
and suffering of the family during the illness or shock
of sudden death; we have met for prayer with the family, pledging our support to the family for the times
ahead. In the Christian community, there ought to be
no unattended loneliness; death should bring deeper
bonds of support and friendship.

In summary, we acknowledge that vigil is a prayerful
and active experience. In a person's dying moments,
the Church gathers with the family to keep watch at
the bedside with special prayers, blessings, and eucharistic Viaticum. At death, we celebrate the Christian's
participation in the Lord's *Pascha* (Passover).[10] While
preparing the body for the funeral liturgy, we reflect
on the irony that our deepest respect for a fellow human is often shown when that person is lying so
peacefully in death. Nothing commands more awe
and gentleness than a dead person before us. At such
a moment, prayers are offered for that person and for
the family, and we relive many of our memories of the
one around whom we have gathered. As we visit with
the family and perhaps share refreshments, we are
keeping watch, mindful of one very special thought:
vigil celebrates a dead person who, in our faith-filled
sight and memory, is alive in God and fully present to
us.

In this frame of mind, we gather in the home, the
funeral parlor, or the church for our formal vigil liturgy. In the age-long custom of the Church, we light
our evening candle, the candle of baptism, the candle
of resurrection, to remind us that Christ is among us,
whose promise is that we shall live forever. In the se-

lections from Scripture (psalms and readings), we draw on our memory of covenant with God which guarantees that life will someday be changed for us, too, for the better. And in our concluding intercessions, we pray not only for, but with, all God's people living and dead. Once again, vigil has reminded us of our hope for fullness of life in Christ.

Related Rites and Prayers
Besides the vigil for the deceased and the devotional prayer of parish groups during the wake, there are other critical times in the period soon after death when clergy and parish ministers wish to pray with the family and close friends of the deceased. The related rites and prayers are models of liturgical pastoral care that the minister will adapt according to the circumstances of time, place, and culture (Nos. 98–100). Here, the *Order of Christian Funerals* transforms a recommendation of the American *Rite of Funerals* (1970) into proper pastoral models.

Such critical times occur when news of death has been received, "when the body is prepared and placed in the coffin, when the coffin is placed on the bier, when the family first comes together for prayer at the coffin, when the coffin is closed, or . . . before the body is taken to the church" (ROF, Introductory Note to Chapter 1). In the *Order*, they are identified and structured as follows:

"Prayers after Death" (Nos. 101–108) include an invitation to prayer, a Scripture reading (with a preference for the Gospels), the Lord's Prayer, a concluding prayer, and blessing by the presider, with appropriate forms provided for both an ordained minister and a lay person. "Gathering in the Presence of the Body" (Nos. 109–118) begins with the sign of the cross, a Scripture verse, sprinkling with holy water, a psalm, the Lord's Prayer, a concluding prayer, and a blessing

173

(by an ordained or lay person). "Transferring the Body to the Church or Place of Committal" (Nos. 119–127) begins with an address of gathering, followed by a Scripture verse, a litany for God's healing presence, the Lord's Prayer, a concluding prayer, an invitation to procession, and the procession, accompanied by a pilgrimage psalm of approaching God's house.[11]

Most people never share these moments when the intimate family and friends of the deceased may begin to confront realistically the meaning of death and loss— times when they begin to feel grief and pain deeply. At such moments, the *Order of Christian Funerals* recognizes the need for paschal faith and the consolation of Christian hope as well as the support of the entire community embodied in the presence of the minister.

These are times when a parish priest, deacon, or lay minister offers a needed presence in witness to paschal faith. These ministers represent for the bereaved the value of Christian community, the experience of Church that unites them and the deceased to Jesus dead and risen and to those countless others who share their baptismal life in the body of Christ.

However professional and competent the funeral counselor may be, he or she does not replace the priest or other designated ministers of the faith. Catholic lay persons offer a very worthwhile ministry as funeral directors and bereavement counselors, and it is important that they should be good at their profession. In the absence of other Catholic parish ministers, their special familiarity with, and sensitivity to, the funerary needs and desires of Christians prepares them well to stand by the bereaved in their need for prayer during these critical moments soon after death.

The ministry of gathering the believing Church at prayer around the bereaved is the responsibility of the ordained, yet the *Order of Christian Funerals* not only

174

provides for those times when lay women and men share that ministry but also recognizes how often it falls to the funeral director to fulfill the roles of both minister and Christian friend in addition to caring for the business of the funeral. Nevertheless, renewed priorities will allow the Catholic parish community of the future to be by the side of the bereaved in the person of its priest or deacon or special minister(s). By way of example, let us review one of the models for such presence now provided by the *Order of Christian Funerals.*

Gathering in the Presence of the Body—a model:
The service of washing, preparing, and laying out of the body is no longer a Christian ministry carried out by family and friends. Rather, since the beginning of this century, it has become a paid-for professional service rendered by a mortician. Frequently, the bereaved do not even see the body of the deceased after it is removed by the funeral director, until it is laid out in a funeral parlor. It is encouraging to hear of funeral directors who invite bereaved family members who so desire to assist with certain details of arranging the body: dressing the deceased, giving instructions about posture or themselves arranging the body in the casket, putting the final touches on dress, "tucking in" the deceased, closing the casket, and the like.[12]

When bereaved family members and intimate friends first see the deceased laid out in the casket, it is a moment of utter reality and a Christian time for prayer. The priest or other minister might arrange to meet the family at the funeral home before going in to see the body. He or she might offer to accompany them, should they wish, or to come in a little later, if they prefer. The point is that the priest or another minister be there for them. The minister would then invite the family to share a brief time of prayer together in

175

some agreed-upon manner.[13] The basic model for that short service follows the common pattern of reading, response, prayer, symbolic gesture, and blessing; it should be adapted to the specific circumstances (Nos. 109–118). "In prayer and gesture, those present show reverence for the body of the deceased as a temple of the life-giving Spirit and ask, in that same Spirit, for the eternal life promised to the faithful" (No. 110).[14]

At an opportune moment and in an atmosphere of calm and recollection, the one who is there on behalf of the Church would call the gathering to prayer with something that is very meaningful at this time of suffering: the cross, the sign of the cross. "In the Name of the Father, and of the Son, and of the Holy Spirit. . . ." This is the same cross as these people are experiencing.

After a moment (often powerful) of prayerful silence, God's word, short and to the point, places that cross in a context of divine compassion. The minister might say simply: "Jesus said, 'My brothers and sisters, come to me all you who labor and are overburdened, and I will give you rest.' " Even if this were the only bit of Scripture they heard at that moment—a small part of a larger suggested reading—it might be adequate. Or, continuing, "Shoulder my yoke and learn from me, for I am gentle and humble in heart, and you will find rest for your souls. Yes, my yoke is easy and my burden light." A brief period of silence might be especially appropriate at this point.

Liturgy happens at all kinds of levels at once. That's the function of symbol. Two layers of reality are reflected in that reading of Scripture: something felt about the dead person as well as the bereaved.

Following an invitation to prayer and the word of God, these rites include ritual gesture. The ritual gesture proposed here is a sprinkling with holy water. Some may find another gesture more appropriate, such as signing the deceased with holy water by hand on the breast and offering it to others present who might make the sign of the cross on themselves. Sprinkling holy water should be used with great care where the mortician's cosmetic work could be marred, a source of both distress and embarrassment.[15] Gesture is important in ritual action to spell out what we are doing, what has meaning to us. In selecting gesture, the minister should be sensitive to the occasion and the appropriateness of the gesture. For better or worse, those things are remembered.

Frequently, a short psalm, especially one of lament, is an appropriate symbolic word to fill out the ritual gesture or allow it to linger in the participants' imagination. Such a psalm will also frequently express the prayerful sentiments of the bereaved who are present or far away. When circumstances recommend it, members of the family sometimes find it helpful to recite the psalm on behalf of the others. Finally, the prayer of all present is expressed in the familiar ritual words of the Lord's Prayer, and a concluding prayer that fits the circumstances reminds the sad gathering that theirs is indeed the prayer of the Church. For example, in this description where Matthew 11:28–30 had been selected as scripture verse earlier in the rite, the following concluding prayer seems fitting:

Lord God,
you are attentive to the voice of our pleading.
Let us find in your Son
comfort in our sadness,
certainty in our doubt,
and courage to live through this hour.
Make our faith strong
through Christ our Lord. Amen. (No. 399,5)

After these short moments of prayer, the minister has a good opportunity to discuss briefly some choices and arrangements for the vigil, eucharistic celebration, and committal liturgy with both the bereaved and the funeral director.

The Funeral Liturgy (Nos. 128–203 and 264–315)
"The funeral liturgy is the central liturgical celebration of the Christian community for the deceased" (No. 128). Following the vigil, or nightwatch liturgy, the parish family gathers once again, spiritually united with that selfsame assembly which gathered at the empty tomb to proclaim, "Jesus is risen!"

One cannot help noticing the importance that the Introduction to the 1969 *Ordo* places on the liturgy of the word, the eucharist, and final commendation. Similarly, the unity between the celebration of the eucharist and burial (or other disposition) is a paradigm for other forms of funeral liturgy. Recognizing the legitimacy of different cultural patterns, the ritual is primarily interested in how these may kindle paschal faith and Christian consolation. Historically, these funeral rites have christianized many different cultural patterns, always drawing ultimate inspiriation from the paschal mystery, no matter how "pagan" or "unlikely" the customs being assumed. The *Order of Funerals* (1969) allows pastoral priorities to mold the ideal in order to serve different situations. This applies to the local parish as well as the universal Church. Thus, the *Ordo* is normative and descriptive of pastoral practice without being obligatory in its detail. It says with authority, "This is the way Catholics take leave of their dead." Priests and other ministers of the funeral are expected to discern, together with the bereaved, the best way the *Ordo* can give form to their specific funeral. This does not imply that planning a funeral becomes a burden to the faithful; nor should the *Order of*

178

Christian Funerals be regarded as one among an "anything goes" collection of rites.

It is best to think of the *Order of Christian Funerals* as the normative *resource book* for celebrating the Catholic funeral rather than as a *rituale* of the post-Tridentine era. Although it presents models to guide ordinary practice in most cases, fluidity in the selection and celebration of the rites will depend on the particular needs of the funeral.

The liturgy in the church, especially the celebration of the eucharist, remains the principal Catholic proclamation of paschal faith and source of Christian consolation. It deserves primary attention in planning the various services of the funeral. Even if the eucharist be celebrated at a time other than that between death and burial, it should take place as closely as possible to burial or other form of final disposition.

Two forms of the funeral liturgy are provided: the funeral liturgy (that is, funeral Mass) and funeral liturgy outside Mass. In all circumstances, a funeral Mass is the paradigm. However, certain reasons exist for celebrating a liturgy outside Mass (No. 178). The funeral liturgy outside Mass includes all elements of the funeral liturgy except that of the eucharist.

Besides the familiar exceptions stemming from the liturgical calendar,[16] selecting this form, centering on the liturgy of the word, would be determined by circumstances when the eucharist is not possible (no priest available) or not desirable (pastoral reasons judged adequate by the pastor and the family, such as ecumenical sensibilities). In the latter case, pastoral sensitivity must discern carefully both the need and impact of not celebrating the funeral Mass. Mixed-religion families, and families within which the religious practice of the elders is no longer shared by the adult children, increasingly choose a funeral liturgy outside Mass as the least challenging to the sensibilities of the participants and the best way of avoiding complications surrounding intercommunion. While these motives obviously have their pastoral value, one should not be too quick to reject the power of the funeral Mass to evangelize or to invite nonpracticing Catholics to reconciliation. Celebration of the eucharist at a Christian funeral is too important an issue to be a mere pawn in a game of compromise. There should be no "soft options" at such an important moment where time and eternity overlap.

When the bereaved happen to be elderly parishoners, it is worth remembering the stigma once attached to being "refused" the funeral Mass at burial. Wisely, the *Order of Christian Funerals* states: "When the funeral liturgy is celebrated outside Mass before the committal, a Mass for the deceased should be scheduled, if possible, for the family and friends at a convenient time after the funeral" (No. 128).

Because of traditional usage, the funeral liturgy with Mass has been termed simply funeral liturgy. Accepting that convention, we now consider this larger collection of rites, which cover the ritual time between the preliminary vigil (with related rites) and the rite of committal. The central liturgical action of the Catholic funeral, held preferably in the parish church, includes the reception of the body at the church (whether that takes place immediately before the funeral Mass or earlier), the Mass itself (liturgy of the word and of the eucharist), final commendation and farewell (which may be celebrated here with the Mass or later with the rite of committal), and the procession to the place of committal. The only difference between this funeral liturgy and the funeral liturgy outside Mass is that the liturgy of the eucharist (preparation of the gifts, eucharistic prayer, and communion rite) is not celebrated. However, to remind us of the essential place the eucharist holds in observing the death of a Christian, funeral liturgy outside Mass includes the recitation of the Lord's Prayer. Where funeral liturgy is celebrated outside Mass solely because of the shortage of priests, holy communion outside Mass could be appropriate, and the *Order of Christian Funerals* includes the rite (Nos. 409–410). This option will often fall to the lay presider.[17]

Reception of the Body
The reception of the body at the church is a significant homecoming. This is where Christian life begins in baptism and is nourished in the eucharist. This is also the place where the Christian family gathers to celebrate other "growth points" in life: confirmation, marriage, reconciliation, anniversaries.

The assembly that welcomes the body is the host community tracing its unbroken line to the assembly of the Apostles. Here, the communion of saints is made visible. The person whose body is solemnly carried into the church is present among us in the communion of the baptized. The symbols which greet the casket are reminders of a living faith, which cannot be quenched by death.

We greet the family and loved ones accompanying the coffin, welcoming them as pilgrims who have chosen "to walk in the presence of the Lord in the land of the living" (Psalm 116:9). The dead person is as much part of that procession as are those who have gathered at the entrance. Those who are already assembled within the church are likewise involved in this liturgy of welcome. The sprinkling with holy water, the placing of the pall, the lighting of the Easter candle, are all signs of baptism, to celebrate the rite of passage not from but into the land of the living. To emphasize the importance of these symbols and the equality of all the baptized before God, all other flags and insignia are removed from the casket upon arrival at the church (No. 38). These may be replaced after the coffin is taken from the church.

In these rites of gathering, the liturgical assembly meets as the communion of saints. We come together in a geographical place at a specific time in history. Yet, when we do this, we are also joined in fellowship by all who have lived before us. We greet the dead person as one we believe to be alive in God's presence and newly arrived in the company of the Apostles, the Martyrs, and all the Saints.

Singing an entrance song during the procession is recommended to draw the community together (No. 135). This is a song of gathering, of approaching God's house in faith, as well as of intercession for the deceased. Examples from Scripture of such songs of faith in resurrection and eternal life are given in the *Order of Christian Funerals* (No. 403).

What is the mind-set of the entrance song? In the company of those ancient Jewish pilgrims, making their festive journey to the temple, we can sing, "Let us go to God's house rejoicing" (Psalm 122). Our hero in this pilgrimage is the dead person among us who, "now rejoicing in the Courts of the Lord" (Psalm 84), reminds us that life and our hope in the future are not in vain. As we "come before the Lord, singing for joy" (Psalm 100), we not only express our hope but are also formed into a people of expectation. To long for God's presence "as the dry land craving water" (Psalm 63) or "as the deer yearning for running streams" (Psalm 42) becomes the song of the living who have gathered to honor those who have gone before them and now enjoy "the resting place of the Lord" (Psalm 95). The opening song is not the triumphant entrance of the ministers but the liturgical action which makes real the gathering of the community in eucharistic assembly.

Liturgy of the Word

In the liturgy of the word, the faith community renews its belief in the resurrection. The assembly meets once again to hear the retelling of those stories upon which it bases its hope. In this liturgy, those who have gathered to mourn a dead person also meet to celebrate the promise of life without end, made by Jesus Christ, one who was once dead but who is now alive. In this coming together, we celebrate a baptism (as symbolized by the white pall) and a wedding feast (one from our faith community has gone to the banquet of the risen Lord). The risen Lord is already returning to the Church of expectation (awaiting the endtimes) as we gather to hear the word of God and enact the eucharist.

The readings are to be chosen according to pastoral circumstances (No. 138). There may be one or two readings before the Gospel. Part III of the *Order* provides a selection of scriptural texts,[18] all of which are interchangeable (No. 344). The minister is responsible for making the choice in consultation with the family and close friends of the mourners.

Two factors should determine our number and choice of scriptural passages. The first is the actual circumstance of our gathering. Why are we here? Who has actually gathered? Our decisions should be based on quality rather than quantity. Some assemblies, for example, whether large or small, may be more spiritually mature and require a more substantial liturgy of the word. The second factor pertains to the theology contained in the readings. The homilist should develop the thread of the liturgy from a sensitive and imaginative choice of readings. Each passage of scripture is a fragment from the past of a certain faith community's level of theological understanding. The chosen readings and the homily invite the present-day faith community to share the perceptions of our forebears about their God, encouraging the assembly to make its own response in faith.

Although the Hebrew Scriptures do not represent the same highly developed belief in afterlife as appears in intertestamental and New Testament literature, they witness firmly to a belief in the covenant between the people and their God. The very title of "Yahweh" implies "I shall be there for you," especially in moments of deepest need. In an age where king gods lived and died, Israelites believed firmly in a God-King who, despite their lapses, was always there for them, a God "who never slumbered, but kept watch over them" (Psalm 121). In the Hebrew mind, "life" included more than physical life and meant being in communion or friendship with God; "death," in turn, meant being absent from God, turning one's back on God.

The earliest Christian community, too, was not concerned about afterlife. The community of the Apostles and their successors believed that the Lord, who had risen from death, would very soon return to the fellowship of believers. On that day of judgment, those who had been vigilant and faithful to the Lord would be drawn together into unending fellowship with God. This hope was central to the community's understanding of baptism. Even in the gospels, those earliest faith communities attached more importance to the "coming of heaven on earth" than to merely "going to heaven." Israel's restoration hopes were made articulate in gospel tradition: "Your kingdom come on earth as in heaven" (Luke 11:2; Matthew 6:9). The strongest command in the gospels is for vigilance, to be awake and ready to greet the risen Lord when he returns to reclaim the new Israel. See also, for example, Paul's admonitions in 1–2 Thessalonians.

The psalms are the most important songs or hymns we sing in our liturgy. The songbook of Israel is, to this day, the basic hymnbook of the Christian community. These songs of trust in a personal God express our deepest joys and anxieties. The very words tell us of God who is always there for us. They are full of joy in a living God, celebrating even in moments of great sorrow and distress our constant hope that God is a God of promise who will never abandon us. These are the love songs of a covenant people for whom this life is but one great step closer to God. A pilgrimage people who have known the exile of the desert will one day know fresh green pastures, confident in God's safekeeping (Psalm 23). In the psalms, we are able to give God a name: "You who are life for us," "You are our future," "Hope of the forsaken," "You who are our freedom," and so on.

The gospel alleluia is the song of our resurrection hope. We sing alleluia because we are an Easter people, the people of a living God. In Psalm 150 we acknowledge that everything with life and breath praises God in unending alleluias. "Alleluia" must never become a word of "private" adoration or contemplation; it is the voice of the living, assembled in praise of the one who is always there. On the lips of the early church, "alleluia" was the only fitting response for the news "the Lord is risen!" In our most ancient Easter hymns, we keep alive that echo, "Christ the Lord is risen; now he lives to die no more. Alleluia!" Hallelujah is an ancient liturgical invitation to praise "Yah" as "You who are here and now present for us."

Various suggested forms of intercession are provided. In the model liturgy of Part I (No. 167), two forms are given, and in the Alternative Texts, Part V, seven forms are provided (No. 401). These include prayers for the deceased according to "status" (whether the person be lay or ordained, adult or child) and for the mourners. "The following intercessions and litanies may be used during a liturgy of the word or a Mass

and should be adapted according to the circumstances" (No. 401).

Liturgy of the Eucharist
Having assembled to hear God's word, we now gather
at the eucharistic table. The procession with the gifts
should not be focused on the gifts alone (a false focus), for this is a symbolic movement that encourages
a procession in the minds and hearts of each of us:
Having heard the word and responded, we are mov-
ing in procession to a new mode of celebration. This is
a transition from *listening* to *giving thanks*. Presenting
the gifts is not insignificant; it is a visual means of
preparing us for the second stage of celebration. We
have heard the proclamation that Jesus has indeed
risen and is coming again, and we have renewed our
faith in the living Lord, who has transformed death
into a victory for life; we now gather to give thanks by
sharing the bread and cup of life and "calling to
mind" God's promises made on our behalf.

The liturgy of the eucharist takes place in the usual
manner. The General Introduction invites special participation by members of the family, and encourages
due reverence to the casket as a focal symbol of this
liturgy. Eucharistic Prayers II and III are recommended
for use at the funeral Mass "because they provide special texts of intercession for the dead. Since music
gives greater solemnity to a ritual action, the singing
of the people's parts of the eucharistic prayer should
be encouraged. . ." (No. 144).

The memorial acclamation that the people sing expresses the great belief of the early church: Christ has
died, Christ is risen, Christ will soon come again.
Theological emphases in the Church have changed
across the centuries; but in light of this earliest belief,
everything else enjoys relative significance (or insignifi-
cance); only the imminent return of the risen Lord mat-

186

tered. All who died before the return of the Lord are already in God's safekeeping (1 Thessalonians 4:13–18; Wisdom 3:1–9). In the memorial acclamation, we are proclaiming the return of the risen Lord to the Church.

Intercessions are made for the whole church, living and dead. This invocation, both of and by the whole communion of saints, draws special attention to the dead person with whom we are praying and who is mentioned by name.

In conclusion, a doxology, or hymn of praise, is proclaimed, again acknowledging God as author of all life and our certain future. God as our future! What a wonderful way to end our acclamations of thanksgiving. The "great amen" is much more than a simple word of affirmation. "Amen" comes from a verb that means "to depend on totally." Our very being is dependent on the existence of a God who is our hope for the future.

In the communion rite, the Lord's Prayer is a reminder of God's kingdom coming to earth; we who pray "Your kingdom come" share responsibility for making that happen. The dead person lying before us also has accepted some share in building the kingdom and, indeed, will continue to work alongside us as we wait in joyful hope for the return of Jesus, one whose name means "I shall be there with you to save." The prayer for peace acknowledges that Jesus' presence and wholeness is gathering us into one people around our risen Lord of life.

During the breaking of the bread, which follows, the litanic Lamb of God sings of hope in resurrection. Jesus is the paschal lamb, whose high feast awaits all who live faithful to his name. To understand these images of shepherd and lamb better, we may return to the Psalter. The title "Shepherd of Israel," Psalm 80, reminds us of the covenant by way of a ballad and a litany for the God of the powers to be here among us as our shepherd (see also Ezekiel 37:15–28 about the great hope of reunification of Israel at the end of time). Psalm 23, "The Lord is my shepherd," is itself the song of a messianic people, who live in the hope of God's coming among us. In Psalm 100, we gather to worship as the flock "who have been gathered into God's house," an allusion to the messianic age already arrived. Psalm 95 rejoices in the fact that in gathering for worship, we are called to conversion by the one who has "guided us to these pastures."

The communion sharing of the bread and cup does not exclude the dead person. We share in the same heavenly banquet. In this life, we still rely on ordinary things, such as bread and wine, to remind us of who God is for us. In death, we no longer need reminding because we no longer depend on our senses, being fully in the presence of God. Every time we gather at the table of the Lord to share the bread and cup, we are gathering with all who now enjoy God's presence face to face. We rely now on signs and wonders; the day will come when we no longer need such things.

Our communion with the saints is further emphasized in the proclamation/acclamation accompanying the distribution. "The body of Christ, amen," and "The blood of Christ, amen," do not refer simply to the bread and the cup. They also refer to the assembly gathered at this table. *We* are the body and blood of Christ. Included in this "we" is the deceased member who continues to enjoy fellowship with the Church but now in a totally new and different way. During the communion procession, suitable songs include those of coming into God's presence, going up to God's house, and songs of God's presence among us. The General Introduction recommends Psalms 27, 34,

63, and 121 as communion processional songs (No. 144).

The thanksgiving, which follows, is a time for reflection and stillness. Liturgy, while prayerful, can be busy. It is good to take a moment in community to be at rest. The vision of the Old Testament was to enjoy the Lord's rest (Psalm 95), to sit and enjoy God. Perhaps, at occasional moments during the day in the weeks, months, and years to come, we could pause for a moment and be with our departed loved one, who is likewise taking delight in being with God. Such pleasures need not be postponed until our own funeral liturgies.

The presider draws the liturgy of the eucharist to a close with the presidential prayer after communion. This thanksgiving asks for God's presence among us, as at this very moment our dead brother or sister is enjoying God's presence.

Final Commendation (Nos. 145–147)
The final commendation now takes place.[19] This rite has the same ritual form, whether following the funeral Mass (Nos. 170–175) or funeral liturgy outside Mass (Nos. 197–202). In both cases, where committal is to follow immediately, the procession to the place of committal provides the rite of transition from the church to the place of final disposition (Nos. 176 and 203). In situations where the funeral liturgy is celebrated after committal, the final commendation is part of the rite of committal; here, again, the same ritual form for the commendation is observed (Nos. 224–232).[20] In some cases, because of extraordinary pastoral circumstances, where no other rites of the *Order of Christian Funerals* would be appropriate, the rite of final commendation might be the only liturgy celebrated prior to interment or cremation.

What is so important about this short rite of final commendation? Why is it an indispensable part of all the funeral rites of the *Order of Christian Funerals?*

The 1969 Introduction teaches us first what the rite is not. "The meaning of the rite does not signify a kind of purification of the deceased . . ." (OF, No. 10). This strong negative assertion is meant to counteract remnants of past funeral theology that continue to confuse this rite with an absolution from sin. The Introduction reminds us that any such "purification" is accomplished through the eucharistic sacrifice, although even there sacramental absolution is not implied. This rite is understood rather "as a farewell by which the Christian community together pays respect to one of its members before the body is removed or buried" (No. 10). These words of Cardinal Lercaro, president of the liturgy *Consilium* in 1969, articulate the current theological interpretation of what was formerly the *absolutio* after the funeral Mass. This renewed understanding derives from early Byzantine practice that christianized the ancient, cultural gesture of a "farewell kiss" for the deceased. The Introduction cites "The Order of Burial" of Simeon of Thessalonica. In death, Christians are not truly separated from one another, Simeon explains, because all follow the same path to the same destination, namely communion with Christ where all the faithful will be together in Christ.[21] Thus, while expressing hope and consolation through paschal communion, this rite also graphically marks the end of the human relationship severed by death. When this rite enhances faith, it can be one more spiritual moment of beginning to "let go," of closure, and initial grief work. Human grieving and the rite of farewell blend in mutual service, not in isolation from one another but as an integration of life and faith.

The final commendation is also found in Part II of the *Order of Christian Funerals* as one of the Funeral Rites for Children. Ritual structure is the same as above, with the Scripture readings, prayers, and gestures adapted to the special circumstances (Nos. 288–292, 309–314, and 327–336). The rite of final commendation for an infant[22] (Nos. 337–341), as recommended in recent pastoral care literature, deserves particular attention in the light of increasing sensitivity to the specific bereavement needs of parents and siblings mourning a newborn or stillborn infant. ICEL editors are to be congratulated for their pastoral foresight in including this short rite; it will provide an invaluable model in parish and hospital ministry where bereaved parents are more and more being encouraged to hold a simple funeral or memorial service.[23]

The *Consilium* intended that the rite of final commendation stand out as a permanent and recognizable moment of faith not to be omitted. Not only does this renewed rite differ in spirit and theology from the former absolution after Mass, it is also no longer viewed as an appendage to the funeral Mass. Like the liturgy of the word, the rite of final commendation and farewell is an essential liturgical element of the *Order of Christian Funerals*.

Many English-speaking Catholics have not yet grasped this new understanding of the rite of final commendation. In some cases, the American Catholic funeral, for example, has simply replaced the former absolution with the new rite, a mere change of words to accompany the former gestures. The *Ordo*, however, is attempting to introduce something different, and pastoral renewal has acknowledged its potential for the further enrichment of the funeral liturgy.

The rite of final commendation is very simple, yet preparation and care are needed for it to be most effective. It combines two basic elements of the liturgical renewal: active participation and prayerful silence.

Both are difficult to realize in the very mixed congregations that usually gather for a funeral. Sensitivity to the particular assembly, especially the bereaved, and a sense of timing are crucial. The degree of participation and the occasions for silence are determined by whether the rite immediately follows Mass or the liturgy of the word or is celebrated at the cemetery.

Invitation to Prayer and Silence
The commendation begins with an invitation to prayer (Nos. 171 and 198). Two models of prayer are provided (along with a further five in No. 402). This invitation to pray in trust to a living God is a formal way of articulating our sadness at saying farewell. Words alone are inadequate; a period of silence and signs of farewell follow (Nos. 172 and 199).

The invitation to prayer alerts all present to the uniqueness of the moment, and the silence that follows allows them to enter personally into this final commendation and expression of last farewell. Here is an interplay of active participation and silence. This invitation to prayer is to ensure that what follows is truly an opportunity for faith-filled prayer, commending the deceased to God while at the same time proclaiming paschal faith and consoling hope. The presiding minister's words are important, the invitation having been prepared as thoughtfully as the funeral homily. They are to include both an introduction and brief explanation (OF, No. 10; OCF, No. 147).

What better time to experience the power of such prayer-filled silence in the liturgy than the closing moments of a funeral! Devotional silence in church is not foreign to Catholics; this old, treasured habit is now called upon to serve the Church in a new way. The psychology of prayer once again interweaves with the psychology of grief. At this significant moment, silent prayer allows the assembled community to experience the Christian faith of committing their dead to the mercy of God through Jesus dead and risen, while providing the opportunity to accept the human finality of death. Both in faith and in life, the bereaved begin to say farewell. The presider makes no concluding "collect" prayer to close the silence. That occurs in the prayer of commendation following the song of farewell.

Signs of Farewell
After the invitation to prayer and appropriate silence, signs of farewell are made (Nos. 173 and 200). These include sprinkling the coffin with holy water and honoring it with incense. Water as a symbol of passage (Red Sea, Jordan River), cleansing, and giving of life is familiar from baptismal liturgy (No. 36). The symbolic use of incense is more dependent on history for its funerary interpretation, as we observed above. Although these symbolic actions have been part of the Christian preburial rites in the West since early medieval times, they seem anachronistic to many people today. Nonetheless, the *Ordo* (1969) and the *Order of Christian Funerals* have preserved the use of holy water and incense in the funeral liturgy, specifically for the rite of final commendation. The reason for keeping them is rooted in their natural symbolism and long tradition. However, their significance as signs of farewell is a further interpretation proposed by the drafters of the Introduction (OF, No. 10).[24]

Song of Farewell
The least understood part of this short rite is the song of farewell (Nos. 174 and 201). The *Ordo* intends this song of farewell to be experienced as the climax of the entire rite of commendation. Some churches have not even attempted it on a regular basis; yet the text and melody of the song should be such that it may be sung by all present (OF, No. 10). The text "Saints of

God," with its venerable history in Christian funeral rites discussed in Chapter One, is recommended, and six other texts are provided (No. 403) as litanies and songs of a baptismal people. Any appropriate *valedictio*, or farewell song, in the popular religious traditions of a parish may serve this purpose.[25] Ethnic parishes might explore the rich treasury of familiar songs of farewell and hope "till we meet again." Without blunting the edge of sadness, such songs serve to sharpen our senses to the fundamental belief that Christ is risen and we, too, shall rise with Christ.

Why is the song of farewell, as climax of this rite, sung so infrequently? Though never formally rejected, the song has simply never been fully understood or widely encouraged. Even before the *Rite of Funerals* made its official appearance in English in 1970, the song of farewell was practically doomed to failure.

Hindsight reveals that the proposed Roman funeral ritual issued as a guide for official experimentation in 1967 does not mention the song of farewell by title or indicate its specific importance.[26] The responsory "Saints of God" was already included there, but it seems to serve more as a traditional replacement for the responsory *"Libera me"* than as a new climactic song of farewell. By 1968, the so-called Chicago rite, developing this Roman experimental rite, was published and likewise gave no hint of the importance of a song of farewell. In addition to a responsory proposed by the Roman experiment, the widely used Chicago rite offered a short litany "expressive of the better sentiments in the former responsory *Libera me* but better relating our 'deliverance' through the power of Christ's mysteries."[27]

This Chicago rite greatly influenced the provisional American version of the *Rite* (1970). By that time, the experimental rite of commendation and farewell already took root in American soil and, although included only as a substitute in the ritual of 1970, it was destined to become the usual practice. Meanwhile, the subcommittee of the *Consilium* collected similar experiments and reactions to experiments from across the world and during 1968 prepared the typical edition of the *Ordo*. It was apparently during this final year of revision that the song of farewell emerged as the appropriate climax of the rite of final commendation. Unfortunately, it came as something quite new to the parochial experience when it appeared in the 1970 *Rite of Funerals*. Not only were other forms already more familiar, but introducing such an important sung piece met with the resistance that greeted all "new music in the liturgy" during those difficult times. Indeed, as time went on, no one missed it. Nevertheless, because it is a major expression of the faith embodied in the rite (commendation and farewell in hope of resurrection), omitting the song has had an effect on the understanding and appreciation of the entire funeral liturgy.

Now, however, all this is history, and liturgical renewal cannot any longer claim the prerogatives of a necessary interim. "Strong and effective songs of farewell," as they were prophetically described in 1970[28] are now available. Much work still needs to be done, however, for the song of farewell to characterize the rite of final commendation and thus allow it to express more fully the paschal faith and be a greater source of consoling hope through community song.

Prayer of Commendation
"A prayer of commendation concludes the rite. In this prayer, the community calls upon God's mercy, commends the deceased into God's hands, and affirms its belief that those who have died in Christ will share in Christ's victory over death" (No. 147). The final prayer

195

of commendation (Nos. 175 and 202) is full of tenderness and hope, as are the six additional texts (No. 403). The sad moment of farewell has arrived. Yet, as a pilgrim people, we should expect no resting place until our own time has come to enter God's rest.

The prayer of commendation, like the other liturgical elements of the final commendation, bridges the centuries of many different funerary variations and unites Christians of today with those of history. Commendation has been a constant means whereby the Christian mind and heart gives flesh and blood to paschal faith in life with God after death. For example, it is the foundational concept underlying expressions of belief in the communion of saints.[29] Commendation is likewise a point of Christian faith enjoying renewed ecumenical interest. In his *Introduction to Christian Worship*, Methodist liturgical scholar James White cites the commendation of the deceased to God as one of the two principal possibilities for understanding the function of Christian burial beyond the purely utilitarian order.[30]

At these closing moments of public farewell, the prayer of commendation places two very important assertions on the lips of the community of faith for all to hear, including, and perhaps especially, the most intimately affected of the bereaved. One is the assertion of reality that the deceased is indeed dead, and the other is the assertion of belief that a continuity of relationship with the deceased is an acceptable source of consolation when the reality of the loss erupts in all the emotions of grief during the months ahead. Finally, the prayer of commendation also proclaims with confidence that the time will come when the bereaved will no longer grieve in the same way as during this time of mourning, and that, too, is as it should be, for life with God in the communion of saints is founded on bonds of faith, not on emotions.

Like the invitation to prayer, which introduces this rite of final commendation, the prayer of commendation, which closes it, plays an important role in funeral ritualization. With this prayer, the end of any direct association with the body of the deceased is in sight. The moment of final closure approaches. Whether this transition is experienced as welcome or dreaded by the bereaved according to the circumstances, it is almost universally an emotionally loaded moment. It is, therefore, a point in the ritual where faith and life meet dramatically and where faith, as expressed in the liturgy, has power to shape the meaning of this death for the bereaved and the assembly. As such, it, too, requires careful preparation. Certainly, all the selections provided in the *Order of Christian Funerals* should be reviewed to confirm their appropriateness in the specific circumstances of the funeral, and where necessary and authorized, they should be pastorally adapted.

Limits and Exceptions
The rite of final commendation is to be held only as part of the funeral celebration itself, that is, with the body present, except where such presence is physically or morally impossible. Obviously, a rite of giving the deceased over into God's hands and of leave-taking makes no sense if the liturgy being celebrated is not strictly speaking a funeral. In consequence, this eliminates the former anomalous practice permitting the *absolutio* after anniversary and memorial Masses for one or many of the faithful departed. That rite, carried out around a token bier or catafalque, was a remnant of medieval memorial services. Because the service was primarily one of intercessory prayer for the dead, the dramatic effect of such a catafalque was apparently believed to elicit greater devotion and prayer. The practice, still familiar not so long ago on All Souls Day, no longer holds the same meaning and

has disappeared quietly into liturgical folklore with the coming of the liturgical renewel.

Quite a different matter is the situation where it is physically or morally impossible for the body to be present. Because the liturgy celebrated in such circumstances is every bit a "funeral" in the common understanding and sensitivity of people, a service of commendation is appropriate. Although the body cannot be physically present, the paschal faith ritualized by prayer of commendation and a song of farewell deserves nonetheless to be expressed. The consoling hope, thus celebrated and deepened, and the opportunity for leave-taking ought not to be minimized, especially when the reality of death is rendered all the more concealed due to the absence of the corpse. Nevertheless, the *Ordo's* concluding principle regarding the commendation liturgy (OF, No. 10) must govern the adaptation of the rite to situations where the body is not present. Under no circumstances would the use of holy water or incense be appropriate. The invitation to prayer and the commendation prayers themselves need to be adapted to the circumstances. In such exceptional situations, again, the song of farewell and the prayer of commendation clearly constitute the ritual high point of the liturgy of commendation.

Procession to the Place of Committal (Nos. 148–149)
In the procession to the place of committal, the *Order of Christian Funerals* has restored the spirit of the funeral procession. It is well to remember that the procession from church to grave noted in the earlier Christian tradition ordinarily would not have been much longer than the recessional of today's funeral and the walk with the casket to the grave. It is not distance but a sense of movement with the deceased as liturgical action that creates a funeral procession.

The procession to the place of committal is to be tailored to suit the circumstances (Nos. 176; 203; 315). A hymn or chant may accompany the procession from the church. Verses from Psalms 25 and 116 are recommended, with familiar antiphons for the people to sing. Both psalms speak eloquently of God's saving power. The Scripture section of the *Order of Christian Funerals*, Part III, provides appropriate psalms and selected verses. The chant *In paradisum*, for example, which in the 1969/1970 rituals served as a recessional antiphon in the post-Tridentine pattern, has been restored to its traditional place of preeminence with Psalm 25.

The funeral procession as such is no longer common in most first world nations because of urban congestion, the distance between church and cemetery, a change in public mourning customs, and the like. Yet, the appropriate symbolism and long tradition of these psalms deserve pastoral attention. For example, by means of simple repetition, they can beautifully express the continuity of faith professed in a procession which begins with the movement of the casket from the church to the waiting hearse and then continues at the cemetery for the short walk with the casket to the graveside or cemetery chapel. Furthermore, arrival at the cemetery is often an awkward moment. The symbolic language of our authentic ritual tradition is available to render that difficult moment of today's funeral a processional of faith rather than an uncomfortable experience of not knowing how to behave.

Rite of Committal (Nos. 204–233 and 316–336)
"The rite of committal, the conclusion of the funeral rites, is the final act of the community of faith in caring for the body of its deceased member" (No. 204). There are two forms of the rite of committal for adults. Most familiar is the rite celebrated when final

199

commendation takes place at the conclusion of the funeral liturgy (Nos. 216–223); committal with final commendation (Nos. 224–233), although less common, is a pastorally valuable option, particularly in view of funerals involving cremation.[31] Likewise, there are two parallel forms for funerals of children (Nos. 319–326 and 327–336). The pastoral introduction to the two forms for adults (Nos. 204–215) is reiterated in the introduction to the rites for children (Nos. 316–318).

"Whenever possible, the rite of committal is to be celebrated at the site of committal, that is, beside the open grave or place of interment, rather than at a cemetery chapel" (Nos. 204 and 316). Included as places of interment are "grave, tomb, or crematorium." Locating the celebration of the rite at a crematorium is consistent with the understanding implicit in the *Order of Funerals* that cremation constitutes a technologically accelerated form of physical decomposition. At a crematorium, the rite of committal with final commendation serves well pastorally, and an adapted version of the standard rite is recommended for ritualizing the interment of the ashes at a later time (No. 212). The rite of committal (often with final commendation) is recommended for "burial at sea," and a model prayer is included among additional prayers to inspire and guide pastoral care under those extraordinary circumstances (Nos. 406, 3).

"In committing the body to its resting place, the community expresses the hope that, with all those who have gone before marked with the sign of faith, the deceased awaits the glory of the resurrection" (No. 206). In the always dramatic and emotionally charged setting of final disposition, the rite of committal extends the faith expressed in the final commendation and bonds the Church on earth with the Church in heaven, celebrating the farewell of the faith community here with the simultaneous welcome by the community who now see God face to face.

Nowhere do the paschal faith of Christians and the crosses of human mortality meet more explicitly than beside an open grave or other final resting place (No. 209). It is the authentic tradition of the Church to be present there.[32] The liturgy of committal thus embodies the consolation of faith, which gives meaning to this seemingly most meaningless experience of human loss, and promises the continued presence of the Church.

Lament
In this context it may be helpful to consider the prayer form of lamentation, already alluded to in the funeral liturgy of the word. Lamentation in Old Testament times was born of grief and anxiety. For the community or individual, emotionally exhausted, grief was ritualized in common.

The ritual of lament included a statement of the reasons for grief. To expressly articulate the causes of deep sadness can in itself be therapeutic and an initial step in the healing process. After this open confrontation with the cause for grief, the next stage was one of expressing anger. If God is a God of mercy, then why should such misfortune be allowed to happen? Where is this God of ours? An expression of anger, even against God, can likewise be a giant step on the road to healing. At this point in the Temple Liturgy, a priestly oracle would have been given, a reminder of God's faithfulness. Realization dawns. Why have we expressed such anger, given vent to such feelings? Do we not have higher expectations of God? God is loyal and to be trusted. Out of this realization is born the final stage of trust and confidence in the God who is here for us in these times of our greatest need.

The strength of lamentation as a prayer form lies in its being a communal prayer. Even the so-called individual laments have become part of the community heritage. As we share one another's grief, so we share in the process of healing and rebirth. The death of a family member, friend, or colleague has shock effects beyond our immediate family and circle of friends. The healing process also embraces those who more remotely have shared in the sadness.

The liturgical use of lamentation also reveals a hidden dynamic. In the psalter, most psalms of lamentation were used as processional songs, in preparation for entering God's presence. In the context of the rite of committal, having been accompanied in the funeral procession by such chants as Psalm 42/43, our dead fellow pilgrim is presented as coming before the Lord with excitement and joy.[33]

Cemetery

The rite of committal and the inherent unity among the rites of the *Order of Christian Funerals* provide a clear perception of the place of committal, with the traditional Catholic cemetery as its paradigm. Because this understanding has been discussed at some length in a separate monograph,[34] several summary points may suffice here.

First, cemetery as understood by the *Order of Christian Funerals* is a traditional cemetery, where death is accepted as a reality and final hope in the paschal mystery is professed. In the second place, the *Order* is committed to normative cemetery liturgy, especially graveside liturgy and participation in the actual committal (lowering of the casket or entombment) when appropriate to the experience of the bereaved. Another expectation is the availability of a cemetery chapel to be used for certain funeral rites and memorial celebrations. The cemetery chapel does not replace the graveside as the place for the liturgy of committal or the parish church as focal location for the celebration of the funeral Mass.[35]

The primary objective of the cemetery, according to the *Order of Christian Funerals*, is ministry. In radical distinction to the secular cemetery, the Catholic cemetery of the *Order of Christian Funerals* is not primarily a provider of services for profit, although most Catholic cemeteries are a major source of income for the works of charity in many a diocese. Service rendered by the Catholic cemetery would distinguish itself, above all else, as the genuinely person-centered work of the Church, extending the very saving, healing mission of Christ. Just as bereaved Catholics hope to find in their parish ministers the compassion of Jesus toward the widow of Naim at the funeral of her only son (Luke 7) and the love of Jesus toward Lazarus, Martha, and Mary (John 11), so, too, are they invited by the *Order of Christian Funerals* to find Joseph of Arimathea and Mary Magdalene with the other women of Easter morning ministering to them in the Catholic cemetery. When one realizes that Catholic cemeteries in the United States alone number in eccess of 6000, this is a considerable opportunity for witness and catechesis.[36] Catholic cemetery personnel are to make what happens at the cemetery a genuine continuation of the funeral liturgy at church. For example, the procession with the body from the church is the same procession as enters the cemetery and proceeds to the grave or cemetery chapel/mausoleum, no matter how short or long a drive from church to cemetery. Although surprising perhaps, this procession with the deceased from church to grave is known through interdisciplinary research to play a very significant role in Catholic experience of grief today. Is it a coincidence that this spiritually and psychologically meaningful moment of continuity between church and cemetery, the appropriate liturgical expression of which is in the hands of the Catholic cemeterian, is precisely the classic early Christian funeral? Perhaps, but one is surely tempted to explore here also something of that archetypal human symbol of leave-taking.

Catholic funeral directors and cemetery personnel likewise will play a major role in helping to shape this new Catholic experience of cremation in continuity with our faith-filled tradition. That tradition will help the Catholic cemetery stand in firm opposition to current immediate disposal propaganda, which tempts the uninformed faithful away from the salutary values, both spiritual and therapeutic, of the full liturgical expression of our Easter faith. It may, in fact, be time for the Catholic cemeteries—especially diocesan cemeteries in larger cities—to have their own cremation retorts. Whatever worth this suggestion might have, it is clear that as Catholic consumers of cremation services, we must make our values known if we are to preserve the authentic inculturation of the faith in the 21st century.

The invitation of the *Order of Christian Funerals* to enflesh the theological unity of the funeral rites in praxis will take some further education, training, and collaboration between cemetery personnel and parish clergy and lay staff—or, as we should say, between cemetery ministers and parish ministers.[37]

In summary, the *Order of Christian Funerals* (Nos. 207–209) provides a concise description of each of the several rites of committal.[38] In all of these forms of the liturgy, we are not only celebrating the passage of a dead person from our earthly community to that of heaven; we are also strengthening our own faith. There is a sense of joy as our farewell joins with the song of welcome of those who are now with God. But there is also an acknowledgement of the profound grief that remains with us. Encouraged by our hope of resurrection, we are ministers of comfort and support to each other. This brief liturgy is but a prelude to a life that must henceforth be readjusted. The liturgy now points beyond the committal and announces the commitment of the assembled Church to walk with the bereaved on the long, painful process of healing.

NOTES

1. See, for example, Howard C. Raether, "The Place of the Funeral: The Role of the Funeral Director in Contemporary America," *Omega* 2 (1971), pp. 131–149, and the extensive bibliographies on funeral ritualization in Beverley Raphael, *The Anatomy of Bereavement* (New York: Basic Books, 1983) and Marian Osterweis et al., eds., *Bereavement: Reactions, Consequences, and Care* (Washington, D.C.: National Academy Press, 1984).

2. See Alfred C. Rush, "The Rosary and the Christian Wake," *American Ecclesiastical Review* 152 (1965), pp. 289–297. Fr. Rush's suggestions deserve serious attention, for they well illustrate the place of devotions in relation to the liturgy. One example of the "Scriptural Rosary" at the wake is found in *Holy Cross Funeral Liturgy* (Notre Dame, Ind.: Congregation of Holy Cross, 1976), 31–32.

3. See Rutherford, "Funeral Liturgy," pp. 85–86.

4. When the vigil liturgy is separated from the principal funeral liturgy by a short time, morning or evening prayer of the liturgy of the hours (depending on the time of day) would seem preferable to repetition of the liturgy of the word. (See below and Appendix III.) The scriptural rosary, with the singing of psalms in response to short biblical verses between decades, may serve as a transitional service in the process of educating toward celebrating the liturgy of the hours.

The rationale for this directive concerns ritual integrity. Culturally, theologically, and therapeutically, the liturgies of the

OCF encompass a process. Analogous to the process celebrated in the RCIA, death, the funeral, and bereavement also constitute a process that unfolds by means of rites of passage. Each of these rites—or, better, sets of rites—in the OCF enjoys an inner coherence and an integral relationship to the other sets. Together, they give ritual expression to the Catholic way of death and bereavement.

Temptations to telescope these rites into one streamlined gathering for the believing community undermine the explicit faith of Catholic funeral liturgy. Furthermore, beyond theory, such often well-meaning practices rob the bereaved of one of the principal opportunities offered by the Church today to enjoy the consolation of their faith. One place such telescoping is apparent is when the vigil (sometimes collapsed into the recitation of a rosary only) immediately precedes the funeral liturgy.

5. "The funeral Mass is ordinarily celebrated in the parish church, but at the discretion of the local Ordinary, it may be celebrated in the home of the deceased or some other place" (OCF, No. 155). Cf. OF, Nos. 59 and 78).

6. In the morning hour, we celebrate the resurrection, the rising of the Son of Justice (Psalm 72) over the face of the earth. This is also the time when, filled with the zeal of new creation, we reflect on the expectations of the messianic community, the prophetic nature of the *koinonia* (new community) and the missionary vocation of the Church. Our primary purpose of evangelization is to proclaim that Christ is risen and that the community of Christ's chosen ones will not see death. During the evening hour, we are reflective in our thanksgiving, offering praise because of Christ and praying for Christ's continued presence among us. Traditionally, this was the time of evening sacrifice, and hence the priestly nature of the *koinonia* is given greater prominence. Both liturgies are celebrated at prime times of light and darkness. The evening liturgy celebrates the kindling of the evening lights as a reminder that Christ, our risen Lord, is the light in our darkness. Morning prayer celebrates new dawn, the moment of sunrise when we greet Christ at his hour of resurrection. Prime times of light and darkness are interchangeable

with life and death. In both instances, light and life are triumphant, defeating both darkness and death.

7. See, for example, Therese A. Rando, ed., *Parental Loss of a Child* (Champaign, Ill.: Research Press, 1986) and Elaine Ramshaw, "Ritual for Stillbirth. Exploring the Issues." *Worship* 62 (1988), pp. 533–538.

8. Beyond the literal reference to "little children," the larger meaning of the term *paidia* may be referring to "neophytes," those newcomers to the faith who are both evangelizers and servants of the community. In their sense, the "small, insignificant people" (e.g., the *anawim*, poor ones of Israel) are the ones who proclaim the kingdom of God. Is not the death of an infant, likewise, a proclamation of a living God who welcomes all who have become "children" for the sake of the kingdom? See Mann, C. S., *Mark* (Anchor Bible, Vol. 27), New York: Doubleday, 1986, p. 376.

9. One of the major reasons that liturgical practices survive to this day is pastoral requirement. Tradition is a living activity of "handing on." Far from preserving or fossilizing, tradition is a creative process of contributing viable forms to ancient customs.

10. See Rutherford, *Pastoral Care.*

11. For an excellent practical discussion of these model services see Michael Marchal, *Parish Funerals* (Chicago: Liturgy Training Publications, 1987), pp. 25–32, and for further analysis of the importance of these moments in the functioning of funeral ritual in the bereavement process, see Rutherford, *Pastoral Care.*

12. See, for example, an early and widely publicized affirmation of such involvement by the bereaved: Roy Nichols and Jane Nichols, "Funerals: A Time for Grief and Growth," in Elisabeth Kübler-Ross, ed., *Death: The Final Stage of Growth* (Englewood Cliffs, N.J.: Prentice-Hall, 1975), pp. 87–96.

13. American funeral directors have suggested that an appropriate time for this short rite with the bereaved might be the last 15 minutes of the hour set for private viewing, which

frequently is scheduled immediately before public viewing or visitation.

14. This sample description has been developed in conjunction with many workshop participants and published also in Rutherford, *Pastoral Care*.

15. Here as elsewhere, communication between the ministers of the Church and funeral service personnel is critical. See also Chapter Six for further details on this point.

16. "During the Easter triduum, on solemnities, and on Sundays of Advent, Lent, and the Easter season," the very nature of these days prohibits the funeral Mass. The second typical edition of the *Roman Missal* (1974) spells out the principle clearly in a positive light: "The funeral Mass has first place among the Masses for the dead and may be celebrated any day except solemnities, which are holy days of obligation, *Holy Thursday, the Paschal Triduum,* and the Sundays of Advent, Lent, and the Easter season." See *Missale Romanum,* Editio typica altera 1974, No. 336. This edition contains the third official revision of the *GIRM*. The italics indicate parts of the text added to the first edition. In *BCL Newsletter* 12 (1976), p. 56. Note the misprint of "now" for "not" in the reference to the revised *Roman Missal:* "days on which funeral Masses are now [corr: not] to be celebrated."

Even on these days, however, the body is brought to the church for the celebration of the liturgy of the word and the rite of final commendation and farewell (OF, No. 6). Nourishment and consolation are offered through the word of God in the very place where the table of God's word is joined in worship with the table of the Lord's Supper. As at the baptism of infants outside Mass, where the worshipping community is invited to move from the baptistry to a position around the altar for the Lord's Prayer (in anticipation of full eucharistic participation), the Church still desires, on occasions when Mass cannot be celebrated, to gather the community around the deceased in the place where it ordinarily celebrates the eucharist. In all such cases, however, the *Ordo* leaves no doubt that the eucharist itself "must, if possible, be celebrated on another day within a reasonable time" (OF, No. 6).

17. See again Kathleen Hughes, *Lay Presiding: The Art of Leading Prayer* (Washington, D.C.: Pastoral Press, 1988).

18. These are divided into four sections: Funerals for Adults (seven readings from the Old Testament, 19 from the New, 10 psalms of response, 11 acclamations and 19 gospel texts); Funerals for Baptized Children (two Old Testament, seven New Testament, four psalms, three acclamations, six Gospels); Funerals for Children who die before Baptism (two old Testament, one psalm, two acclamations, three Gospels); and a Collection of Psalms (16 psalms with responses, with Psalm 119 divided into 22 sections, giving a total of 37 selections).

19. If there has been no eucharist but only a liturgy of the word, the Lord's Prayer is recited (No. 194), and there may be the opportunity for holy communion with a concluding prayer (No. 195). Then the rite of final commendation takes place.

20. The Rite of Committal with Final Commendation will be treated together with the Rite of Committal below.

21. Simeon of Thessalonica, *De ordine sepulturae* in PG 155, 685B.

22. This is a short rite of prayer to comfort the parents and entrust their infant to God. The rite itself is a model, and the minister should adapt it to circumstances. This form may be uséd in the hospital or place of birth or at the time of committal of the body (No. 318). A brief address (No. 337) reminds us of the three short days Jesus spent in the tomb before resurrection. Two choices of scripture verse encourage us to hope (No. 338). A blessing of the body with a short responsory and litany (No. 339), leads to the Lord's Prayer (No. 340), two prayers of commendation (No. 341), and a choice of forms of blessing (No. 342) conclude the rite of commendation for an infant.

23. See above, note 8, and consult the local chapter of the national support group, The Compassionate Friends, for further specific details.

24. See Gy, "Le Nouveau Rituel," p. 27.

25. *Ibid.*, pp. 25–27.

26. *The Order of Funerals for Adults.* Experimental Rite for use by permission of the Holy See (Washington, D.C.: National Council of Catholic Bishops, 1967), pp. 29–30 (Nos. 30–34).

27. *The Rite of Christian Burial.* Adapted for use in the Archdiocese of Chicago by the Commission on the Sacred Liturgy. (Chicago: Archdiocese of Chicago, 1968), pp. 31 and 33–35.

28. McManus, "Funeral Rite," p. 133.

29. For a thorough review of the tradition of the communion of saints in ecumenical perspective, see Michael Perham, *The Communion of Saints,* Alcuin Club Collections, No. 62 (London: SPCK, 1980).

30. "It is only natural to wish to commend those we love to God's keeping. Concepts of purgatory are very unlikely for modern Protestants (and probably for many Roman Catholics, too, today). But the hope of resurrection in Christ is so central in Christian faith that we can hardly refrain from praying that God will accomplish God's purpose for the deceased. It is most unnatural to pray for a person up to the moment of death and then be dumb. God's love continues after death as well as before. . . ." See James F. White, *Introduction to Christian Worship* (Nashville: Abingdon, 1980), pp. 269–270.

31. See Chapter Six.

32. See Chapter Two.

33. For further consideration of the role of lament in pastoral care and funeral rites, see Sparkes and Rutherford, "Lament."

34. See Rutherford, *Pastoral Care.*

35. Large metropolitan areas and regions of extreme cold winters face special logistical concerns in this matter of graveside committal. Cemetery personnel in those circumstances are invited to be sensitive to these norms, as exemplified by guidelines such as those in the Archdiocese of Chicago (Patrick J. Pollard, ed., *Christian in Death*).

210

36. In this context, one might follow the leadership of Joseph B. Sankovitch, Director of Cemeteries for the Archdiocese of Seattle. Several publications from his office include: *A Mission Statement* (1988), *Why Catholic Cemeteries?* (1988), *Why Preneed in the Catholic Tradition?* (1988), and *Cremation* (1987), all published in Seattle by the Associated Catholic Cemeteries, Archdiocese of Seattle.

37. In this context, one should be aware of the work of the National Catholic Cemetery Conference and its official magazine, *The Catholic Cemetery* (Des Plaines, Ill., 1960–).

38. See Appendix IV for a more detailed guide to the resources in the *Order* for celebration of the various forms of the rite.

Present and Future

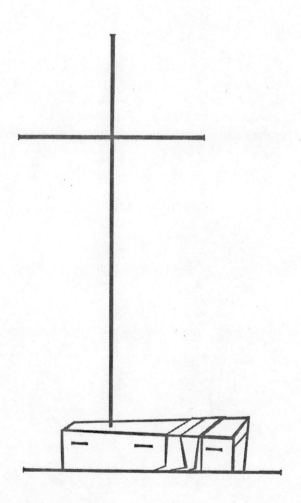

Chapter Six

The Present: Reform and Renewal

This final chapter documents some pastoral experiences of celebrating the funeral liturgy. It is not the result of a systematic survey but the fruit of conversations and observations during the past two decades. Some of them have been subjected to more rigorous study, and where appropriate, the results of that empirical research are included here as well.[1]

ENVIRONMENT AND ART
One of the most immediate agenda of contemporary funerary renewal concerns the spaces in which we celebrate the funeral rites. In the United States, for example, the Bishops' booklet *Environment and Art in Catholic Worship* has awakened widespread attention to liturgical environment and artistic appointments in general. Such supplementary directives are necessary, for the role that art and environment play in the total funeral liturgy is only implicitly addressed in both the 1969 *Ordo* and the *Order of Christian Funerals*. In our gleanings throughout the decade between these two ritual books, however, nearly every discussion about liturgical space, whether to be newly designed or renovated, has included sensitivity to the placement of casket and the bereaved in the various rites of the funeral liturgy. Design concerns have involved, for example, ensuring that the entrance aisle is wide enough for a procession with pall bearers *carrying* the casket and the appropriate location for an urn of cremated re-

mains in the church (perhaps on a portable plinth in or near the baptistry?).[2]

Frequent questions about the appropriateness of certain funeral parlor settings, artistic appointments for the funeral liturgy, and liturgical space in church design for wakes and funerals, for example, are part of the liturgical design agenda. The psychological and sociological answers that have guided much of funerary practice during the past quarter century will in the coming era be complemented by new poetic questions. With regard to the *Order of Christian Funerals*, one recalls as well the inherent association between place and time as constituent elements of the three ritual moments that gave shape to the Christian funeral throughout history.

One recurring, successful application of this spirit is the placement of the casket for vigil or reception of the deceased near the baptismal font, often a full baptismal pool. The gathering of the assembly near the waters of baptism, which presently the presider will sprinkle over the casket of the deceased, cannot help but richly engage the religious imagination in the symbolic association between Christian initiation and funeral liturgy. Such an arrangement likewise fosters an entrance procession with the casket involving all the assembly rather than the often self-conscious walk of the bereaved into a sea of watching eyes.

One example from close to home well illustrates the value of these considerations. Recently, the remains of a University of Portland graduate, who had been shot down over Vietnam and missing in action for nearly 20 years, were returned to his widow, children, and elderly, also widowed father. For many appropriate pastoral reasons, it was decided that the military funeral would be celebrated at the University of Portland in the Chapel of Christ the Teacher, which serves a

216

well-integrated role in the life of the canonical parish nearby. Two environmental and artistic highlights are noteworthy.

The first concerns the funeral procession with the casket draped with the American flag. Because replacement of the flag with the white pall of baptismal remembrance is sometimes viewed as patriotically insensitive, this occasion of a hero's welcome—with extensive local television news coverage—was perceived to be an important pastoral and pedagogical moment.

The flag-covered casket was met at the hearse as it arrived at the head of a campus walkway leading to the chapel. The cross and candle bearers, the pall bearers (both in military and civilian garb), an honor guard of student ROTC cadets, the deceased's family, and the presider made up the entourage. Following a brief, prayerful welcome, the procession made its way in solemn pace along the several hundred yards of familiar campus sidewalks to the *portico* of the chapel, where the rest of the assembly had been gathering.

Welcome was extended to the larger community. There, with the eyes of all fixed on the flag-decorated casket, the color guard of student cadets solemnly removed and folded the American flag, presenting the familiar triangular form to their commanding officer for safekeeping during the liturgy of the Church. Immediately, the wide portal was opened, and the liturgical procession led the body of the patriotic hero and faithful Christian into the baptistry, situated in the narthex of the chapel.[3] This leads to the second point of environmental interest.

Just as family and friends had dramatically marked his death in service to his country with symbols of national honor, now all gathered around the baptismal pool to remember his entrance into life that knows no death. With the casket arranged between the portal

217

and the font, the presider, positioned across the font from the casket, began the rite of reception. Holy water was drawn from the font for the sprinkling, and pall bearers spread the white pall ceremoniously over the casket. Although the optional prayers of the then-current *Rite of Funerals* accompanied these actions, the gestures themselves in their natural environment spoke much more forcefully than any words. An opening hymn was sung as the procession of the entire assembly led the deceased into the principal chapel space, the banquet room of word and sacrament, for the celebration of the funeral Mass.

At the end, following the final commendation and farewell, the casket was met at the door, where the funeral director removed the pall and the color guard replaced the American flag for the recessional to the hearse and cortege to the national cemetery. There, further traditional military honors complemented the rite of committal.

Needless to say, the balanced attentiveness to the appropriate rituals of both nation and Church, each with full yet nobly simple gesture and straightforward use of natural and architectural environment, did not go unnoticed. Respectful media coverage commented on both sets of funeral rituals as appropriate and meaningful, and many participants remarked later at the reception how pleased they were that so many values dear to the deceased and his family, friends, and colleagues found expression. In contrast to some other experiences of military funerals, no one complained that the American flag had been treated disrespectfully by removing it in favor of the white pall. Perhaps we have relearned an old lesson: "Render unto Caesar the things that are Caesar's. . . ." In any case, the attention paid to space, appointments, and gesture in this unique set of circumstances affirmed the thesis of the U.S. Bishop's Committee on the Liturgy: "Like the covenant itself, the liturgical celebrations of the faith community [Church] involve the whole person. They are not purely religious or merely rational and intellectual exercises, but also human experiences calling on all human faculties: body, mind, senses, imagination, emotions, memory. Attention to these is one of the urgent needs of contemporary liturgical renewal."[4]

Parishes where the funeral liturgy is truly communal are, for the most part, parishes where considerable effort has been devoted to remote preparation. This has included parishwide catechesis, especially about death itself in the 20th century, Catholic faith and contemporary teaching in face of death, and about the liturgy of death and burial. More than one parish priest has insisted that the best vehicle for such effective funerary catechesis is the funeral liturgy itself. Good, consistent liturgical example demonstrates in practice what is taught in homily, school, or parish education classes.

A plan of action has also been part of successful education programs. Although they differ in detail and approach, most include means to attain the following goals: a parish guide to funerals, a parish cantor and funeral musicians, explicit channels of communication with funeral directors who serve the parish, and appropriate participation aids for all liturgical services.

The Parish Handbook for Funerals
One of the best ways to further the parish's understanding of funerals is to provide every family with a simple handbook or guide to funeral practice in the parish. As a companion to a more comprehensive diocesan manual, the handbook offers the family a brief theology of death in the Catholic community, gives explicit directives on what to do when someone dies in the family, and provides information about the funeral

liturgy as celebrated in that parish. Through its information about the liturgical customs of the parish, the handbook serves as background for planning the funeral with the parish priest or other minister. It can facilitate family discussions about planning ahead, especially in the case of terminally ill patients, or help elderly Christians, often realistically in touch with death's immanence, to talk about their death and funeral preferences with younger members of the family. This booklet would treat only those items specific to the particular parish and include references to the several excellent general planning pamphlets and self-help guides available commercially.[5]

The handbook would urge parishioners to inform the pastor of the death as soon as possible *and* to involve both the parish ministers and the funeral directors at the same time in the process of making arrangements for the funeral. This helps establish priorities for a funeral that is founded on Christian values and facilitates the choice of options offered by the *Order of Christian Funerals* and parish custom, both of which could affect arrangements with the funeral home.

Furthermore, experience has shown that uncertainties about song and music at funerals and fears about denial of Christian burial, stemming, for example, from presumed canonical irregularities or a longtime absence from regular church attendance, are often unfounded and can be alleviated by appropriate pastoral care when people approach the parish priest at the same time as they inform the funeral director. This is especially true when the mortuary in question is not Catholic. Similarly, funeral directors who serve Catholic parishes exercise an essential part of their service when, familiar with current liturgical and canonical legislation, they assist Catholics through accurate information to seek the consolation of their faith in face of death.[6]

All such necessary information is available to the parish pastoral team and funeral director both in the *Order of Christian Funerals,* the Code of Canon Law, and generally in regional or diocesan guidelines for funerals. The parish handbook for funerals makes essential information available in an uncomplicated manner to the larger parochial community.

Also important is the handbook's emphasis on music as an integral part of funeral liturgy in the parish. Here, again, the matter of music and song will not come as a surprise to the bereaved, and the question is no longer whether to have music but which hymns, songs, and other musical selections are most appropriate to this funeral.

Music and Song at the Parish Funeral
The musical passivity so characteristic of funeral rites among English-speaking Catholics is gradually being transformed into appropriate and sensitive liturgical participation. How is this happening?

One way is the formation of a special funeral choir or *schola.* Frequently made up of older, often retired men and women, as well as younger homemakers whose children are in school, such choirs exercise a valuable music ministry. The diverse groups that assemble for funerals render congregational singing exceedingly difficult without a choir's musical support. Yet the choir alone without a cantor to direct congregational participation, often becomes a performing group instead of a liturgical choir. Sometimes the leadership of a cantor alone may work. Yet the best solution employs both choir and cantor, a route taken by parishes where music is a liturgical priority, thoroughly endorsed by post-Vatican II liturgical renewal.

Several examples from widely different geographical locations in the United States affirm that the funeral choir (often called "resurrection choir"[7]) is becoming a truly viable option. Experiences shared by many pastoral musicians may be summarized in the following observations by two parish choir directors representing urban and rural centers.

"When I came to the parish, a funeral choir existed. These were senior citizens who wanted to do something to help people through the process of grieving, so they all volunteered to sing at a funeral whenever it occurred. During the past two years, we have developed a good repertoire of service music and new hymns, beyond the seven traditional ones (e.g., *How Great Thou Art*) with which we began. Special requests by the bereaved family and friends are worked into the program prepared by the choir, and guest soloists and instrumentalists cooperate with us. In fact, most professional musicians I have worked with have liked the arrangement; they appreciate the accompaniment and know that the overall result will be much finer for the bereaved. It works well; it sounds well, and it looks like you practiced it forever, but you really haven't, and that's really my experience.

"Local funeral directors advise people planning a funeral at St. Syms of our policy, and usually a member of the choir or I will meet with the family to confer on the program and any special requests. Teamwork and communication is extremely important—for example, letting the funeral directors know the policy. When I first came into the parish, we began to talk to the funeral directors, and they got used to my style . . . that really helps . . . communicate with them, and say "thank you" for services they render. For example, when there have been special requests involving outside professionals, I'll say, 'The musician you hired was very accommodating, and thank you for making the arrangements.'[8]

222

"Finally, one of the choir members has added a further dimension to his bereavement ministry. He always makes an audio tape of the funeral liturgy and, upon request by the family, gives it to them as a *memento*. Many have commented on how much they appreciate the choir and that gesture—a real means of memorial for them. St. Syms is a caring parish; we are blessed with a wonderful pastor, and he even sings with us."[9]

From rural Washington another successful pastoral musician explains the work of the funeral choir. "The focus of music in the funeral liturgy is not on grief, mortal grief, but very much on hope, thanksgiving, and praise. There is an element in it that reflects on our own life, our own death, our own hope of salvation; we are not speaking only on this person who is being buried, but we are speaking of ourselves; it is a communal sharing of the theological dimension of death in regard to ourselves.

"Funerals differ, depending on how the person died and how the family can accept it. Songs and music are chosen differently, too, depending on circumstances, but the elements of hope and of thanksgiving are always there. Some families just don't want music at all. Even then, we explain the parish commitment to observe the norms of Catholic liturgy and sing at least the ritual parts.

"Our 'resurrection choir' consists of 12 men and women, generally those who do not have full-time jobs or are retired. The parish organist is the head accompanist for this group. Both she and her substitute have the list of members. They meet once a week for an hour after morning Mass, having refreshments and building community. These choir members are mostly older people who sing for all funerals, even if a soloist has been hired by the family. They sing all the acclamations, etc.; they support the congregation in their song. If there is no soloist, they serve as cantor but don't take the place of a hired soloist. Their function is to represent the parish community and to support the assembly in singing the responses and acclamations that belong to the ritual. That is primary. They are "on call," so one person in the choir is responsible for calling all the other members when there is a funeral. They meet 45 minutes before the funeral. Normally, the pastoral musician works on preparing the liturgy with the families or with the priest. If she is not there, the organist makes these plans with them.

"It used to be the funeral directors who arranged the music, but not any longer. The musician of the parish or the director of music ministry exercises this responsibility because that person has the knowledge, background, and source of materials to use. The funeral liturgy is not just another event where music is plugged in to add entertainment. Part of the job is to see that all liturgies are events in accordance with the directives of appropriate liturgical expression. That expression is very communal in nature. So when funeral directors take over and hire a soloist to sing two songs (mostly at the presentation of gifts and at communion), usually it destroys the community aspect of mutually shared support within the family structure, within the community structure. They, too, become spectators set apart, and are not allowed to come into the grieving process, or the healing process of which the liturgy affords in these days. Now, when a parishoner dies, all the funeral directors know the first thing they do is call the pastor. The next thing they do is leave a message to the director of music ministry to give a call. Often, they will include in their message some of the desires of the family, but they have learned now not to recommend any musical choices. Where appropriate, we incorporate the family's desires into the liturgical service; if it is not appropriate, as gently as possible, we suggest alternatives. If it is an adamant matter for them that particular pieces must be done, we suggest that they be done in the vigil or rosary service the night before. In extreme cases, we have included less appropriate selections before or after the liturgy.

"The next step is for our parish and the Cathedral to get together and then to meet with the funeral directors to prepare a pamphlet on Music Ministry for Catholic Funerals."[10]

Another way some parishes are making music a more integral part of the funeral liturgy is by working systematically toward a familiar parochial repertoire of good, singable hymns. Many hymns appropriate for Sunday eucharist can be sung equally well at funerals. If the funerary repertoire is kept small and simple, certain pieces will become sufficiently familiar for people to overcome their longtime reluctance to sing at funerals.

Many parish musicians looked forward to a revised English-language edition of the *Ordo* that would offer music selections for the funeral, following the example of the French, Irish, and—to a certain extent—the Canadian editions. Yet the ICEL editors of the *Order of Christian Funerals* chose rather to stress the importance of music and song in the funeral rites, while leaving selection of repertoire to the compilers of hymnals and parish muscians. Hymns for the Office for the Dead, Part IV, form an exception to this general principle. Familiar hymn texts, together with tune indications, are proposed in the context of the morning and evening hymns (Nos. 375 and 387), and four additional hymns are incorporated at the end of Part IV (No. 396).

It has been suggested that to include further music and hymnal selection in the *Order of Christian Funerals* would incur a certain editorial bias, most certainly inhibiting further musical development in some parishes. On the other hand, not to include a limited repertoire of more songs and chants misses a wonderful teaching opportunity. Although not every parish would use the music in the same way, its very presence in the printed *Ordo* would demonstrate the principle that music is normative for the fullness of liturgical celebration. The example of the musical notation for presider's parts in the *Sacramentary* is often cited as a worthwhile approach for the *Order of Christian Funerals* as well.[11]

Another advantage of including music in the national ritual is the fostering of a national musical tradition for funeral liturgy. Mobility is such that people come from all parts of the nation to "attend" funerals. A national repertoire, however small, of funerary compositions could further help transform "attending" funerals into "liturgical participation." Likewise, a regional or diocesan music supplement could make local and ethnic favorites readily accessible to every parish. The *Ordo* does encourage many different musical forms, especially of an acclamatory or litanic nature. Such pieces derive immediacy within the liturgy from their basic, elementary refrain style of singing, requiring no prior knowledge or advance practice.

Perhaps a most encouraging development of music at funerals is the experience of the paschal character of Christian death, promoting more than exuberant alleluias and exclusively Easter hymns. A widespread *use* of joyful but sensitive psalmody, sung responsorially, as well as recent compositions specifically for the funeral, is giving greater balance to the enthusiasm of the early renewal. This is apparent in certain diocesan and parochial participation booklets, where a balanced selection of music is included for appropriate moments in the *Ordo*. This complies with the intention of the *Order of*

Funerals (No. 21, 4), which recommends that suitable texts and melodies for singing be made available "wherever appropriate."[12]

One particularly pressing pastoral problem is the insistence by family members and friends that certain specified music items be "played at the funeral" because they had been requested by the deceased or those closest to the deceased.[13] Apart from putting undue pressure on parish musicians, this approach to selecting the music of the assembly for the funeral liturgy can deprive the community of the right to celebrate the faith of the Church in the resurrection of Jesus as source of consolation and meaning in the midst of despair and meaninglessness. Although the time of death is not the appropriate pedagogical moment to reach the immediately bereaved, this issue points up the importance of consistently appropriate celebrations of the Catholic funeral, ongoing parish education, and clearly communicated parish guidelines. Liturgy is communal, not private; personal preferences for music indicated by the family of the deceased should not be allowed to force the music director to compromise his or her integrity as a liturgist responsible for providing liturgical song for the parish assembly. The handbook mentioned above might clearly spell out not only the right but the duty of the parish music director to recommend appropriate alternatives and on certain occasions to be prepared to say no. Here again, examples such as the story of the Chicago bagpiper and the recommended assertive but caring planning in conjunction with funeral directors noted above point the way to discretion and compassionate pastoral care.

Communication with Funeral Directors
Successful celebration of the *Order of Christian Funerals* depends on the understanding and cooperation of funeral directors and other mortuary personnel. Where

this does not yet exist, it is seldom because of ill will but frequently the result of poor communication and misunderstanding. This can be especially troublesome in large cities where many different funeral directors serve the same parish. Both parish priests and morticians have spoken of their frustrations with an obvious failure to cooperate in liturgy. In other cases, both parties unfortunately seem satisfied with the *status quo* of routine funerals.

The *Order of Christian Funerals* is a valuable guide to relieve some of those frustrations, as the film *Of Life & Death* on the 1970 Rite by the National Funeral Directors Association has demonstrated.[14] No rite of funerals can succeed, however, where liturgical renewal is thwarted by ministerial carelessness or unprofessional commercialism. Both groups would appreciate greater communication but are unclear about areas of mutual responsibility and often uneasy about where to begin a dialogue. Joint sessions to facilitate implementation of the *Order of Christian Funerals* and ongoing professional education among funeral service practitioners and clergy as well as among seminaries and mortuary schools has proven a most effective approach to better communication and cooperation.[15]

Funeral directors are in the business of burying the dead. Because that business involves grieving persons, the funeral industry has extended its service to include "grief counseling" in conjunction with the funeral. Sometimes, this service involves generic religious rites, analogous to the "humanitarian funeral" for the religiously unaffiliated. The funeral industry is concerned with the *end of life*, and the mortician's art leaves no doubt that *this life* is its object.

The concern of the Church as expressed liturgically in the *Order of Christian Funerals* is broader. It embraces the genuine service rendered by the funeral director in a pastoral context that begins with life and continues long after death. Thus, many parish priests have taken the responsibility to approach funeral directors with a knowledge of, and appreciation for, their professional service, offering to assist them with the peculiarities of Catholic funerals. Rarely do funeral directors desire to "take over" the liturgy of funerals, but most appreciate information about its celebration so that they can do their job efficiently and effectively. Where efficiency or professionalism interferes with Catholic funerary values, however, it is again the Catholic client who has the responsibility to insist on appropriate service. Catholics who realize that their faith values are not the primary concern of the funeral industry and who have learned to do business with funeral homes accordingly, find channels of mutual communication remarkably clear. The result can be the kind of collaboration that makes the funeral liturgy a memorable ecclesial event in the life of the bereaved and a worthy commemoration of the deceased by all participants.

A valuable alternative to the familiar commercial approach of the funeral business, to the memorial society options, and to the most recent suggestions of "do it yourself funerals,"[16] is the concept of funeral service performed primarily as a ministry. While many religious funeral service personnel consider their caregiving ministerial in a broad sense, one mortuary in particular stands out as existing primarily as a ministry to the community. Corinthian Funeral Service of Portland, Ore., was founded in 1982 as an ecumenical service agency to provide mortuary care at reasonable cost for clients for whom the church, synagogue, or meeting house is the preferred location of funeral ritualization and "who are concerned with spiritual rather than material values at the time of death," according to the statement of purpose. In addition to direct mortuary competence at the time of death, Corinthian supports pastoral care in the clients' religious communities and educational programs to bring about a change in national attitudes toward death and grief.[17]

Participation Aids
The *Order of Christian Funerals* (No. 12) wisely calls the minister's attention to the almost universal fact that all kinds of people gather for funerals. Priests and other ministers are reminded that they are to bring Christ's gospel to all people. Pastorally, one is of course respectful of opinions and religious convictions different from those manifest in the funeral liturgy. Nevertheless, the ministers' faith in that which marks the Catholic funeral as Catholic should always guide the manner of celebrating the liturgy.

There are times when a large percentage of those present are from such varied backgrounds that a serious pastoral challenge arises. Such times test the presider's ability to express the inherent meaning of Catholic funeral symbolism authentically. A further degree of sensitivity is needed when members of the immediate family itself are not of the Catholic faith or are separated from the Church. The French edition of the 1969 Introduction advises concisely that one should be sensitive to their way of thinking and welcome their legitimate desires but at the same time help them understand the meaning of what the Church does.[18]

There is a concern that Catholic faithful themselves no longer know what to expect at the liturgy. In the special circumstances of the funeral (grief, infrequency, people from different parishes, ecumenical mix, and the like), the *Order of Funerals* allows great freedom and variety in its manner of celebration. The variety and lack of familiarity with the responsory parts of the funeral rite often seem to disorient people so that they will not give even the most ordinary responses.

One must remember that this is the first time since the early Middle Ages that active participation in the funeral liturgy is expected of the faithful. It is believed, nevertheless, that a certain sense of ritual pattern and continuity is beginning to assert itself. The process will take time, given the special context of death and burial. Consequently, from a pastoral point of view, one does not compel participation at funerals; one can only educate people and foster good liturgical practice. On the other hand, there is no reason to be defeatist about this matter. Participation in the funeral liturgy does not come about by itself; that it is actually happening is a sign that the patient effort at liturgical renewal is beginning to have a transforming effect.

There are two opposing positions among funeral ministers regarding participation aids for vigil and funeral services. One position insists that ministers ought not to confuse the bereaved with service sheets because they are not necessary.[19] The other holds that appropriate participation aids are necessary if one desires participation that is more than the intermittent recitation of familiar prayers.

In unfamiliar situations and surroundings, such as vigil or funeral, people appreciate knowing what is going to take place. A good participation aid, therefore, presents a clearly understandable *order of service*. Otherwise, the natural reaction is to do nothing. Thus, the service sheet should indicate in clear type both nonverbal and verbal participation in the liturgical action: stand, be seated, kneel, respond, silent prayer, sing, and the like. These may be conveniently printed in the margin of the page—clearly but so as not to distract from the order of service itself.

This basic format also allows for personalization. The name of the deceased can be printed in the title. The names of those who take part in the liturgy, such as readers, pallbearers, et al., along with specific references to the liturgical readings may be mentioned. The words and music of the chosen hymns or hymnal references are usually inserted in their appropriate places. In this way, the service sheet also becomes a *memento* of the liturgy for the participants. This implies printing work for each funeral, but when a basic printmaster is used and only the specific references are inserted, it is no more complicated than printing the personalized holy cards already quite common at Catholic funerals. And it ensures that liturgical participation at funerals becomes a priority.[20]

Both adherents and opponents of participation aids agree on the principle of "noble simplicity." Unfortunately, many service sheets are unnecessarily complex and frequently verbose. The proposed printmaster indicates the plan for a simple aid, which need be no more than a single page (5½ by 8½ inches), to guide the assembly in meaningful participation while serving as marker for the hymnal. At other times, it can be a self-contained booklet of several pages. The challenge is finding a suitable simple format that fosters participation and allows personalization. In its simplest form, personalization involves choice of readings, interventions, and prayers by the presiding minister(s) and hymns and responses by the people. The most successful booklets, for example, provide the order of service, indicate by title the variable parts, and print out in full only the congregation's parts.

The Funeral Workshop
An approach that integrates all of the above concerns about remote preparation and participation is the parish funeral workshop. One example of a funeral work-

shop sponsored by a parish liturgy committee illustrates what is becoming a more frequent occurrence in quite a few locations around the country.

Generally, three speakers are invited to make presentations: a funeral director, an attorney, and a parish priest. The funeral director is to give a careful explanation of the services provided by the mortuary, including the many options available. He or she may speak about the costs involved and some legal aspects pertaining to the funeral. In this latter section, the state's funeral requirements, such as those pertaining to embalming and other means of preserving the corpse for funeral services, are noted, and mistaken notions are dispelled. The attorney discusses what is involved in preparing a last will and testament, pointing out who handles it, how it is written, and what must be in it. The third part of the workshop takes up the role of the priest and parish ministers at the time of death. The priest explains what they do when a parishioner has died. He impresses upon the participants that parish personnel take the news of a death in the ecclesial family very seriously and go to the home as soon as possible, remaining there as long as necessary. Here, too, the priest or other minister can introduce the parish funeral handbook and discuss the important place that planning for funeral liturgy holds in the parish.

Following these remarks by the three presenters, a question-and-answer period closes the session. A wide range of persons may gather to participate in this kind of funeral workshop. Some may be very young. Some may come with families, some without. Some will be concerned about a terminally ill relative, and there may even be a few who are in very bad health themselves and may die in the year ahead. These workshops are successful, and some parishes plan to offer them annually, especially where funerals are frequent. They have been found helpful in familiarizing parishioners generally with funeral liturgy and pastoral care while providing them with necessary information about other practical matters relating to death in the family. In the group discussions or question sessions, those who care for the deceased and their bereaved families likewise gain valuable insights into the expressed concerns of the participants.

All these things—the best of participation aids, the most talented funeral choir and cantor, fluid communication between parish ministers and funeral directors, and the most helpful parish funeral handbook and workshop or other forms of parish education—are merely the context within which the funeral liturgy itself takes place. They constitute the backdrop on the stage of parish life that suddenly becomes crucial when death occurs. They are the remote preparation for the pastoral visit and liturgical planning that follow upon announcement of death.

VIGIL AND RELATED RITES

The Pastoral Visit
The first visit by the priest or parish minister(s) with the bereaved after a death is a pastoral challenge second to none. Genuine pastoral presence, the presence of the Church, is primary. Ministers with years of experience describe this visit as more a time of listening than speaking. Listening is part of liturgical planning for the funeral. Much is said about the deceased that can enable the minister to ask the right questions at the opportune time to firm up specific details for the liturgy. Special and favorite scriptural themes surface; particular names emerge. Listening helps the priest or other minister begin to prepare a mental outline. Some pastors explain that at such a visit, they try not to begin to plan the funeral liturgy as such but rather extend the invitation to the bereaved to help plan the liturgy and indicate that they or a member of the pas-

toral team will come by at another time to do that. In some parishes, it is the custom to close this visit by offering to celebrate a vigil service or Mass at home with the family and their relatives sometime before the actual funeral.

At the agreed-upon time or opportune moment during the first visit, the priest or other minister requests time to concretize, as much as possible, the plans for vigil, funeral liturgy, and committal. Many ministers use a simple planning sheet for this.[21] On it, there's the order of service, with blanks to fill in appropriate personal choices. Most experienced ministers find it helpful to assist the bereaved to complete as many choices as they can at the time of this visit; the vigil and related rites especially need to be determined immediately. Frequently, people will want to think about the Scripture readings and choice of readers for the funeral Mass. In that case, the priest sets a time when they will give him those choices. Clarity and delicate attention to the desires of the family and other bereaved friends, while preserving the liturgy of the Church, are essential for successful pastoral visits. This time of pastoral attention to the bereaved often determines whether they are going to be merely passive recipients of the ministrations of others or active participants in the liturgy as something they and the Church community can do for the deceased and themselves.[22]

The Vigil
How do people experience the vigil? From the opinions collected, the majority of Catholics view the vigil liturgy, whether scriptural vigil or rosary, as an opportunity to pray *with* the bereaved *for* the deceased. The context for this prayer is usually a visit to the funeral home intended to be a sign of "last respects" to the deceased (whether viewed in an open casket or not)

and thereby a sign of condolence to the bereaved. Frequently, people who never knew the deceased will go to the funeral home to offer sympathy and support to the spouse or members of the family whom they do know. Or, they will pay respects to a deceased friend without knowing any of the bereaved and offer their support all the same.

Within this varied context, more and more Catholics seem to be planning their condolence visit during the vigil. Without much explanation, they indicate that attending this service seems to be the appropriate Catholic way of showing sympathy and paying last respects. Those who cannot conveniently take time away from work to attend a morning funeral appreciate this liturgical opportunity to pray with the family rather than "merely" view the deceased, say a personal prayer at the casket, and offering condolences.

Some have pointed out that they feel more positive about the liturgical vigil service than about the rosary, which many describe as the prayer service of special groups such as the Altar and Rosary Society and Knights of Columbus. They are comfortable with it because it is familiar but prefer the vigil service as the more meaningful time of prayer. Others insist that a wake without the rosary is just not a wake for them. Although some parish teams have observed that they have the rosary more often than the scriptural wake, increasing numbers of Catholics and of non-Roman Catholic participants at vigil services no longer understand the rosary devotion. While not opposing it for others, they feel uncomfortable when asked to take part in its traditional form as the community's prayer at a wake. Some tolerate reciting the rosary at wakes because "that's what the deceased would have wanted."

Obviously, pastoral practice requires sensitivity to the wishes of the deceased and of the family, but it also requires carefully educating people of faith about the values of the funeral liturgy and the faith of the broader Catholic and Christian community. There are sufficient moments during the hours spent in vigil for group devotion. Recent pastoral experience reveals that the fruit of such education over time has led to a new level of participation, so that *both* the scriptural vigil, usually at church, *and* the rosary, often at the funeral home, are well attended, even by many of the same people.[23]

The Vigil at Church
Celebrating the vigil in the church is becoming more and more common. Sometimes this entails bringing the body to the church on the evening before the funeral liturgy and making provision for its security. Such provisions may include an opportunity for friends and family members to take turns spending time in reverent vigil with the body of the deceased throughout the night.[24] Specific details for this arrangement need to be worked out with the funeral director. It entails an extra round trip for vehicles and personnel to the parish church: once to deliver the body and once to remove it to the cemetery. The funeral directors interviewed indicate a willingness to contract for this service, generally an "extra" to the ordinary Catholic package.

Among the many excellent vigil services at church that one hears about today, an example from rural Oregon is described most vividly by the pastor who prepared it and presided at its celebration. On the occasion of the tragic death of a young farmer, a father of three, after setting out the details of things to be dealt with and reviewing the pastoral planning visit, the priest describes the vigil as follows (references to the *Order of Christian Funerals* have been inserted in parentheses to facilitate comparison with the present rite):

237

"We brought the body to the church Tuesday evening, where we celebrated the formal entrance into the church, usually held before the funeral Mass (Nos. 82–85). The casket was taken to its usual place for the funeral liturgy; it was positioned facing the congregation and opened for the wake. Hymns were sung at appropriate times during the service.

"Because there were many non-Catholics present, I gave the homily as part of the entrance rite. I explained the water, white pall, and paschal candle as primary symbols of baptism, when the deceased was plunged into the whole mystery of Christ's death and resurrection, which now in death were no longer symbols.

"Since the deceased had just recently harvested his grain, his wife got the idea of making a wreath of unharvested wheat that would be set next to his casket (cf. No. 86). Draped down from the wreath was a scroll, and on it the principal text of the vigil and funeral Mass (I Corinthians 15:35–44), written in calligraphy by the wife. The deceased's wife read this passage at both the vigil and funeral liturgy. The gospel selection for the vigil was John 12:23–26. Both these readings involve wheat as a basic symbol. There were long pauses after each reading, as well as after the intervening psalm. The church was stone-quiet during the long pauses. (I had mentioned in the introduction that the vigil was a time for the community to renew its own faith in the death and resurrection of the Lord and in their meaning for all of us.)

"The vigil ended with everyone passing by the coffin into the wing of the church for refreshments and a chance to meet the deceased's family. The many children at play during the refreshments really added in their own way to the overall point of the funeral."[25]

In interviews, it is notable how much people relate the time of vigil to the funeral home and to the presence of the body. This deeply rooted tradition has moved, along with the earlier wake over the body of the deceased, from the family home to the mortuary. Personal and devotional prayer surrounding the preparation and wake in the domestic setting have been embraced by the larger liturgy of the vigil. Although funeral homes have taken over such domestic care and seek to serve religious customers as prayerful places for it, mortuary chapels are not liturgical spaces and substitutes for or extensions of the parish church. Pastors seeking ways to render the vigil more spiritually fruitful than sometimes experienced in the funeral home need to take both ecclesiology and the religious sensibility of the faithful into careful account. Understanding the historical development of the funeral liturgy around home and church provides an essential context for practical solutions that are both contemporary and authentic to the Catholic tradition.

THE FUNERAL LITURGY AT CHURCH

Reception of the Body
Because the station in the home of the deceased had already been replaced in the earlier national versions of the Roman Ritual by a rite of reception of the body at the church entrance, the revised opening rite in the church fell on good soil. It can be affirmed without hesitation that its use in the United States, for example, is almost universal and well liked by the faithful. Few parish priests think of it as optional. While some have occasionally included other symbols (such as the bible or gospel book), the use of holy water, paschal candle, and white pall to relate this death to life through initiation into the paschal mystery has become a universal expression of the American Catholic funeral. Some commentators found the reception rites of the *Rite of Funerals* (1970) contrived, however, and an exaggerated use of baptismal symbolism, especially

with the cumbersome and difficult text from Romans 6 incorporated into the liturgical action. Others were critical of the manner in which the reception rite is "executed." Perhaps too many presiders felt obliged both to read all of the rite as printed (despite the frequent rubric "or in similar words") *and* to add further lengthy commentary to explain the symbols. A concise account of what is about to happen before the liturgy begins may be especially helpful for those of other faiths. Yet, simply sprinkling the body with holy water, placing the white pall on the coffin, and performing the other ritual actions in silence have also been known to speak more meaningfully than explanations, particularly when the presider refers to them again in the homily. One priest in particular pointed out that the more Catholic communities experience the symbolism of full Christian initiation, particularly in the *Rite of Christian Initiation of Adults,* and live what is symbolized there, the more they will be able to appreciate the impact of water, paschal candle, and white robe/pall at the funeral.

Interviews as well as more rigorous empirical studies[26] demonstrate emphatically that the rite of reception of the body has indeed become part of American Catholic funeral custom during the past two decades. The greater verbal simplicity of the rite in the *Order of Christian Funerals* (Nos. 159–164) provides a balance between spoken and visible words. Although an option in both the 1970 *Rite* and the *Order of Christian Funerals,* the ritual of spreading the funeral pall, generally white, has become a Catholic custom, especially in the United States. Readily perceived as a reminder of the baptismal garment of the deceased, the white pall marks the dignity of the person and the equality of all before God in death and resurrection (No. 38). It is appropriately spread after the baptismal sprinkling with holy water before the entrance procession and removed only after the coffin has been returned to the church portal for the transfer to the place of committal. In this manner, it functions differently from other optional symbols such as cross, bible, or gospel book. Those symbols, carried in the entrance procession and then placed on the coffin (No. 163), are removed before the beginning of the procession to the place of committal (No. 176). Occasional attempts to discourage the use of the pall or to remove it before the recessional from church in favor of displaying the casket do not respect local custom in the United States, the meaning of the pall as symbol, or the noble simplicity of Catholic funeral liturgy today.

Although all the American parish priests interviewed use this reception rite, most have developed their own way of celebrating it effectively. Their adaptations have to do with space, audibility, and visibility. Relatively few older parish churches are equipped with audio jacks in the vestibule; even where sound is no problem, space and visibility frequently are. Thus, some have moved the rite of reception from the entrance of the church to inside. Positions range from inside the church door to halfway down the main aisle to down front at the place where the casket usually rests. All of these adjustments are pastorally understandable. Yet, in effect, the rite at the entrance runs the risk of becoming an opening rite for a funeral liturgy in church, and that is not its liturgical function. It is designed as a solemn greeting and reception of the deceased and bereaved upon arrival at the church, whether for wake, vigil, or funeral liturgy. Analogous to the reception of candidates for Christian initiation, followed by a solemn final entrance into the church, it is reminiscent of that first sacramental entrance.

Rather than move the rite into the church, some pastors have instructed the people who gather before the funeral party arrives to take places in the rear of the church where they may turn and observe all clearly. Where there is insufficient room even for the funeral party to stand around the casket (or for reasons of convenience), the last pews would be reserved for the bereaved. After the rite of reception, the presider leads the casket (preferably carried by the pallbearers rather than rolled) into the body of the church. The funeral party follows first, and the rest of the congregation completes the entrance procession. In this way, the community-forming symbolism of the opening processional hymn takes on greater meaning. Pastors who have taken this option note that such a procession, with all participating, relieves the uncomfortable feeling of the bereaved as they otherwise walk through a forest of eyes focused on them. It also eliminates the gap in the seating that usually forms between the funeral party and the rest of the congregation.

Still others do not believe it is necessary for all the participants to see and hear everything that takes place at the entrance. In their opinion, the simple rite at the entrance is primarily meaningful for those attending the deceased; the others experience the special symbols sufficiently throughout the liturgy.

This last opinion is similar to that embraced by the Canadian version of the 1969 *Ordo*. There, the reception of the deceased and bereaved and the covering of the casket with a white pall was handled very simply. Only a short prayer marked the liturgical moment, and the entrance procession followed immediately. The reception of the body in the 1990 Canadian edition of the *Order of Christian Funerals* follows the ICEL rite of reception, now paralleling the edition used in the United States more closely.[27]

All this points to the creative potential of the now customary and popular rite of reception at the entrance to the church. The pastoral efforts to involve all present in its celebration are praiseworthy. Our research reveals many different levels of participation and demonstrates the pastoral sensitivity required to direct such participation at the outset of the funeral liturgy in the church.

A valuable part of these introductory rites that supports the pastoral task is the opening, or gathering, song. Pastoral practice affirms the assumption of the *Order of Christian Funerals:* "To draw the community together in prayer at the beginning of the funeral liturgy, the procession should be accompanied, wherever possible, by the singing of the entrance song" (No. 135, with examples given in No. 403).

The Funeral Mass
The liturgical center of Catholic funeral liturgy is, of course, the funeral Mass. At funerals, perhaps more than any other occasion, both laity and clergy emphasize the impact on them of instruction and communion, word and eucharist, of the funeral Mass. People remember "what father said" or at least "how nice he spoke" and "how beautiful it was to see so many receive holy communion." Many older Catholics comment favorably on the difference from the past when there was neither a homily nor the opportunity for the faithful to receive communion at funerals. This change alone relegated "the 18-minute funeral" to the annals of history, for it takes time to celebrate word and sacrament in a manner that nourishes the faith of those present and to bid farewell to the dead. Our inquiries have revealed that great attention is paid to the homily and communion at the funeral Mass.

Homily
We have already discussed the homily-eulogy tension.[28] People expect to hear something about the deceased, many insist. Yet they know that nourishment

243

at the table of God's word is essential to true Christian consolation. Furthermore, the faithful repeatedly confirm the personal benefits of a good funeral homily.

All concede the need to duly recognize the Christian whose funeral Mass is being celebrated. This should not be a eulogy in praise of the deceased, and it is something different from a preached biography, frequently contrived and lacking details that are more familiar to the assembly than to the homilist—not to mention inevitable errors. One associate pastor collected many of the various homily aids that have been published and made up a funeral homily kit for the use of his parish team. Others discuss and evaluate specific funeral homilies given in the parish. One pastor prints the text of his funeral homily as a *memento* for the participants and especially as a continued source of prayerful consolation for the bereaved. And, finally, another adds the suggestion that the homilist should be honest with the assembly.

At this point it is appropriate to take up the thread of the pastoral account above, relating the funeral of a young father. The presider's description continues as follows:

"At the funeral next morning, the deceased's wife (dressed completely in white) and the children met everyone at the door of the church. They then went forward to close the casket. The children had made a little bouquet to put in their father's hands. His wife pulled some of the wheat stalks from the wreath and placed them in his hands. The three children kissed their daddy goodbye, and the casket was closed.

"I introduced the Mass by calling attention again to the wheat near the coffin and briefly summarized the service of the previous evening. The dead man's wife again read the passage from I Corinthians; for the Gospel, we selected Matthew 25:31–40. The homily contrasted funerals of the past with the present (black vestments/white vestments; black pall/white baptismal pall; six orange candles around the casket/white paschal candle dedicated on Easter at the head of the casket; dirgelike music/hope-filled lyrics; no flowers/ flowers, etc.) and then went on to explain why this is the case; not a morbid preoccupation with death, but because it's all linked with, and almost overwhelmed by, references to the resurrection. It's hard to summarize what I said, but apparently it hit hard and made a point." (The thread of this account will be continued later.)

Holy Communion
Another special moment in the funeral Mass for many people is the reception of holy communion. Neither priests nor lay persons have offered much commentary on this, except to insist that it is a very appropriate manifestation of shared faith in resurrection. One non-Roman Catholic person has likened holy communion in the liturgy of the Christian community to the family potluck meal after burial services. One cannot help recall the origin in ancient Christian tradition of the funeral eucharist.

In this context, one of the most sensitive issues is the matter of intercommunion among Christians of different traditions. Catholic directives governing occasions when other Christians may be admitted to eucharistic communion generally exclude intercommunion at funeral or memorial Masses, because such participation is not regarded a matter of "grave necessity."[29]

However painful this experience of separation in faith, it is not considered sufficient reason to deviate from the Roman Catholic theological principle that in practice, eucharistic communion is a sacrament of unity manifest in ecclesial communion. Exceptions are permitted under specified conditions only because eucha-

245

ristic nourishment is held to be a source of divine grace that ought not be refused if necessity so requires or genuine spiritual advantage is suggested. The Secretariat for Christian Unity interprets this principle strictly, but Church law leaves the decision to the "judgment of the diocesan bishop or the conference of bishops" (Canon 844, 4–5).

Pastorally, very few dioceses explicitly recognize a funeral as a case of grave necessity; yet the official interpretation is not universally observed. As a result, considerable confusion exists among Catholics and other Christians alike. Such a state of confusion only aggravates the pain of separation. Some pastors believe, however, that the Christian unity between the bereaved and the deceased, together with the hardship of ecclesial separation at the time of death, is sufficient pastoral reason to invite non-Catholic members of the funeral assembly, especially family and close friends, to receive communion, should they wish to do so according to their own consciences. There are those who do this delicately and with adequate explanation during the funeral liturgy. Still others offer invitations to all present indiscriminately just prior to holy communion.

Recognizing that there are exceptions to the current law on intercommunion, this author advocates following the pastoral directives and interpretation of the Secretariat for Christian Unity—but with two action-oriented recommendations. First of all, whether for funerals or other situations, pastoral care demands that the faithful and others involved be advised delicately but clearly how Catholic Church law regards intercommunion. Careful parish-wide catechesis, including especially the Catholic belief underlying the directives, is urged as the best way to dispel present confusion. One ought to include also some emphasis on the sensitivity involved in dealing with ecumenical pastoral needs and the need to discern whether the exceptional nature of the Christian funeral might constitute sufficient gravity of reason to warrant a further exception. It is good to explain also the canonical tradition that any person approaching communion in good faith will ordinarily not be refused without grave reason. With this reminder, Catholics will be better prepared for those occasions, not so infrequent anymore, when other Christians, who share a faith in the eucharist, approach and are given holy communion.

The second recommendation concerns the nature of the Christian funeral and its consequences in ecumenical pastoral perspective. It is an invitation to competent ecclesiastical authority to study the exceptional nature of the Christian funeral itself in view of sacramental intercommunion. Appendix V takes up this invitation in detail.

Incense
The use of incense during the funeral Mass is another matter of mixed feelings among clergy and laity alike. As we saw above, an American annotation to No. 22, 5 of the Introduction to the *Rite of Funerals* (1970) states that its use is optional in the United States. Also, as in the case of holy water, it is not to be multiplied. In practice, this refers to the use of incense at the preparation of the gifts, during the final commendation and farewell, and at the cemetery. The last use is almost extinct, and the other practice, of honoring the gospel book with incense, falls under the guidelines of the *Order of Mass*. Of the remaining two uses, our research indicates about an equal representation of both.

The American version of the 1970 *Rite* (No. 43) continued the practice of including an incensation of the body during the rite of preparation of the gifts, followed by an incensing of the presider and congregation. Some parishes where this practice is customary, reflecting on what is being symbolized by these different incensations and how people experience them, discovered quite a confusion among parish personnel and faithful.

Not many are willing to consider incensation at this time to be a symbolic purification, a further gesture of preparation of gifts and people, including the deceased, to enter into eucharist. Yet that seems to be its primary intention at this point. Moreover, the practice of going to incense the casket (purification and honor) while making the round of incensing the altar (a blend of sanctifying space and honoring Christ and the martyrs, whose relics rest in the altar) confuses the meaning of the gesture. A minor point, to be sure, but if incense is going to be used, it ought to be used in accord with the sign being expressed.

The *Order of Christian Funerals* (No. 144) dissolves the confusion all together. Following the interpretation of the Roman Congregation for Divine Worship and the general principle that the "liturgy of the eucharist takes place in the usual manner at the funeral Mass" (No. 144), the *Order* discontinues the practice of incensing the body during the rite of preparation of the gifts. The final revised text reflects the General Instruction on the Roman Missal: "Before the priest washes his hands, he may incense the gifts and the altar. Afterward, the deacon or other minister may incense the priest and the congregation" (No. 144). Taking all this into consideration, one cannot miss the distinct overall impression that contemporary Catholics are satisfied with the liturgy of the funeral Mass. Despite an occasional, reasoned plea for the return of the sequence, *Dies irae,* the balance found in the new prayers for Mass in the Sacramentary[30] and the wide choice of readings in the *Lectionary* are termed welcome changes. Some have indicated a desire for greater recognition for the use of contemporary literature, especially poetry, as an extension of the scriptural word. And finally, there is the recommendation to request one or more proper Eucharistic Prayers for the funeral Mass. In practice, the third Eucharistic Prayer, with its proper commemoration, is the one most frequently prayed—for many Catholics, the only one they ever hear, even on Sundays.

New Eucharistic Prayers would render the funeral Mass memorable, while not jeopardizing its continuity with the other celebrations of the eucharist. One already hears how attentively people listen during the special commemorations. There is a further reason still. Analogous to the Eucharistic Prayers for Masses with Children and those for Reconciliation, proper Eucharistic Prayers for funerals would further enrich the theology of paschal mystery and, potentially at least, encourage a more attentive personal participation in the celebration of the eucharist on behalf of the deceased. Preference has been indicated also for a structure that invites acclamatory prayer by the people throughout the canon, similar to Eucharistic Prayer II and III for Masses with Children. Such proper Eucharistic Prayers with special acclamations, some argue, would only take people further away from the expected and confuse them with more variety. Although our inquiries indicate that participation during the Eucharistic Prayer might indeed be slow in coming, experience gives good reason to assume that actively practicing Catholics would pay special attention to a proper Eucharistic Prayer at the funeral Mass.

This is an appropriate context to note the 1976 decree by the Congregation for the Doctrine of the Faith on "Public celebrations of Mass in the Catholic Church for other deceased Christians." This decree has been incorporated in the new Code of Canon Law (1983).[31] Although these are not funeral Masses properly speaking, people often think of them in the same context as a funeral. This is especially true when such a Mass is celebrated for a person of national renown. When a very diverse group gathers for the occasion, the presider and those responsible will want to be especially attentive to the kind of ecumenical, pastoral needs noted earlier in this chapter.

The commentary on the Code reads: "There are three conditions for a non-Catholic to be given an ecclesiastical burial: (1) the prudent judgment of the local ordinary, (2) the absence of a contrary intent on the part of the deceased, and (3) the unavailability of the proper minister of the deceased."[32]

Final Commendation
The full title for the traditional short service at the casket after the funeral Mass well represents both the intention of the service and the way people experience it: final commendation and farewell. Although the cemetery or other place of final disposition remains the true site of last farewell in the ordinary experience of people, it has been argued by not a few priests and people that this short service is the farewell of the full worshiping community. The cemetery service, frequently celebrated by only a few and under less than ideal conditions for worship, is rather the explicit close of the funeral following the eucharist and farewell.

American Catholics generally feel that the commendation liturgy does what seems liturgically appropriate and ritually necessary. That is, it brings the celebration of the paschal mystery, as it touches the life of this dead Christian, to an explicit close and provides a transition to the final moment of disposition, whenever that takes place and with whatever number of the community present.

The option to celebrate the final commendation and farewell at the cemetery or crematorium hall (before cremation) is considered unrealistic by most parish priests interviewed. (For the laity, the question is almost purely academic.) Implied in the option, of course, is the proximity of the place of burial or cremation. Rural parishes that maintain a churchyard and cemetery have used the option quite meaningfully, especially in good weather, as have religious communities whose cemeteries are near the church or chapel where the funeral Mass is celebrated. Similarly, in cities where a chapel at the cemetery is customarily used for the entire funeral service (mostly without the eucharist), celebrating the commendation rite at the graveside has also been described as liturgically effective.

In all these situations, however, one must be attentive to the rhythm of the funeral liturgy. The rite of committal with final commendation has a different liturgical dimension than the simple rite of committal. It not only seals, as it were, the climactic funeral liturgy, but it encompasses ritually the power-laden final moment itself of leave-taking at the grave. Presiders have commented on the need to approach the rite differently in these two different settings; they insist that there is far more than a mere change of physical location to consider.

Although this option is ordinarily not possible and, where possible, not always practical, it is worthy of attention. Among other things, it illustrates how the Catholic funeral can be concluded in different ways, depending on differing pastoral circumstances and needs. The emphasis here is on *difference*, not mere *preference*. The commendation rite functions differently according to its place in the liturgical rhythm of the rite; either use is equally good. Where it concludes the funeral liturgy in the church, an appropriate cemetery service (not a duplication) follows; where it takes place at the cemetery, it replaces the ritual function of a

251

burial rite. The criterion for a choice is a pastoral one. It answers the question: Under the circumstances, which manner of conclusion is pastorally better for this funeral?

Liturgical expression at the final commendation and farewell differs, too, depending on place, although only because of circumstances. Our responses show that incense is frequently used at the commendation in the church but rarely outside the church. The difficulties of transporting a lighted censer or lighting it again at the cemetery are cited as reasons for the latter situation. Holy water, on the other hand, is often used in both situations, although less frequently at the commendation in church, especially if holy water was sprinkled during the rite of reception.

Most responses pertaining to these actions suggest simply that water and incense are remnants from the former absolution service. Some priests have dropped both as too identified with purification and only contrived gestures of commendation or farewell. They strive to give new meaning to the commendation rite by taking a position close to the casket; by resting one's right hand on it during prayer; by preparing the transitional invitation to prayer specifically for this deceased person; by incorporating in the commendation and farewell the gesture of removing and giving the traditional casket cross (at the cemetery) or the deceased's bible (if it was on the pall-covered casket) to a member of the family; by allowing one of the bereaved to speak a word of thanks to the assembly and to invite all to the funeral reception after burial; and the like.

Our pastoral account from above concludes the liturgy at church briefly: "After Mass and the final commendation, we all gathered around the casket and, while we sang the oft-repeated refrain 'And I will raise him up,' we carried the young father's body out of the church to the waiting hearse."

LITURGY AT THE CEMETERY

The most general impression from our responses reflects how widely the great freedom provided by the *Order* is indeed exercised, not so much within parishes but from parish to parish. This phenomenon and the suppleness required of the liturgy at the cemetery because of outside circumstances frame our observations. One need think only of the differences in liturgical practice that climate implies; that urban, suburban, or rural residence implies; that differing cemetery regulations, laws, and the like imply, to mention but a few. We note here, therefore, only those of most general interest.

Real Earth

All our research points to a concern about the cemetery industry and its apparent control of liturgy at the cemetery. Just as dialogue with funeral directors has proven helpful to clarify Catholic funeral values, so, too, there is an urgent need for parish priests and cemetery personnel to discuss the spiritual and liturgical needs of the people they serve. Modern management of cemeteries is essential, and the legitimate demands of those served are part of such management. A legitimate and minimal demand of the Catholic *Order of Christian Funerals* is to celebrate the cemetery service "at the grave or tomb" of the deceased. More and more, this minimum expectation is becoming an exception. Often, one must request it explicitly and pay extra for the service.

Certainly, in large city cemeteries, it is less expensive to wait until several bodies are ready for burial and then inter all of them at one time, efficiently and without bereaved spectators present. But are the consequences worth the cost benefit to the bereaved? To be sure, all-weather cemetery chapels are provided for the comfort and convenience of mourners, but what if comfort and convenience are not the most important values to the bereaved? Efficient handling of services, crowd control, and easy parking are undeniable priorities for which people are grateful, and for which they pay, but does that make them into a "parking-lot civilization"?

One is reminded of the practice in eastern Canada where the priest who accompanies the bereaved to the cemetery remains behind, standing next to the grave until the last person is out of sight. People comment that they cherish this custom very much. It is a sign of the Church's presence to them, a source of great comfort to the family. In some parishes in the United States, it is likewise becoming the practice of certain parish priests to plan the committal service with interment at its recommended place (No. 209) unless the bereaved explicitly request otherwise. This involves thorough liturgical catechesis but over time becomes the expectation among parishioners.

Apropos of these remarks, our continuing account of one rural funeral closes on the note of real earth: "The young family's farm is adjacent to the local cemetery. Thoughtfully, the widow bought a plot overlooking their home and land—with the site of the fatal accident looming in the distance. Everyone was invited to the home for lunch after the burial, and most people actually came out. It was a festive afternoon, even though I noticed several people watch from the living-room windows to see the dead man's grave being filled in."

Cremation
Catholic people and their priests alike frequently ask what is liturgically appropriate for the disposition of

254

ashes, or cremains. There is, of course, a prior question: "What is the Catholic way of celebrating the paschal mystery in funeral liturgy when cremation has been selected as means of final disposition?" To guide our discussion in light of responses gleaned from current pastoral praxis, the *Order of Christian Funerals* sets out for us an attitude and an approach.

The appropriate Roman Catholic attitude toward cremation, as noted in the revised funeral liturgy, is rooted in the longstanding Catholic tradition that the death of one of our community is not an isolated event. We bring the body of our deceased loved ones to their final place of rest in a spirit of love and care, and support for those left behind.

Where does cremation fit into all of this? Perhaps the most important thing to recognize is that the choice of cremation does not limit us to immediate cremation at death, with liturgical expression of our faith left to a memorial service sometime after the fact. Yet, already, this seems to be a growing trend in those Catholic parishes where cremation is selected frequently. Why is this? From pastoral interviews, the main reason seems to be that this is the widespread general practice surrounding cremation outside the Catholic community. Because we have so little Catholic experience with cremation, we find ourselves following the trends of the world around us.

The *Order of Christian Funerals*, however, as a liturgical document embracing for us the tradition of the Catholic Church, assumes that cremation is a process that takes place after the deceased has been committed to God and bidden farewell. From the perspective of Catholic faith and liturgical practice, cremation is what happens after the body has been delivered to its place of final rest, that is, after the committal services. As described above, cremation is understood in liturgical

255

law as a technologically accelerated process of physical decomposition.

The attitude we are invited to hold in a Catholic practice of cremation places high priority on the long tradition of keeping the memory of our dead, especially in the Catholic cemetery. Prior to cremation, it is the body that holds our faithful attention. After cremation, it is the grave or niche where the cremains rest.

What are our options in celebrating the full Catholic funeral liturgy, even when cremation is selected for its economic benefit? Perhaps the most common option thus far combines the selection of embalming (in itself an *inexpensive* procedure) with the use of a simple casket. Casket manufacturers have also begun to provide an attractive and appropriately simple temporary casket, which is, in effect, an outer frame, or shell, around a removable inner box, complete with traditional casket lining and pillow.

In the latter case, for example, upon completion of the liturgy in the church and committal at the crematorium, the inner box is removed from the temporary casket, and cremation follows. With this option, the funeral liturgy follows our traditional Catholic pattern in honor and memory of the deceased and in support of the bereaved by the community of faith.

Where even these costs are an economic disadvantage to our faithful, still other options are possible. In such cases, members of the Church community and the parish itself might recall the corporal works of mercy and assist their fellow parishioners. Some parishes have discussed, for example, the option of purchasing such a temporary casket shell so that the cost to the needy bereaved in the parish would be even less.

To select cremation without embalming is another option. To do so, one might consider refrigeration of the body until the time of services. Some state laws, however, require that a body be cremated or buried within hours after refrigeration. That timing makes it difficult to provide a full celebration of the funeral liturgy and procession with the body to the crematorium. Nevertheless, it is possible when the liturgical community and funeral service practitioners are willing to cooperate.

More detailed consideration of the growing practice of cremation among Catholics and of liturgical attitudes and approaches has been taken up in a specific monograph on the topic.[33] There, practical issues such as ashes in church, memorial services after the fact, options in the *Order of Christian Funerals* itself, and some suggestions for the future are given the attention that space constraints render impossible in this revision.

In all that, it is clear that one of the greatest qualities of the *Order of Christian Funerals* is its ability to provide an appropriate expression of faith for Catholic funerals even under these newest of circumstances. With sound pastoral judgment, founded on knowledge of the 1969 *Ordo* and its interim renderings, such as the *Rite of Funerals*, and with commitment to the faith they proclaim, parish priests and their pastoral teams may hereby serve the faithful with greater flexibility and inspiration. Once again, the liturgy is inviting us to be somewhere none of us has ever been; it is our pastoral responsibility to translate this invitation into living liturgy for an ever-growing number of Catholics who request cremation. That Western Catholics have discovered cremation will probably not surprise historians of the 21st century. How we respond to the invitation extended us by the revised *Order of Christian Funerals* and to the cultural challenge to christen cremation will, however, be among the touchstones whereby future generations will measure our fidelity to the Catholic tradition and the renewal of Vatican Council II.

It has become an axiom in pastoral care literature and conversations that the attention of the Church toward bereaved members does not end with the funeral liturgy and committal. Yet follow-up visits to the many persons touched by death in parish life is decried by clergy and other ministers as service more often characterized by goodwill than actuality. Parochial ministry to those in more immediate need, as it seems, is so demanding that there is little or no time left to reach out to the bereaved.

Empirical research has confirmed the importance of attentive pastoral care on both sides of the liturgy surrounding death. Despite the real impediments to such care just noted, priests and other ministers are more likely to be considered helpful in face of death when their availability includes an attentiveness toward planning and also extends to the time after the funeral. Ministers themselves confirm this perception.[34] This is clearly an even more imperative invitation to continue or to undertake the development of lay bereavement ministry groups. Furthermore, much work remains to be done in the formulation of specific liturgical ways to follow the direction of the *Order of Christian Funerals* as a model for rituals of memorialization. Recalling the remembrance of the deceased at Mass at one month (the "month's mind") and annually on the anniversary of death, parochial celebrations on All Saints' and All Souls' days, and the like, a growing number of parishes with lay bereavement groups have successfully introduced contemporary adaptations of these ecclesial opportunities for liturgy beyond the funeral. One familiar example may suffice to represent this necessary effort to bridge the gap between goodwill and actuality in the pastoral care of bereaved parishioners:

"In August of 1987, we celebrated our first parish Memorial Mass. Records of weekly Mass intentions and parish deaths supplied me with a list of those who had died during the previous year. Three weeks before the date of the Mass, I sent out handwritten notes to the families of those whose names appeared there, announcing our desire to remember the parish dead of the past year, explaining that the names would be entered onto a special "memorial scroll," and inviting them to a Memorial Mass and reception afterward. We also published the announcement in the parish bulletin.

"The time of the memorial was set on a weekday at the daily 12:05 p.m. Mass. Ours is a downtown parish, and elderly parishioners are hesitant to come out at night. Although this daily Mass draws people from the businesses in the downtown area who belong to other parishes, we did not perceive this to be a conflict.

"The scroll was displayed at the back of the church on a table. (The scroll? I bought two wooden rolling pins and had butcher paper cut to the proper width at the art store. It is an easy matter to add lengths of paper to the scroll as space is needed, with the added benefit of preserving the already entered names.) It was close at hand for the parishioners to write the names of those whom they wanted to remember. The physical act of writing the names had meaning for them, and we had no idea how many parishioners would participate the first time.

"At the time of the memorial Mass, the scroll was placed in the sanctuary in front of the altar on a small table. The pastor used incense during the Mass and incensed the scroll. After the Mass, members of the congregation came into the sanctuary to see and to touch the scroll. Afterward, it was placed between two candles on a table in the hall where the reception was held, for it was obvious that those too frail to come to the sanctuary earlier also wanted to see and touch.

"I had butterflies in the pit of my stomach. I knew people would come to the Mass. But would they take the time to be community and console one another? It was beautiful, a time of sharing and healing. Everyone responded to my handwritten note in one way or another. If a member of the family was unable to attend, a friend came instead. Those who were able to come even for a quick cup of coffee did so; those who attended from the downtown businesses were pleased to be included and to participate in this memorial Mass.

"The second memorial Mass was November 11, 1987. Once again, the announcement went into the bulletin three weeks before the date. This time, I sent handwritten notes only to those families who had suffered a death within the last six months. The weather had turned cold and rainy. Also, we had just celebrated All Saints' and All Souls' [days]. Would there be a need?

"The scroll was once again in place at the back of the church. There were fewer questions but many more names than before. I was thankful the scroll was so adaptable. The Mass was again celebrated at the daily noontime hour, and the scroll was placed in the sanctuary in front of the altar. We had a larger crowd than in August, even though it had only been four months since the initial memorial Mass.

"The pastor and I were both struck by the way the congregation reacted and responded to this Mass in contrast to the Mass for All Souls' Day. There were tears and genuine communion with one another. That this was a very personal and meaningful time full of faith and prayer was obvious—a time for the broken-hearted, and it was appreciated and needed. We decided that such a parish Memorial Mass filled a real need in the parish life of our worshiping community."[35]

Throughout this study, and especially this chapter, the temptation to project the *ordo exsequiarum* of the 21st century has been great. It is our conviction, however, that such a projection would violate all that has been discovered here. Research may indeed herald the future but only because it represents the real situation in which today's funeral liturgy brings the death of an individual Christian into touch with the paschal mystery of Christ. Tomorrow's funeral must do the same in tomorrow's world, and renewal will remain the key to a continuity of paschal faith.

As the recent history of the genesis of the 1989 edition of the *Order of Christian Funerals* itself revealed, debate among those charged with the *magisterium* of the Church as to precise details of meaning in such expression seems eternal. Taken as a whole, the tradition, the debate among shepherds, scribes, and scholars, and above all the liturgy itself, constitute the context that must shape the liturgy of the future. Strong images and symbols of the past, especially those from sacred Scripture, will continue to be reinterpreted to enflesh the paschal mystery in ways consonant with Christian faith in the 21st century. Classic renderings, such as *In Paradisum* and "the bosom of Abraham," speak differently about death to our religious imagination than to Christians of the 4th century or to those of the Middle Ages. It falls to us to keep that faith alive and pass on the euchological tradition to the next generation. If the agenda of the previous two decades has been to identify and make available the funeral liturgy of the authentic Catholic tradition, the publication of the *Order of Christian Funerals* in 1989 ushered in the more significant agenda of affirming the praxis of authentic Catholic faith that continues to shape its formation and without which it will not be received into the Church of the future.

Wherever the Catholic funeral today is still but a vernacular rendering of the late medieval post-Tridentine liturgy of burial, it is but a mirror of the past longing toward the future. There, the present must yet be made ready to receive the fertile seed of renewal. Where the spirit of renewal has gone hand-in-hand with liturgical reform in word and rite, there the seed has found good soil and reveals in embryo the form of future experience with funeral liturgy. Although rite and word will change, they will be recognizable from their roots in present faith and liturgy. We cannot project ritual detail. We do believe, however, that in the 21st century, word and sacrament will continue to express an ever-new Christian faith in paschal life where only death is visible.

NOTES

1. See Rutherford and Kandelman, *Religious Ritual*, and Rutherford, "Funeral Liturgy."

2. Development of proper liturgy involving cremains that respects the concerns of the Holy See's directive not to perform over the ashes liturgy directed toward the deceased body will surely be an important item of pastoral liturgical renewal in the coming decade. See below for further remarks and bibliography.

3. An article with description and photos of this baptistry by David Clark, Director of the Archdiocesan Office for Worship, Portland, Ore., has been prepared for *Environment and Art Letter* (Chicago: Liturgy Training Publications). In press.

4. Bishops' Committee on the Liturgy *Environment and Art in Catholic Worship*, Washington, D.C.: 1978) No. 5. See also James F. White and Susan J. White, *Church Architecture: Building and Renovation for Christian Worship* (Nashville: Abingdon, 1988).

5. A traditionally popular aid has been *The Lord is My Shepherd: A Book of Wake Services* and *Toward a New Life* (complete with Funeral Rite Selection Sheet) both published by Ave Maria Press, Notre Dame, Ind., 1971, and frequently reprinted. Plans for a revised *Order of Christian Funerals* edition are in process. Other planning guides prepared as companions to the *Order of Christian Funerals* are available from the publishers of the *Order*. Very comprehensive and helpful is *Now and at the Hour of Our Death*, Chicago: Liturgy Training Publications, 1989.

6. A practical example of such information is the generally little known but widely significant change in Catholic Church practice and law not to prohibit funeral rites for deceased Catholics who have entered irregular marriages without public scandal to the faithful. Canon 1184, 3; see James A. Coriden *et al.*, eds., *The Code of Canon Law: A Text and Commentary* (New York: Paulist Press, 1985), pp. 839–840.

7. Although I am uncomfortable with the title "resurrection choir" (a remnant from the recent practice of unfelicitous memory whereby the funeral Mass was called the "Mass of the Resurrection"), it seems to have greater popular appeal than "funeral choir." Just as every celebration of the eucharist is a "Mass of the Resurrection," every choir is a resurrection choir. Furthermore, the theological implication indicating "immediate resurrection" at death and funeral, is a matter of some concern. Perhaps the title "funeral choir" would in fact avoid both euphemism and issues of theological debate?

8. The following anecdote well illustrates the point. "Once a family had an arrangement with the bagpipe player. The funeral director knew he was coming, but I didn't. So, this person arrives about 20 minutes before the funeral and proceeds to tell us he was going to play Irish folk music for the funeral. I just said to him, 'I don't think it's possible because the choir and the organist didn't know you were going to be here; now that you're here, would you like to see what we might be able to do together?' After we had talked for a while, I asked about his repertoire? When he started to name all Gaelic songs, I had no idea what he was talking about and said, 'Can you translate some of it—give me an

idea?' The end result was a perfect solution. He went out-side to meet the hearse as it came to the church, and while people were gathering for the procession on the outside, he stood at the church door playing—I think it was *Amazing Grace*. When the procession arrived at the center of the church for the opening prayers of the reception of the body, he stopped playing. Later he accompanied the choir for fa-miliar tunes, and then he played while the processional re-turned to the cars. That worked out really well." See note 9.

9. Interview with Sr. René Simonelic, C.R., St. Symphorosa Parish, Chicago, Ill., July 1989. Pastor: Rev. John P. McNamara.

10. Interview with Mary Smith, M.M. (1990), parish music director, Holy Family Parish, Yakima, Wash., July 1989. Pas-tor: Rev. John Murtagh.

11. The Liturgical Press, one of the three American publish-ers producing the initial presider's editions of the *Order*, has included a substantial Music Supplement, pp. 386–473, with a helpful index of musical pieces. *Order of Christian Funerals*, Collegeville, Minn.: Liturgical Press, 1989.

12. The Latin reads: *additis, quotiescumque opportunum fuerit, melodiis cantui aptis.*

13. Recently, one pastoral musician reported experiencing the song "Drop Kick Me Jesus Through the Goalposts of Life" as a gathering song (played on cassette tape because the organist was unable to play it)!

14. During a funeral director-clergy consultation sponsored by the Religious Affairs Committee of the NFDA in May 1988, a proposal to prepare a revised version of this educa-tional film in light of the *Order of Christian Funerals* was well received. Consult local members of the NFDA or its national information service for further details about the project.

15. To facilitate such mutual formation and continuing educa-tion, the National Funeral Directors Association maintains a speakers' forum in the form of a *Seminary Resource Program*, directed by the Religious Affairs Coordinator (Paul E. Irion, 149 Kready Avenue, Millersville, Pa. 17551).

16. See for example Continental Association of Funeral and Memorial Societies, *The Memorial Society: A Description* and *Directory of Memorial Societies in the United States and Canada* (Washington, D.C.: CAFMS, 1989); Lisa Carlson, *Caring for Your Own Dead* (Hinesburg, Vt.: Upper Access Publishers, 1987), and the review of this work by Howard Raether, *The Director* 58 (1988), pp. 35–38. See Peter Gilmour, ed., *Now and at the Hour of Our Death* (Chicago: Liturgy Training Publications, 1989), pp. 6–8 for a convenient summary of options for preparation of the body.

17. "The Corinthian Group is committed to bringing about change in national attitudes toward death and grief by 1) de-emphasizing the commercial aspects of the death and dying experience, 2) encouraging funeral services in churches and synagogues, and 3) helping people accept these experiences as a significant part of living. Positive changes and attitudes can occur when misconceptions, myths, and anxieties about current funeral practice are replaced with constructive and meaningful alternatives." The Corinthian Group, Inc. (4424 N.E. Glisan, Portland, Ore. 97213), Brochure, 1983.

18. *La Célébration des Obsèques,* p. 9.

19. For example, Walter Schmitz and Terence Tierney, *Liturgikon: Pastoral Ministrations* (Huntington, Ind.: Our Sunday Visitor, 1977), p. 159.

20. Printing such participation aids might be a further service that funeral directors can offer to their Catholic and other religious clients.

21. See note 5 above.

22. See Rutherford, "Funeral Liturgy," pp. 79–83.

23. Cf. Rutherford, *Pastoral Care,* and see Chapter Five, p. 191 [=ms pp 207–208]

24. This opportunity proves especially helpful pastorally when the death in question has touched the lives of large numbers of people who desire an opportunity to participate in prayerful vigil before the funeral liturgy. For example, fol-

lowing the accidental death of the Rev. Thomas C. Oddo, C.S.C., president of the University of Portland, in October 1989, an extended vigil in the presence of the body (casket closed) was held in the university chapel around the clock from the time of reception until funeral services two days later. Mourning students, faculty, and staff took turns of one-hour intervals to participate in the "wake."

25. Personal correspondence by the Rev. James G. Brady, C.S.C., formerly pastor of St. Patrick's Parish, Independence, Ore., September 1978. The description of this funeral will be continued at appropriate points throughout the rest of the chapter.

26. See Rutherford-Kandelman, *Religious Ritual*, and Rutherford, "Funeral Liturgy."

27. For the Canadian commentary on the 1989 *Order* see J. Frank Henderson, ed., *The Christian Funeral*. National Bulletin on Liturgy, No. 119 (Ottawa: Canadian Conference of Catholic Bishops, 1989).

28. See Chapter Four, p. 147.

29. *Acta Apostolicae Sedis* 64 (1972), pp. 518–525. See also *Code of Canon Law* (Washington, D.C.: Canon Law Society of America, 1983), Canon 841. In this matter of intercommunion, several documents of the Roman Catholic *magisterium* are essential to the discussion: the Decree of Vatican II, *Unitatis redintegratio* (Nov. 21, 1974) in Flannery, *Vatican Council II*, pp. 452–470, esp. no. 8; the Instruction *In quibus Rerum Circumstantiis* (June 1, 1972) in Flannery, pp. 554–559; and the interpretation of this latter instruction, *Dopo le publicazione* (Oct. 17, 1973) in Flannery, pp. 560–563.

30. Henry Ashworth, "The Prayers for the Dead in the Missal of Pope Paul VI," *Ephemerides Liturgicae* 85 (1971), pp. 3–15.

31. *BCL Newsletter* 12 (1976), p. 91. See *Code of Canon Law*, Canon 1183, 3.

32. James A. Coriden, Thomas J. Green and Donald E. Heintschel, eds., *The Code of Canon Law: A Text and Commentary* (New York: Paulist Press, 1985), p. 839.

33. See Rutherford, *Honoring the Dead: Catholics and Cremation* (Collegeville, Minn.: Liturgical Press, in press).

34. Rutherford, "Funeral Liturgy," pp. 81–83.

35. Personal correspondence with Celeste Brendan Granato, lay pastoral minister, Church of St. Michael the Archangel, Portland, Ore., August 1988. Pastor: Rev. Edmond Bliven.

From the *Rite of Funerals* (1970)
to the *Order of Christian Funerals* (1989)

In the decade following the appearance of the *Order of Funerals* (1969), pastoral practice and local custom throughout the English-speaking world expressed the need for indigenous funeral rites. In January 1981, the International Commission on English in the Liturgy (ICEL) published its preliminary consultation document ("red book") calling for a comprehensive revision of the funeral rites. ICEL chairman Archbishop Hurley explains in the Preface: "Because the liturgy is now celebrated in living languages, it places a further demand upon us. Texts must not only be carefully prepared but they must also be periodically reviewed so that the vitality, freshness and immediacy of the vernacular liturgy is maintained."[1]

This 1981 study took three years to prepare and consisted of a translation of existing liturgical texts for presider and congregation. Rubrics and introductory material were not included in this initial program, but descriptive headings were used to situate each text clearly in its proper place in the ritual (e.g., "Prayers for the Deceased Person," "Song of Farewell"). Replies to this document were received by August 1981, and in two years, the ICEL standing committee on texts was able to produce the first draft (September 1983).

A new structure was already emerging in this first draft:

Foreword, Decree and Introduction
PART I: RITES BEFORE THE FUNERAL
Introduction
Chapter One: Announcement of Death
Chapter Two: First Viewing of the Body
Chapter Three: Vigil for the Deceased
Chapter Four: Transfer of the Body to Church or
                Cemetery
Chapter Five: Reception at the Church

PART II: FUNERAL LITURGY
Chapter Six: Funeral Mass
Chapter Seven: Funeral outside Mass

PART III: RITES AT THE GRAVE, OR TOMB, OR
CREMATORIUM

In early 1984, three substantially similar drafts were issued, expanding the above Part III (to include options of committal with and without Final Commendation and Farewell) and adding three new parts ("Funerals of Children," among the most noteworthy) and an Appendix.

A fifth draft followed in July 1984, expanding the opening sections to include a Foreword, Decree and two Introductions (an ICEL General Introduction and the Roman Introduction of 1969). The format of the second draft and the new sectional introductions of the third draft were preserved. In November 1984, the sixth draft appeared, which tightened up the model 1983 draft: One new section was added (IV. Additional Texts), the 1969 Roman Introduction became an Appendix, and a Biblical Index was created.[2]

By this sixth draft, more than a literal revision of text had occurred. The book had begun to assume the shape of a ritual resource book or a pastoral "manual" (similar to those referred to in Chapter Three above) rather than the familiar format of the post-Tridentine *rituale*. Five further draft revisions were to appear between December 1984 and May 1985 before the publication in October 1985 of the ICEL *Order of Christian Funerals* ("gray book"). During 1985, the order took the final shape in form and content that would guide the process of approval and confirmation. Most especially, the introductory format of Part I became "Vigil and Related Rites" and the new chapter "Rite of Final Commendation for an Infant" was included. Helpful additions were also made to other parts, rendering the texts of Sacred Scripture, the Office for the Dead (Morning and Evening Prayer), and additional texts (including the Rite for Holy Communion outside Mass) readily accessible for pastoral use. The Introduction to the *Order of Funerals* (1969), here again at the beginning of the volume preceding the General Introduction of the *Order of Christian Funerals*, would remain an appendix in the 1989 edition.

Thus, the ICEL "gray book" of October 1985 had been born of the manifold stages of consultation and correspondence that accompanied the preparation of 11 drafts. By this stage, the revision was firmly rooted in parish liturgical practice, reflecting the wisdom of pastors, liturgists, parish musicians, and assemblies worldwide.

The following chronology will help the reader appreciate some of the enormous effort that went into preparing the *Order of Christian Funerals*.

A Chronology

1969	*Ordo Exsequiarum–editio typica*
1970	*Rite of Funerals*—a translation
1977–1980	Program for revisions developed
1981 Jan.	ICEL Red Book Consultation on Revision

1983 Sept.	First Draft Edition
1984 Feb.–Dec.	Second–Seventh Draft Editions
1985 Jan.–May	Eighth–Eleventh Draft Editions
Oct.	ICEL Gray Book
Nov.	*Order of Christian Funerals* approved by NCCB
1987 Apr.	OCF confirmed by the Congregation for Divine Worship
1987–1989	Debate between the National Conferences of Bishops, ICEL, and the Congregation for Divine Worship regarding proposed adjustments
1989 Oct.	OCF published by order of the NCCB for mandatory use in the United States, beginning Nov. 2, 1989

NOTES

1. *Consultation on Revision: Rite of Funerals* (Washington, D.C.: ICEL, 1981), p. 5.

2. Table of Contents: sixth revised ICEL edition, November 1984. Reprinted with permission.

Order of Christian Funerals
Sixth Draft Edition
Foreword
Decree
General Introduction

PART I: FUNERAL RITES/Introduction
RITES BEFORE THE FUNERAL LITURGY/Introduction
 1 Vigil for the Deceased
 2 Other Rites and Prayers
  -Prayers after Death
  -Gathering in the Presence of the Body

Masses for the Dead

From early Christian times, the presupposition of faith has been that the deceased in need of atonement benefits from the celebration of the eucharist. This belief is still very much alive in Catholic pastoral life and thus also continues to be a distinguishing mark of Roman Catholic faith in life after death. The *Order of Christian Funerals* clearly affirms this belief, taking into account contemporary sacramental theology and the larger pastoral context of death and bereavement. "At the death of a Christian, whose life of faith was begun in the waters of baptism and strengthened at the eucharistic table, the Church intercedes on behalf of the deceased because of its confident belief that death is not the end nor does it break the bonds forged in life. The Church also ministers to the sorrowing and consoles them in the funeral rites with the comforting word of God and the sacrament of the eucharist" (No. 4).

Roman Catholics today understand the practice of offering Mass for the dead in a traditional way, yet not without a sensitivity to the liturgical and theological renewal of Vatican II. Two attitudes appear operative simultaneously in the religious life of American Catholics. Both proclaim the belief that through the paschal sacrifice of Jesus, God has reconciled the world and, true to his promise, has offered that forgiveness to this faithful Christian now dead.[1] Both reflect the historical Catholic teaching that the merciful God requires atonement for the temporal punishment due sins that have been forgiven. For the traditional Christian, atonement after death implies a state of purgation, usually termed "purgatory."[2] Both current attitudes also continue to reflect the way Catholic teaching about purgatory assimilated to itself the earlier Christian practice of including the faithful dead in the celebration of eucharist.

It is here especially that the two attitudes toward Mass for the dead differ. One conceives the Mass primarily as an act (action) of worship that is celebrated as an end in itself. Its strength rests on Vatican II and postconciliar documents as well as on the renewed liturgical books. The other attitude views the Mass primarily as a means of worship and a channel of grace applicable to other ends. It is rooted in late medieval theology about the value of the Mass and looks to Trent and post-Tridentine practice for its verification. Presently, varying blends of these two views are common, and those responsible for pastoral-liturgical ministry with bereaved families and friends face them almost daily. The importance of the eucharist for the dead in the *Ordo* calls for a brief comment on each of these attitudes.[3]

By its very nature, the Mass is an action—an act of worship of God by the Church through and with the risen Christ. It consists in the sacramental actualization in praise and thanksgiving of the paschal mystery of Christ through which universal salvation was achieved once and for all. The paschal sacrifice was universally effective for salvation and at once an act of worship totally and completely acceptable to God. So, too, the eucharistic memorial of this paschal mystery sacramentally actualizes the saving passover of Christ and his perfect sacrifice of praise. This primary understanding of the eucharist as an action of the risen Christ together with the faithful assembled as Church is acknowledged by post-Vatican II documents to be the model for the "normative Mass" today.[4] Eucharistic liturgy is thus first and foremost worship.

When the eucharist in this sense is offered for a deceased Christian, that person is remembered as one of the baptized who died faithful to the promise of the paschal mystery and whose personal passover the community now celebrates, even if somehow not yet realized in its fullness. The Church continues to reckon among "the faithful" the Christian who during life followed the way of conversion and of faith in Jesus dead and risen. Just as that life was lived in eucharistic community, so, too, does it continue to enjoy the concern of that eucharistic community after death. The name of the deceased is mentioned in the intercessions and the proper prayers of the Mass. These prayers profess the Catholic belief in the communion at worship of the blessed who are with God, of the faithful dead in a state of purgation and of the Church living in time (the "communion of saints"). They recognize that the living Christians can offer atonement vicariously for the punishment due the past sins of the dead who suffer in that interim state. These prayers do not, however, spell out a theology of judgment or punishment, of heaven, hell, or purgatory.

All this demonstrates most clearly in practice that the liturgy is not limited in its expressions of the faith to theological explanations. In the liturgy, time is suspended, mirroring eternity. In the Mass for the dead, the community utters its hope for the deceased in the mode of God's now. There are prayers for forgiveness of sins that speak in the first person on behalf of the deceased Christian standing before God. There are prayers asking God's mercy while atonement for the evil of sin is made. There are prayers looking forward to the final resurrection and fullness of life in God's kingdom.

In the eucharistic celebration, these prayers of the Church that characterize the continuous movement of praise and petition are joined with the worship of the risen Christ. As such, they cannot remain unheard by God, who always accepts the perfect worship of the glorified Christ; as human prayer, however, their effect depends on the faith and devotion of the petitioner. This conviction of faith rests on the very nature of eucharistic worship that is at once the action of Christ and of the Church. This point of faith, together with the paschal mystery that the eucharist commemorates, is why prayer for the dead as part of the eucharistic celebration has always been accorded a special efficacy.[5]

According to this first attitude, therefore, the Church offers the eucharistic sacrifice for the faithful dead not as a means to effect one's salvation or ameliorate one's state in purgatory, but rather to proclaim in faith that Jesus' death and resurrection has reconciled this Christian with God. Thus, the community celebrates the deceased's own passover from the power of sin and death and, taking to itself some of the hardship of the desert passage through purgation, anticipates in hope his or her entrance into the fullness of the promised kingdom of everlasting life in Christ.

The other predominant attitude toward Mass for the dead conceives of the Mass as having ends apart from the act of worship itself. According to this view, celebrating the eucharist ("saying Mass") has an objective value. To explain this view of the value of the Mass, Catholic theology since Duns Scotus has employed the model of "the fruits of the Mass." In our case, one applies the so-called special fruits of the Mass to a deceased person according to the intention of the priest celebrant.[6] Thus, one offers Mass "for the repose of the soul of N." Popularly, this means that the sacrifice of the Mass is offered to God as the greatest of all prayers on behalf of the deceased. God then applies the fruit of the Mass to that person's specific situation.

Such an application of the Mass is secondary to the essence of the eucharistic celebration.[7] It derives from a theology that gives equal significance to all four "ends of the Mass" (adoration, thanksgiving, petition, and expiation). In pastoral practice, an emphasis on petition and expiation continues to qualify requests that "Mass be said for" a certain deceased person. This interpretation of the Tridentine canons on the Mass perceives the Mass itself as a means to these ends.[8]

This is the way many Catholics conceive what "happens" when Mass is offered for a deceased Christian on the occasion of a funeral or at other times. A casual comparison of parish bulletins supports this conviction. One is tempted to interpret the reference in paragraph No. 10 of the 1969 Introduction according to this same theology. Pastorally, one is advised, however, to study Catholic liturgical theology after Vatican II in the full context of all the pastoral instructions that were promulgated together with the new ritual books. There one finds the balance of a teaching Church in touch with both the old and the new of its faith, as the *Order of Christian Funerals* (Nos. 5–6) carefully expresses it.

Prescinding from further discussion about the priority of either theology, one danger deserves mention. That is the misunderstanding caused by confusing a secondary effect of the eucharist with its primary meaning. This occurs when one argues that the value of the Mass as the worship of Christ is infinite (primary) and that it is therefore useless to offer more than one Mass for any given deceased person (secondary). The error here is to apply the infinite value and infallible acceptance of the worship of Christ, sacramentally actualized in the Mass, to either intercessory prayer on behalf of the dead or to the Mass itself as propitiatory prayer for a particular intention. The hoped-for effect of such prayer depends on the dispositions of the petitioner and of the one to receive the favor rather than on the gift itself.

Although more than one Mass for the deceased is consistent with contemporary theology of prayer, exaggerations in either direction are obviously out of place. On the one hand, multiplication of Masses for a dead Christian that is based on a quantitative, quasimagical view of prayer fails to take the primary nature of the eucharist as well as the nature of propitiatory prayer and God's providence into account.[9] Discouraging the faithful from requesting special remembrance of a deceased person at a given celebration of the eucharist fails, on the other hand, to recognize the place of the faithful dead in the eucharistic celebration of the paschal mystery of Christ, according to the ancient tradition of the Church. Sensitivity to genuine eucharistic faith, even when that faith is in need of pastoral correction, remains the only proven approach to fostering the kerygmatic Catholic truth expressed in the words of the 1969 Introduction: "The Church therefore offers the eucharistic sacrifice of Christ's passover for the dead. . . ." (No. 1; cf. OCF, Nos. 3–6).[10]

Because the euchological tradition extends many images, both biblical and popular, from all the ages of the past into the present, it is all the more important pastorally to have a holistic sense of funerary liturgical prayer. Recalling Fr. Gy's observations on the prayers of the Ordo[11] one is urged to build liturgical preaching and catechesis on the Catholic faith expressed in the entirety of the Order of Christian Funerals and its praxis rather than on the theology of a single text.

NOTES

1. Cf. *Rite of Penance,* Prayer of Absolution (No. 46). This work presumes, as the *Rite of Penance* itself does, a community of faith and does not take up the question, however important, of those who die estranged from God.

2. See the reiteration of this teaching by Pope Paul VI in his apostolic constitution on Indulgences ("Indulgentiarum doctrina"), Jan. 1, 1967, in *The Pope Speaks (TPS)* 12 (1967), pp. 124–135.

3. Background to the following includes Paul VI, "Mysterium Fidei" (Sept. 3, 1965) *TPS* 10 (1965), pp. 309–328; Sacred Congregation of Rites, *Eucharisticum Mysterium* (May 25, 1967) (Washington, D.C.: USCC, 1967); Josef A. Jungmann, *The Mass* (Collegeville, Minn.: Liturgical Press, 1976), esp. pp. 97–152; Karl Rahner and Angelus Häussling, *The Celebration of the Eucharist* (New York: Herder & Herder, 1968); and Pierre-Yves Emery, *The Communion of Saints* (London: Faith Press, 1966). An easily accessible summary of these views and others is found in Lucien Deiss, *It's the Lord's Supper: Eucharist of Christians* (New York: Paulist Press, 1976).

4. See, among others, *GIRM,* Introduction, Chapters I and IV and *Notitiae* 3 (1967), p. 195.

5. See, for example, Rahner-Häussling, *Eucharist,* p. 82: "The conception of grace, which is attested by the texts of the Masses for the dead in the Roman liturgy, implies awareness of our communion with those who have died in Christ and the belief that we are able to be close and helpful to them by celebrating Mass *for* the dead. By that Mass, they are drawn afresh into communion with Christ, who overcame death in death and whose communion with the dead leads to resurrection; that is the communion which for early Christians was *pax* and *communio* absolutely. The *pro* in the expression *offerre pro defunctis* does not mean directly 'in order to help'; here, too (as in fact elsewhere), it primarily expresses the occasion for the celebration of the Mass ('on the occasion of the death of the late _____'), then a remembrance (especially when the name is mentioned), and finally a repre-

sentation: We offer sacrifice to God in place of the deceased."

6. Jungmann, *The Mass*, pp. 148–150; see also Nicholas Halligan, *Sacraments of Initiation and Union* I (New York: Alba House, 1972), pp. 166–169.

7. Rahner-Häussling, *Eucharist*, p. 39.

8. DS 1743; 1751–1754. Cf. Jungmann, *The Mass*, pp. 143–144.

9. On this matter, Fr. Jungmann has written that "there is little point in forcing distinctions between fruits of varying value or in arranging the different grades of efficacy in neat categories. For the ultimate success of a prayer does not depend on the one who prays but on the free will of the One who grants, and that One does not need a computer." Jungmann, *The Mass*, p. 149.

10. The 1970 English translation read, "The Church therefore *celebrates* the eucharistic sacrifice of Christ's passover for the dead, and *offers* prayers and petitions for them." (Emphases added.)

11. See above, pp. 149–150.

Office for the Dead

"The vigil for the deceased may be celebrated in the form of some part of the office for the dead. To encourage this form of the vigil, the chief hours, "Morning Prayer" and "Evening Prayer," are provided here" (No. 348). The following commentary is offered to complement the *Order*'s excellent introduction (Nos. 348–372) and to further encourage adoption of the liturgy of the hours as a regular part of funeral liturgy and memorialization.

In Morning Prayer for the dead, the rite of gathering is omitted if it has been replaced by the reception of the body. When the hour is celebrated outside the funeral liturgy, the morning hymn (No. 375) may be replaced by any of the additional hymns (No. 396) or other hymns suited to the occasion or season. The call to worship for the dawn hour as expressed in the invitation of Psalm 95, is also a call to preparation, conversion, renewal of covenant. The regular psalmody for this hour consists of Psalm 51 (a lamentation), Isaiah 38: 10–14, 17–20 (a canticle of entreaty for rescue by God), and either Psalm 146 or Psalm 150 (a hymn of praise). After each psalm/canticle, a period for silent reflection should conclude with a psalm collect, according to an ancient tradition of the Church of applying Old Testament hymns to current perceptions of Christ.[1]

A reading follows the psalms. The extract from 1 Thessalonians 4:14 about belief in the risen Christ may be replaced by any other appropriate text (options are provided in Part III). A homily is recommended to make a brief application of psalm and reading to the people's grief and to rekindle their Christian hope in resurrection. Then follows a short litany of praise, the responsory. The gospel canticle is the Song of Zechariah, the *Benedictus* (Luke 1:68–79).

In continuity with the tradition, one recalls how the *Benedictus* once functioned in the early medieval committal rites. Note also that Morning Prayer in the ancient Church was simpler in form and may help us to appreciate both the liturgy of the hours and contemporary adaptations. Worship began with either Psalm 51 (call to repentance) or Psalm 63 (longing to be in God's courts), a variable psalm, a scripture lesson with Old Testament canticle, a psalm of praise (Psalms 148, 149, or 150), a hymn to light (e.g., the *Gloria*) and intercessions (biddings, Lord's Prayer, blessing), and dismissal with exchange of peace. In Christian antiquity, evening prayer looked something like this: the lighting of the evening lamps/candles (with acclamation, hymn, and thanksgiving "preface") led to the burning of incense in the East Syrian Church to accompany Psalm 141 and its collect prayer, closing with the Intercessions, the Lord's Prayer, threefold blessing, dismissal, and rite of peace. Evidence for this form of worship is to be found in many of the patristic writings but none so relevant for the liturgy of the dead as in St. Gregory of Nyssa, describing the deathbed scene of his sister Macrina in 379. The day before she died, he wished to remain with her during the evening, "but the chant of the singers called to the thanksgiving for the light, and she sent me off to the Church." Then comes a description of the following evening: "And when evening had arrived and the lamp was brought in, she opened her eyes that had been closed until then and looked at the light and made clear that she wished to say the thanksgiving for the light, but since her voice failed her, she fulfilled the offering with her heart and with the movement of her hands, while her lips moved in harmony with the inner impulse."[2]

The final section of Morning Prayer is the rite of intercession. The biddings themselves are based on the prayer "Lord, give us new life in Christ." (In evening prayer, the biddings are addressed directly to Christ.) The texts provided may be modified according to the pastoral situation. After the Lord's Prayer, the concluding prayer is chosen from one of the three provided (No. 382) or from the additional prayers (No. 398). A procession may then take place to the place of committal (No. 384), and several texts of chants, prayers, and psalms are provided for this occasion.

Evening Prayer follows a similar pattern of set text with possible options. The rites of gathering (Nos. 385–387) may be replaced by the rite of reception of the body. Otherwise, the evening hymn (No. 387) may be substituted by other suitable hymns. During the evening psalmody, Psalm 121 is a blessing song for pilgrims "on their way home"; Psalm 130 is a lamentation ending with hope and expectation; and the canticle from Philippians 2:6–11 is a hymn to Christ the suffering servant of God. The reading from 1 Corinthians 15:55–57 may be replaced by another (e.g., from Part III) and the recommended homily is followed by the responsory or short litany which honors God as source of life and hope. The canticle from Luke 1:46–55, the *Magnificat*, is yet another canticle of the early community of Jewish Christians reflecting on the Old Testament fragments of God's promises to Israel.[3]

In the early days, this whole section of psalmody was much shorter, possibly consisting of one psalm only, Psalm 141 ("Let my prayer rise like incense before you, Lord, my hands raised in an evening sacrifice of praise") with a concluding collect prayer. This simple form acknowledges our inability to see God face to face or to come into the divine presence except through the cloud (of incense), which symbolizes not only our repentance but also God's glory. That same shadow hovered over the deep at creation, covered the mountain of covenant, led the pilgrims through the desert at the exodus, overshadowed Mary at Jesus' conception, spoke from the skies at Christ's baptism, descended over the mountaintop at the transfiguration, smothered the earth on Calvary, received the risen Lord at ascension, and hovered over the new creation at Pentecost. Finally, the intercessions address Christ directly, honoring him as our hope and resurrection. The Lord's Prayer leads to the concluding prayer, which, like the intercessions, may be replaced by other appropriate texts.

These two liturgical hours are a more reflective form of praise than the Mass. Generally, the only symbol used is the lighting of the candle. The value of this form of prayer lies more in its content than in its drama or visual appeal. The texts of psalms, canticles, scripture readings, hymns and prayers are full of confidence in God's promise that the dead shall live, and that we shall all one day see God face to face. This form of prayer provides comfort at the time of the death and funeral liturgy, and also in the weeks, months and years ahead. While the Church exercises a ministry of pastoral care after the death and burial, so, too, does it provide the form of prayer to strengthen that ministry of support and healing.

Although the *Order* does not refer to Compline or Night Prayer, this more intimate form of worship is also suitable for celebrating the life and death of the Christian. "I will lie down in peace and sleep comes at once, for you alone, Lord, make me dwell in safety"

(Psalm 4). "Whoever dwells in the shelter of the Most High shall not fear the terror of the night; when you call, I shall answer: I am with you, I will save you in distress and give you glory" (Psalm 91). These psalms are born of our hope and longing to be with God. Likewise, the short responsory "Into your hands, O Lord, I commend my spirit" and the Lucan canticle *Nunc Dimittis* speak of the peaceful, gentle optimism of the pilgrim at twilight and sing of the undying hope of the prophet in his twilight years.

The introductory notes on ministry and participation (Nos. 368–372) speak of the need to educate the faithful in the importance of these liturgical hours. The idea that the Office "belongs to the priest" or "is only for private recitation" (by individuals or communities) was replaced by the emphasis of Vatican II on the role of the whole liturgical assembly in celebrating the liturgy of the hours. Likewise, the introduction acknowledges that the liturgical hour may be celebrated in places other than the church and that it may be adapted accordingly. In addition to the priest or deacon presiding, other ministers have a rightful part to play, including cantor, reader, and acolyte. A lay person may preside where necessary. As with all texts for the funeral liturgy, the family of the deceased should be involved in the planning of this liturgy.

Since the liturgical hours are primarily sung celebrations, singing should always be encouraged. The *Order of Christian Funerals* prioritizes the hymn, the psalmody, and the gospel canticle. Antiphonal or responsorial forms for singing the psalms are provided in the relevant sections of psalmody. The introduction concludes that an organist (instrumentalist) and cantor should assist the assembly in singing, that the parish should provide booklets (sheets) of the texts for all to participate, and that clear indications be given as to the structure of the liturgy and the occasions for participation.

Besides being a virtually untapped treasury of prayer, as parishes that have begun regular celebrations of Morning and/or Evening Prayer during Advent and Lent have discovered, the liturgy of the hours will often provide the most appropriate solution for those ecumenically sensitive situations in search of liturgical expression. Christians of all traditions share the profession of faith inherent in the liturgical hours celebrated at death. "When the community celebrates the hours, Christ the Mediator and High Priest is truly present through his Spirit in the gathered assembly, in the proclamation of God's word, and in the prayer and song of the Church. The community's celebration of the hours acknowledges that the spiritual bond that links the Church on earth with the Church in heaven, for it is in union with the whole Church that this prayer is offered on behalf of the deceased" (No. 349).

NOTES

1. See Balthasar Fischer, "Praying the Psalms in the Light of Christ," *Assembly* 15 (1989), pp. 434–436.

2. See St. Gregory of Nyssa, *The Life of Saint Macrina*, trans. Kevin Corrigan (Saskatoon: Peregrina, 1987), pp. 21–25. The term "thanksgiving for the light" referred not only to the kindling of the lamps and the hymn, but to the whole occasion of gathering for evening praise, a true eucharistic occasion for the presence of the risen Christ within the assembly. See also Robert Taft, *The Liturgy of the Hours in East and West* (Collegeville, Minn.: Liturgical Press, 1986), and for further context, Thaddäus A. Schnitker, *Publica Oratio: Laudes matutinae und Vesper als Gemeindegottesdienste in diesem Jahrhundert* (Diss., Univ. of Münster, pp. 88–91).

3. For further reflections on biblical eschatology in the *Benedictus* and other Lucan canticles from the tradition of the

Anawim messianic communities, see Raymond E. Brown, *The Birth of the Messiah* (Garden City, N.Y.: Doubleday, 1977), pp. 350–355 and 355–392 *passim* on both the Magnificat and Benedictus canticles, and Joseph A. Fitzmyer, *Luke* (Garden City, N.Y.: 1981)), pp. 361 and 378, where the author affirms Brown's interpretation.

Appendix IV

Resources for the Rite of Committal

What follows is a more detailed guide to the resources in the *Order* for celebration of the various forms of committal.

The standard rite of committal for adults and children is made up of three sections: a gathering at the place of committal (invitation to prayer, scripture verse, prayer over the place of committal); the committal itself (committal intercessions, the Lord's Prayer, concluding prayer); and a conclusion (prayer over the people, including blessing and dismissal). In the rite of committal for adults, four scripture verses are provided at the gathering (No. 217), with a choice of seven prayers over the place of committal (three in No. 218, four in No. 405). At the committal itself, six forms are provided (two in No. 219, four in No. 406), with four forms of intercession (two in No. 220, two in No. 407) leading to the Lord's Prayer (No. 221). For the conclusion, the minister has a choice of five prayers (two in No. 222, three in No. 408).

In the rite of committal for children, the invitation to prayer is appropriate for the death of a child (No. 319). The four scripture verses are identical with those given for adults (No. 320). Three selections of prayers over the place of committal are provided (No. 321), the first especially suitable for children, with a further four in common to adults (No. 405). For the committal itself, there are prayers for a baptized or unbaptized child (No. 322), with optional texts (No. 406); the intercessions (No. 323) are suited for children and their families, teachers, and playmates, with the possibility of adaptation and use of other forms (No. 407). The concluding prayer may be chosen from two for baptized children and one for children who have died before baptism (No. 325), with additional choices (No. 408). There are two forms of prayer over the people, whether the minister be ordained or lay (No. 326).

In the rite of committal with final commendation, the liturgy is quite similar to the first form, also falling into three sections. The gathering consists of the same elements of invitation (two forms for adults in No. 224, one form for children in No. 327), scripture verse (four suggestions for adults and children in Nos. 225 and 325), and prayer over the place of committal (three forms each from Nos. 226 and 329, with further options in No. 405).

In this form, the committal itself begins with an invitation to prayer (two forms in No. 227 for adults; three forms for children in No. 330, with options in No. 402). This leads to a silence (Nos. 228 and 331), followed by the signs of farewell (Nos. 229 and 332). A song of farewell is sung, with one responsory given for adults (No. 230) and two for children (No. 333), with a further seven options (No. 403). Then a prayer of commendation is made, two forms for adults (No. 231), two for children (No. 334). The committal takes place in silence (Nos. 232 and 335). The liturgy closes with prayer over the people (Nos. 233 and 336), with the same choice of two forms of blessing as in the standard rite, depending on the ministerial status of the presider.

290

Intercommunion: The Question

Funerals, like weddings, bring people of many different religious and non-religious traditions together around the table of the Lord's Supper. For those who share the faith of Christians, as we saw in Chapter Six, intercommunion on those occasions remains a highly sensitive ecumenical issue. Addressing that concern from Roman Catholic perspective, the following proposal is an invitation to Catholic theologians, canonists and bishops to review the matter in light of the pastoral mandate of the *Order of Christian Funerals*.

For intercommunion at a Catholic funeral to be canonically acceptable, there must exist a theologically valid reason for granting a further exception to the Catholic principle that relates eucharistic communion and ecclesial communion as inseparable sacraments of Christian unity. Does the exceptional nature of communion at the Christian funeral constitute such an exception?

Eucharistic communion at the funeral Mass explicitly manifests belief in the communion of saints into which the deceased has been taken. That unity of believers extends beyond the boundaries of the church on earth and beyond the theological differences that divide the one body of Christ. According to the theology of the funeral tradition, eucharistic communion at the funeral Mass sacramentalizes the unity of the full Christian community, expressing explicitly the belief that the deceased is one with the faithful on earth through the mystery of the communion of saints and enjoys the fruit of their intercession on his/her behalf at the eucharistic commemoration of the Lord's Passover.

On the occasion of a funeral Mass, therefore, it seems that those other Christians among the bereaved who profess the same faith in the eucharist as Catholics and who request to receive eucharistic communion as sacrament of the full Christian unity now enjoyed by the faithful deceased deserve respectful attention. The verity of sacramental communion at the funeral, where it is a manifestation of faith in everlasting life, specifically relating the death of this Christian to the paschal mystery of Christ, demands the fullest possible participation by all who believe as Catholics do in eucharistic communion with Jesus dead and risen. Thus, authenticity to the same Catholic sacramental theology that establishes the ecclesial principle would determine this exception.

In the case of intercommunion at the funeral, the exception would flow from the Christian faith that life after death and the communion of saints transcend the failures of all our earthly churches to embody perfectly the body of Christ. All the other conditions required by the Code of Canon Law (Canon 844) for use of such exceptions would, of course, apply. Sacramental intercommunion at the funeral Mass would be explicitly the sacrament of that everlasting communion with Christ into which the faithful deceased has been received and at once, by exception, the sacrament of longed-for ecclesial communion.

Bibliography

Adam, Adolf. *The Liturgical Year: Its History and its Meaning After the Reform of the Liturgy.* Trans. Matthew J. O'Connell. New York: Pueblo, 1981.

Ambrose, Saint. *Sancti Ambrosii De Bono Mortis.* Ed. and trans. William T. Weisner. Catholic University of America Patristic Studies 100. Washington, D.C.: Catholic University of America Press, 1970.

———. *Sancti Ambrosii Liber de Consolatione Valentiniani.* Ed. and trans. Thomas A. Kelly. Catholic University of American Patristic Studies 58.; Washington, D.C.: Catholic University of America Press, 1940.

———. *Sancti Ambrosii Oratio de Obitu Theodosii.* Ed. and trans. Mary D. Mannix. Catholic University of America Patristic Studies 9. Washington, D.C.: Catholic University of America Press, 1925.

Andrieu, M., ed. *Les Ordines romani du haut moyen âge,* Vol. I. Spicilegium sacrum lovaniense 11. Louvain: Université Catholique de Louvain, 1931.

Ariès, Philippe, "Death Inside Out." In *Death Inside Out: The Hastings Center Report,* eds. Peter Steinfels and Robert M. Veatch. New York: Harper & Row, 1975.

———. *The Hour of Our Death.* New York: Knopf, 1981. (This work develops extensively the thesis set out in the author's *Western Attitudes Toward Death: From the Middle Ages to the Present.* Trans. Patricia M. Ranum. Baltimore: The Johns Hopkins University Press, 1974.)

Ashworth, Henry. "The Prayers for the Dead in the Missal of Pope Paul VI." *Ephemerides Liturgicae* 85 (1971), 3–15.

Atchley, C. *A History of the Use of Incense in Divine Worship.* Alcuin Collection, No. 13. London: Longmans, Green & Co., 1909.

Attreed, Lorraine C. "Preparation for Death in Sixteenth-Century Northern England." *The Sixteenth Century Journal* 13 (1982), 37–66.

Augustine, Saint. *The City of God.* Trans. Gerald G. Walsh and Daniel J. Honan. The Fathers of the Church, Vol. 24. New York: Fathers of the Church, 1954.

———. *Confessions.* Trans. Vernon J. Bourke. The Fathers of the Church, Vol. 21. New York: Fathers of the Church, 1953.

Bailey, Cyril. *Religion in Virgil.* Oxford: Clarendon, 1935.

Baruffaldo, Hieronymus. *Ad Rituale Romanum Commentaria.* Augsburg: J. C. Bencards, 1735.

Baumiller, Robert C., ed. *A Workbook for Pastoral Care of Individuals and Families with Special Needs.* Washington, D.C.: National Center for Education in Maternal and Child Health, 1988.

Becker, Ernest. *The Denial of Death.* New York: Free Press, 1973.

Bendann, Effie. *Death Customs. An Analytical Study of Burial Rites.* New York: Knopf, 1930.

Berger, Placidus. *Religiöses Brauchtum im Umkreis der Sterbliturgie in Deutschland.* Forschungen zur Volkskunde 41. Münster: Regensberg, 1966.

Bernard, John H. and Robert Atkinson, eds. *The Irish Liber Hymnorum.* Henry Bradshaw Society 13–14. London: Harrison, 1898.

Bishops' Committee on the Liturgy. *Environment and Art in Catholic Worship.* Washington, D.C.: United States Catholic Conference, 1978.

Bishops of West Germany. "A Death That Is Worthy and Christian." *Origins* 9 (1979), 145–157.

Bleeker, C. J. *Egyptian Festivals.* Leiden: Brill, 1967.

Boadt, Lawrence. "The Scriptures on Death and Dying and the New Funeral Rite." In *Rites of Death and Dying,* ed. Anthony F. Sherman, 7–29. Collegeville, Minn.: Liturgical Press, 1988.

Boase, T.S.R. *Death in the Middle Ages*. New York: McGraw-Hill, 1972.

Bradshaw, Paul. *Daily Prayer in the Early Church*. Alcuin Club Collections, No. 63. London: SPCK, 1981.

Braet, Herman and Werner Verbeke, eds. *Death in the Middle Ages*. Mediaevalia Lovaniensia, Series I, Studia IX. Leuven: Leuven University Press, 1983.

Brightman, F. E. "The Sacramentary of Serapion of Thmuis." *The Journal of Theological Studies* 1 (1900), 88–113; 247–277.

Brown, Raymond E. *The Birth of the Messiah*. Garden City, N.Y.: Doubleday, 1979.

———. *A Crucified Christ in Holy Week*. Collegeville, Minn.: Liturgical Press, 1986.

———. *The Virginal Conception and Bodily Resurrection of Jesus*. Mahwah, N.J.: Paulist Press, 1973.

Brueggemann, Walter. *The Message of the Psalms: A Theological Commentary*, Minneapolis, Minn.: Fortress, 1984.

Bunzel, Manfred. *Die geschichtliche Entwicklung des evangelischen Begräbniswesens in Schlesien während des 16., 17., und 18. Jahrhunderts*. Lübeck: Verlag "Unser Web," 1981.

Bürki, Bruno. *Im Herrn entschlafen*. Beitrage zur praktischen Theologie 6. Heidelberg: Quelle & Meyer, 1969.

Byrne, Patrick, ed. *Funeral Liturgies*. National Bulletin on Liturgy, No. 84. Ottawa: Canadian Conference of Catholic Bishops, 1982.

Carlson, Lisa. *Caring for Your Own Dead*. Hinesburg, Vt.: Upper Access Publishers, 1987.

Centre Nationale de Pastorale Liturgique. *La Célébration des Obsèques* I. Paris: Desclée-Mame, 1972.

Champlin, Joseph M., and James E. Flynn. *The Lord Is My Shepherd: A Book of Wake Services*. Notre Dame, Ind.: Ave Maria Press, 1971.

295

————. *Toward a New Life*. Notre Dame, Ind.: Ave Maria Press, 1971.

Choran, Jacques. *Death and Western Thought*. New York: Macmillan, 1963.

Clark, James M. *The Dance of Death in the Middle Ages and Renaissance*. Glasgow: Jackson, 1950.

Clercq, Carlo de. *La Législation Religieuse Franque de Clovis à Charlemagne*. Louvain-Paris: Bibliothèque de L'Université-Sirey, 1936.

Collins, A. Jefferies, ed. *Manuale as usum percelebris ecclesiae Sarisburiensis*. Henry Bradshaw Society 91 (1958). London, 1960.

Collopy, B. J. "Theology and the Darkness of Death." *Theological Studies* 39 (1978), 22–54.

Commission on the Sacred Liturgy. *The Rite of Christian Burial*. Chicago: Archdiocese of Chicago, 1968.

Congregation for the Sacraments and Divine Worship. "De celebratione exsequiarum pro iis, qui proprii cadaveris cremationem elegerit." *Notitae* 126 (1977), 45.

Consumer Union. *Funerals: Consumers' Last Rights*. New York: Norton, 1977.

Continental Association of Funeral and Memorial Societies. *The Memorial Society: A Description* and *Directory of Memorial Societies in the United States and Canada*. Washington, D.C.: CAFMS, 1989.

Coriden, James A., Thomas J. Green, and Donald E. Heintschel, eds. *The Code of Canon Law. A Text and Commentary*. Commissioned by the Canon Law Society of America. New York: Paulist Press, 1985.

Corpus Christianorum. Series Latina. Turnhout: Brepols, 1953–. (CCL)

Corpus Scriptorum Ecclesiasticorum Latinorum. Vienna. Gerold's Sohn, 1866–. (CSEL)

Chrichton, Ian. *The Art of Dying*. London: Peter Owen, 1976.

Cumont, Franz. *Recherches sur le Symbolisme Funéraire des Romains.* Paris: Paul Geuthner, 1942.

———. *Lux Perpetua.* Paris: Paul Geuthner, 1949.

Curl, James Stevens. *The Victorian Celebration of Death.* Detroit: Partridge Press, 1972.

Cyprian, Saint. *Treatises.* Trans. Roy J. Deferrari. The Fathers of the Church, Vol. 36. New York: Fathers of the Church, 1958.

Davies, J. G., ed. *The New Westminster Dictionary of Liturgy and Worship.* Louisville, Ky.: John Knox, 1986.

Deiss, Lucien. *It's the Lord's Supper: Eucharist of Christians.* New York: Paulist Press, 1976.

Dillon, Richard. "The Unavoidable Discomforts of Preaching about Death." *Worship* 57 (1983), 486–496.

Dionysius the Pseudo-Areopagite. *The Ecclesiastical Hierarchy.* Ed. and trans. Thomas L. Campbell. Lanham, Md.: University Press of America, 1981.

Dix, Gregory. *The Shape of the Liturgy.* London: Black, 1945; New York: Seabury, 1945, 1982.

Dombeck, Mary. "Death Rituals and Life Values: The American Way." In *Rites of Death and Dying,* ed. Anthony F. Sherman, 30–66. Collegeville, Minn.: Liturgical Press, 1988.

Dreves, Clemens, and Guido Blume. *Analecta Hymnica Medii Aevi* 49. Leipzig, 1906; repr. New York–London: Johnson Reprint, 1961.

Drijvers, Pius. *The Psalms: Their Structure and Meaning.* New York: Herder & Herder, 1965.

Emery, Pierre-Yves. *The Communion of Saints.* London: Faith Press, 1966.

Eusebius. *The History of the Church.* Trans. G. A. Williamson. Baltimore: Penguin, 1965.

Evans, Joan, ed. *The Flowering of the Middle Ages.* New York: McGraw-Hill, 1966.

Feifel, Herman, ed. *The Meaning of Death*. New York: McGraw-Hill, 1959.

Fischer, Balthasar. *"Das Rituale Romanum* (1614–1964): Die Schicksale eines liturgischen Buches." *Trierer Theologische Zeitschrift* 73 (1964), 257–271.

————. "Praying the Psalms in the Light of Christ." *Assembly* 15 (1989), 434–436.

Fitzmyer, Joseph A. *The Gospel According to Luke*. Anchor Bible Series, Vol. 28. Garden City, N.Y.: Doubleday, 1981. (*Luke*)

Flannery, Austin, ed. *Vatican Council II. The Conciliar and Post-Conciliar Documents*. Northport, N.Y.: Costello, 1975. (Vatican Council II).

Fuller, Reginald. "Lectionary for Funerals." *Worship* 56 (1982), 36–63.

Geisey, Ralph E. "The Royal Funeral Ceremony in Renaissance France." (PhD diss., University of California at Berkeley, 1954.)

Gilmour, Peter, ed. *Now and at the Hour of Our Death*. Chicago: Liturgy Training Publications, 1989.

Gorer, Geoffrey. *Death, Grief and Mourning in Contemporary Britain*. New York: Doubleday, 1965; London: Cresset Press, 1965.

————. "The Pornography of Death." Repr. from *Encounter*, Oct. 1955, as appendix to Geoffrey Gorer, *Death, Grief and Mourning in Contemporary Britain*, 169–175. London: Cresset Press, 1965.

Gregory the Great, Saint. *Dialogues*. Trans. Odo J. Zimmerman. The Fathers of the Church, Vol. 39. New York: Fathers of the Church, 1959.

Guardini, Romano. Letter to the Mainz Liturgical Congress, April 1, 1964. *Herder Correspondence*, August 1964, 237–239.

Gusmer, Charles W. *And You Visited Me: Sacramental Ministry to the Sick and the Dying*. New York: Pueblo, 1984.

Gy, Pierre-Marie. "Le Nouveau Rituel Romain des Funérailles." *La Maison-Dieu* 101 (1970), 15–31. ("Le Nouveau Rituel") An English translation, "The Liturgy of Death. The Funeral Rite of the New Roman Ritual," is available in *The Way Supplement* 11 (Fall 1970), 59–75.

Habenstein, Robert W., and William M. Lamers. *Funeral Customs the World Over.* Milwaukee: Bulfin, 1960.

———. *The History of American Funeral Directing.* Milwaukee: Radke Bros. & Kertsche Co., 1955.

Haenni, G. "Un 'ordo defunctorum' du Xe siècle," *Ephemerides Liturgicae* 73 (1959), 433–434.

Hänggi, Anton, and Alfons Schönherr, eds. *Sacramentarium Rhenaugiense,* Spicilegium Friburgense, No. 15. Freiburg, Switzerland: Universitätsverlag, 1970.

Halligan, Nicholas. *Sacraments of Initiation and Union* I. New York: Alba House, 1972.

Harrah, Barbara K., and David F. Harrah. *Funeral Service: A Bibliography of Literature on Its Past, Present and Future, the Various Means of Disposition and Memorialization.* Metuchen, N.J.: Scarecrow, 1976.

Henderson, J. Frank, ed. *The Christian Funeral.* National Bulletin on Liturgy, No. 119. Ottawa: Canadian Conference of Catholic Bishops, 1989.

Holck, Frederick H., ed. *Death and Eastern Thought.* New York: Abingdon, 1974.

Holy Cross Funeral Liturgy. Notre Dame, Ind.: Congregation of Holy Cross, 1976.

Hughes, Kathleen. *Lay Presiding: The Art of Leading Prayer.* Washington, D.C.: Pastoral Press, 1988.

Huizinga, Johannes. *The Waning of the Middle Ages.* New York: Doubleday, 1954. Dutch original, 1924.

Hunt, Noreen, ed. *Cluniac Monasticism in the Central Middle Ages.* Hamden, Conn.: Archon, 1971.

Huntington, Richard, and Peter Metcalf. *Celebrations of Death: The Anthropology of Mortuary Ritual.* New York: Cambridge University Press, 1979.

Inter-Lutheran Commission on Worship. *Lutheran Book of Worship.* Minneapolis: Augsburg, 1978.

Irion, Paul. *Cremation.* Philadelphia: Fortress, 1968.

————. *The Funeral: Vestige or Value?* Nashville: Abingdon, 1966.

————. "Protestant Understandings of the Importance of the Funeral Service." National Funeral Directors Association, *The Director* 58 (1988), 16–18.

Isbell, Harold, trans. *The Last Poets of Imperial Rome.* Baltimore: Penguin, 1971.

Jones, Cheslyn, et al., eds. *The Study of Liturgy.* New York: Oxford University Press, 1978.

Jungmann, Josef A. *Early Liturgy, to the Time of Gregory the Great.* Trans. A. Francis. Notre Dame, Ind.: University of Notre Dame Press, 1959.

————. *The Mass.* Collegeville, Minn.: Liturgical Press, 1976.

————. *The Mass of the Roman Rite: Its Origins and Development.* Trans. Francis A. Brunner. Westminster, Md.: Christian Classics, 1989.

Kaczynski, Reiner. *Enchiridion Documentorum Instaurationis Liturgicae* I. Rome: Marietti, 1976.

Kenney, F. J. *The Sources for the Early History of Ireland.* New York: Octagon, 1966.

Die Kirchliche Begräbnisfeier in den katholischen Bistümen des deutschen Sprachgebietes, hrsg. im Auftrag der Bischofskonferenzen Deutschlands, Österreichs und der Schweiz und des Bischofs von Luxemburg. Einsiedeln-Cologne-Freiburg-Basel-Regensburg-Vienna-Salzburg-Linz, 1973.

Krieg, Robert. "The Funeral Homily: The Theological View." *Worship* 58 (1984), 222–239.

Kübler-Ross, Elizabeth, ed. *Death: The Final Stage of Growth.* Englewood Cliffs, N.J.: Prentice-Hall, 1975.

Kurtz, Donna D., and John Boardman. *Greek Burial Customs.* Ithaca, N.Y.: Cornell University Press, 1971.

Leon-Dufour, Xavier, ed. *Dictionary of Biblical Theology.* Trans. Joseph P. Cahill. New York, N.Y.: Harper & Row, 1973.

————. *Dictionary of the New Testament.* New York: Harper & Row, 1983.

Lewis, C. S. *A Grief Observed.* New York: Bantam, 1976 (orig. 1961).

Liturgical Commission. *Christian Death and Burial.* New York: Archdiocese of New York, 1978.

Liturgical Secretariat, Irish Episcopal Conference. *Christian Burial.* Portarlington, Ireland: Mount St. Anne's Liturgy Centre, 1976.

Lodi, Enzo. *Enchiridion Euchologicum Fontium Liturgicorum.* Bibliotheca Ephemerides liturgicae, Subsidia, Vol. 15. Rome: C.L.V.-Edizioni Liturgiche, 1979.

————. *Enchiridion Euchologicum Fontium Liturgicorum, Clavis Methodologica cum Commentariis Selectis.* Bononiae: 1979.

Löwenberg, Bruno. *Das Rituale des Kardinals Julius Antonius Sanctorius. Ein Beitrag zur Entstehungsgeschichte des Rituale Romanum* (PhD diss., 1937; Teildruk). Munich: Druk der Salesianischen Offizin., 1937.

Mansi, Giovanni D., ed. *Sacrorum conciliorum nova et amplissima collectio.* Paris: H. Welter, 1900–1927.

Marceau, Paul. "Death as a Religious Experience." *American Ecclesiastical Review* 168 (1974), 363–371.

Marchal, Michael. *Parish Funerals.* Chicago: Liturgy Training Publications, 1987.

Martène, Edmond. *De antiquis Ecclesiae ritibus*, Vol. III. Antwerp: J. B. de La Bry, 1736–1738.

Martimort, A. G. *The Church at Prayer: The Liturgy and Time*, Vol. 4. Collegeville, Minn.: Liturgical Press, 1986.

Martos, Joseph. *Doors to the Sacred: A Historical Introduction to the Sacraments in the Catholic Church.* Garden City, N.Y.: Doubleday, 1982.

McKenzie, John L. *Dictionary of the Bible.* Milwaukee: Bruce, 1965.

McManus, Frederick R. "Liturgy of Final Commendation." *American Ecclesiastical Review,* 162 (1970), 405–408.

————. "The Reformed Funeral Rite." *American Ecclesiastical Review,* 166 (1972), 45–59; 124–139. ("Funeral Rite").

Mead, Margaret. "Ritual and Social Crisis." In *Roots of Ritual,* ed. James Shaughnessy. Grand Rapids: Eerdmans, 1973.

Meier, John P. "Catholic Funerals in the Light of Scripture." *Worship* 48 (1974), 206–216.

Melloh, John Allyn, S.M. *Order of Christian Funerals: A Commentary.* Collegeville, Minn.: Liturgical Press, 1989.

Miller, Albert J., and Michael James Acri. *Death: A Bibliographical Guide.* Metuchen, N.J.: Scarecrow, 1977.

Moos, Maria Fabianus, O.P., ed. *S. Thomae Aquinatis Scriptum Super Sententiis Magistri Petri Lombardi,* Tome IV. Paris: P. Lethielleux, 1947.

Morgan, Ernest. *Dealing Creatively with Death: A Manual of Death of Education and Simple Burial.* Burnsville, N. C.: Celo Press, 1988[11].

Morenz, Siegfried. *Egyptian Religion.* Ithaca, N.Y.: Cornell University Press, 1973. German original, 1960.

Mowinckel, Sigmund. *The Psalms in Israel's Worship.* Nashville: Abingdon, 1962; Oxford: Blackwell, 1962.

Murphy, Marie. *New Images of the Last Things. Karl Rahner on Death and Life after Death.* New York: Paulist Press, 1988.

Morley, John. *Death, Heaven and the Victorians.* London: Studio Vista, 1971; Pittsburgh: University of Pittsburgh Press, 1971.

Mossman, B. C., and M. W. Stark. *The Last Salute: Civil and Military Funerals 1921–1969.* Washington, D.C.: Department of the Army, 1971.

302

National Catholic Cemetery Conference. *The Catholic Cemetery.* Des Plaines, Ill.: NCCC, 1960–.

National Center for Education in Maternal and Child Health. *A Guide to Resources in Perinatal Bereavement.* Washington, D.C.: NCEMCH, 1988.

National Funeral Directors Association. *The Director.* Milwaukee: NFDA, 1931–.

National Office for Liturgy. *Catholic Funeral Rite.* Ottawa: Canadian Catholic Conference, 1973.

Nichols, Roy, and Jane Nichols. "Funerals: A Time for Grief and Growth." In *Death: The Final Stage of Growth,* ed. Elisabeth Kübler-Ross. Englewood Cliffs, N.J.: Prentice-Hall, 1975.

Ntedika, Joseph. *L'Evocation de l'au-delà dans la prière pour les morts Etudes de patristique et de liturgie latines (IVe–VIIIe S.).* Recherches Africaines de Théologie 2. Louvain-Paris: Nauwelaerts and Beatrice Nauwelaerts, 1971. (L'Evocation)

The Order of Funerals for Adults. Experimental Rite for use by permission of the Holy See. Washington, D.C.: National Council of Catholic Bishops, 1967.

Osterweis, Marian, et al., eds. *Bereavement: Reactions, Consequences, and Care.* Washington, D.C.: National Academy Press, 1984.

Ottosen, K., N. K. Rasmussen, and C. Thodberg, eds. *The Manual from Notmark.* Bibliotheca Liturgica Danica, Series Latina I. Copenhagen: G.E.C. Gad, 1970.

Parkes, Collin Murray, and Robert S. Weiss. *Recovery from Bereavement.* New York: Basic Books, 1983.

Patrologiae cursus completus, Series Graeca. Ed. J. P. Migne. Paris: Privately printed, 1857–1866. (PG)

Patrologiae cursus completus, Series Prima [Latina]. Ed. J. P. Migne. Paris: Privately printed, 1844–1864. (PL)

Paul VI. "Indulgentiarum doctrina." *The Pope Speaks* 12 (1967), 124–135.

———. "Mysterium Fidei." *The Pope Speaks* 10 (1965), 309–328.

———. "Sacrum diaconatus ordinem." *The Pope Speaks* 12 (1967), 237–243.

Pelikan, Jaroslav. *The Shape of Death. Life, Death and Immortality in the Early Fathers.* Nashville: Abingdon, 1961.

Perham, Michael. *The Communion of Saints.* Alcuin Club Collections, No. 62. London: SPCK, 1980.

Pieper, Josef. *Death and Immortality.* Trans. Richard and Clara Winston. London: Northumberland Press, 1969.

Pittenger, Norman. *After Death Life in God.* New York: Seabury, 1980.

Prudentius. *Aurelii Prudentii Clementis Carmina.* Ed. M. P. Cunningham. CCL 126. Turnhout: Brepols, 1966.

Puckle, Bertram S. *Funeral Customs. Their Origin and Development.* London: T. Werner Laurie, 1926; repr. Detroit: Singing Tree, 1968.

Quasten, Johannes. *Music and Worship in Pagan and Christian Antiquity.* Washington D.C.: Pastoral Press, 1983.

Raby, F.J.E. *A History of Christian-Latin Poetry from the Beginnings to the Close of the Middle Ages.* Oxford: Clarendon, 1973.

Raether, Howard C., ed. *The National Funeral Directors Association Resource Manual.* Milwaukee: NFDA Learning Resource Center, 1981.

———. "The Place of the Funeral: The Role of the Funeral Director in Contemporary America." *Omega* 2 (1971), 131–149.

Rahner, Karl. *On the Theology of Death.* New York: Herder & Herder, 1961.

———and Angelus Haüssling. *The Celebration of the Eucharist.* New York: Herder & Herder, 1968. (*Eucharist*)

Ramshaw, Elaine. *Ritual and Pastoral Care.* Philadelphia: Fortress, 1987.

———. "Ritual for Stillbirth. Exploring the Issues." *Worship* 62 (1988), 533–538.

Ramshaw, Gail. "The Place of Lament within Praise." *Worship* 61 (1987), 317–322.

Rando, Therese A. *Grief, Dying and Death. Clinical Interventions for Caregivers.* Champaign, Ill.: Research Press, 1984.

———, ed. *Parental Loss of a Child.* Champaign, Ill.: Research Press, 1986.

Raphael, Beverley. *The Anatomy of Bereavement.* New York: Basic Books, 1983.

Ratzinger, Joseph. *Eschatology.* Trans. Michael Waldstein; ed. Aidan Nichols. Washington, D.C.: Catholic University of America Press, 1988. German original, 1977. (The state of the question has been updated in a foreword and two appendices for the the English translation.)

Riemer, Jack, ed. *Jewish Reflections on Death.* New York: Schocken, 1974.

Rite for a Catholic Wake. Ottawa: Canadian Catholic Conference, 1973.

The Rite of Christian Burial. Adapted for use in the Archdiocese of Chicago by the Commission on the Sacred Liturgy. Chicago: Archdiocese of Chicago, 1968.

Rite of Christian Burial in the Diocese of Albany. Albany: Liturgy Center, 1976.

Rite of Christian Initiation of Adults. Washington, D.C.: United States Catholic Conference, 1988.

Rite of Funerals. Celebrant's Manual for the Church Service. With Pastoral Directives for use in the Archdiocese of Chicago. Chicago: Liturgy Training Program, 1971.

The Rites of the Catholic Church as Revised by the Second Vatican Ecumenical Council. New York: Pueblo, 1976.

Rituale Romanum ex decreto sacrosancti oecumenici Concilii Vaticani II instauratum auctoritate Pauli PP VI promulgatum, *Ordo Exsequiarum.* Rome: Typis Polyglottis Vaticanis, 1969.

Rituale Romanum Pauli V. Pont. Max. iussu editum. Rome: Typis Polyglottis Vaticanis, 1916.

Rituale Sacramentorum Romanum Gregorii Papae XIII Pont. Max. iussu editum. Rome, 1584.

Robinson, J. Armitage, ed. *The Apology of Aristides. Texts and Studies* 1. Cambridge: University Press, 1893; repr. Nendeln, Liechtenstein: Kraus, 1967.

Roguet, A.-M. *The Liturgy of the Hours.* Collegeville, Minn.: Liturgical Press, 1971.

―――. "La prédication de la mort." *La Maison-Dieu* 44 (1955), 104–110.

The Roman Missal revised by decree of the Second Vatican Ecumenical Council and published by authority of Pope Paul VI, *General Instruction of the Roman Missal.* English translation of the fourth edition (1975) prepared by the International Commission on English in the Liturgy. In *Liturgy Document Series* 2. Washington, D.C.: United States Catholic Conference, 1982. (GIRM)

The Roman Ritual revised by decree of the Second Vatican Ecumenical Council and published by authority of Pope Paul VI, *Pastoral Care of the Sick: Rites of Anointing and Viaticum.* Collegeville, Minn.: Liturgical Press, 1983.

The Roman Ritual revised by decree of the Second Vatican Ecumenical Council and published by authority of Pope Paul VI, *Rite of Funerals.* Study Edition. Washington, D.C.: United States Catholic Conference, 1971.

The Roman Ritual revised by decree of the Second Vatican Ecumenical Council and published by authority of Pope Paul VI, *Rite of Penance.* Washington, D.C.: United States Catholic Conference, 1975.

Rowell, Geoffrey. *The Liturgy of Christian Burial.* Alcuin Club Collections, No. 59. London: SPCK, 1977. (*Christian Burial*)

Rush, Alfred C. *Death and Burial in Christian Antiquity.* Catholic University of America Studies in Christian Antiquity 1. Washington, D.C.: Catholic University of America Press, 1941. (*Christian Antiquity*)

————. "The Colors of Red and Black in the Liturgy of the Dead." In *Kyriakon. Festschrift für Johannes Quasten*, Vol. II, eds. Patrick Granfield and Josef A. Jungmann, 698–708. Münster: Aschendorff, 1970.

————. "The Eucharist: The Sacrament of the Dying in Christian Antiquity." *The Jurist* 34 (1974), 10–35.

————. "The Rosary and the Christian Wake." *American Ecclesiastical Review*, 152 (1965), 289–297.

Rutherford, Richard. *The Death of a Christian: The Rite of Funerals*. New York: Pueblo, 1980. (*Death*)

————. "Funeral Liturgy—Why Bother?" In *Rites of Death and Dying*, ed. Anthony F. Sherman, 67–102. Collegeville, Minn.: Liturgical Press, 1988. ("Funeral Liturgy")

————. *Honoring the Dead: Catholics and Cremation*. Collegeville, Minn.: Liturgical Press, in press.

————. *The Order of Christian Funerals. An Invitation to Pastoral Care*. Collegeville, Minn.: Liturgical Press, 1990. (*Pastoral Care*)

————and Harriet A. Kandelmann. *The Role of Religion in Spousal Bereavement: Roman Catholic Funeral Rites*. In *Research Record*. Evanston, Ill.: National Research and Information Center, 1985. (*Religious Ritual*)

Sabourin, Leopold. *The Psalms: Their Origin and Meaning*. New York: Alba House, 1974.

Sacred Congregation of Rites. *Eucharisticum Mysterium*. Washington, D.C.: United States Catholic Conference, 1967.

Saint Andrew Bible Missal. Bruges: Biblica, 1962.

Sankovitch, Joseph B. *A Mission Statement*. Seattle: Associated Catholic Cemeteries, Archdiocese of Seattle, 1988.

————. *Cremation*. Seattle: Associated Catholic Cemeteries, Archdiocese of Seattle, 1987.

————. *Why Catholic Cemeteries?* Seattle: Associated Catholic Cemeteries, Archdiocese of Seattle, 1988.

————. *Why Pre-need in the Catholic Tradition?* Seattle: Associated Catholic Cemeteries, Archdiocese of Seattle, 1988.

Sandmel, Samuel. *Judaism and Christian Beginnings.* New York: Oxford University Press, 1980.

Saxer, Victor. *Morts, Martyrs, Reliques en Afrique Chrétienne aux Prèmiers Siècles.* Paris: Editions Beauchesne, 1980. (*Morts, Martyrs, Reliques*)

Schillebeeckx, Edward. *Christ: The Experience of Jesus as Lord.* New York: Crossroad, 1980.

————. *God Among Us: The Gospel Proclaimed.* New York: Crossroad, 1983.

Schmaus, Michael, *Dogma VI: Justification and the Last Things.* Kansas City-London: Sheed & Ward, 1977.

Schmitz, Walter, and Terence Tierney. *Liturgikon: Pastoral Ministrations.* Huntington, Ind.: Our Sunday Visitor, 1977.

Schnitker, Thaddäus A. *Publica Oratio: Laudes matutinae und Vesper als Gemeindegottesdienste in diesem Jahrhundert.* (PhD diss., University of Münster, 1977.)

Schreiber, G., ed. *Das Weltkonzil von Trient,* 2 vols. Freiburg: Herder, 1951.

Schrott, Aloys. "Die Trienter Reform im Spiegel der nachfolgenden Andachtsliteratur." In *Das Weltkonzil von Trient* I, ed. G. Schreiber, 349–350. Freiburg: Herder, 1951.

Serapion of Thmuis, Bishop. *Bishop Serapion's Prayer-Book.* Trans. John Wordsworth. Hamden, Ct.: Archon, 1964; repr. of 1923 rev. ed.

Sicard, Damien. "The Funeral Mass." In *Reforming the Rites of Death,* ed. Johannes Wagner. Concilium, Vol. 32, 45–52. New York: Paulist Press, 1968.

————. *La liturgie de la mort dans l'église latine des origines à la réforme carolingienne.* Liturgiewissenschaftliche Quelle und Forschungen, No. 63. Münster: Aschendorff, 1978. (*La liturgie de la mort*)

Sprandel, Rolf. "Alter und Todesfurcht nach der spätmittelalterlichen Bibelexegese." In *Death in the Middle Ages,* eds. Herman Braet and Werner Verbeke, 107–116. Leuven: Leuven University Press, 1983.

Sparkes, Robert, and Richard Rutherford. "The Order of Christian Funerals. A Study in Bereavement and Lament." *Worship* 60 (1986), 499–510. ("Lament")

Staniforth, Maxwell. *Early Christian Writings. The Apostolic Fathers.* Baltimore: Penguin, 1972.

Stanley, D. M. *The Apostolic Church in the New Testament.* Westminster, Md.: Newman, 1967.

Stannard, David E., ed. *Death in America.* Philadelphia: University of Pennsylvania Press, 1974.

Storey, William et al., eds. *Morning Praise and Evensong.* Notre Dame, Ind.: Fides, 1973.

Sullender, R. Scott. *Grief and Growth. Pastoral Resources for Emotional and Spiritual Growth.* New York: Paulist Press, 1985.

———. *Losses in Later Life. A New Way of Walking with God.* New York: Paulist Press, 1989.

———. "Saint Paul's Approach to Grief: Clarifying the Ambiguity." *Journal of Religion and Health* 20 (1981), 63–74.

Szöverffy, Josef. *Die Annalen der Lateinischen Hymnendichtung: Ein Handbuch,* Vol. II. Berlin: E. Schmidt Verlag, 1965.

———. "Folk Beliefs and Mediaeval Hymns." *Folklore* 66 (1955), 219–231.

Taft, Robert. *Beyond East and West: Problems in Liturgical Understanding.* Washington, D.C.: Pastoral Press, 1984.

———. *The Liturgy of the Hours in East and West.* Collegeville, Minn.: Liturgical Press, 1986.

Taylor, Michael. *The Mystery of Suffering and Death.* New York: Alba House, 1974.

Thiry, Claude. "De la Mort Marâtre à la Mort Vaincue: Attitudes devant la Mort dans la déploration funèbre française." In *Death in the Middle Ages,* eds. Herman Braet and Werner Verbeke, 239–257. Leuven: Leuven University Press, 1983.

Tissier, Marcel. "L'Homélie aux Funérailles." *La Maison-Dieu* 101 (1970), 117–126.

Toynbee, J. M. C. *Death and Burial in the Roman World*. Ithaca, N.Y.: Cornell University Press, 1971. (*Death and Burial*)

van de Walle, A. R. *From Darkness to the Dawn. How Belief in the Afterlife Affects Living*. Mystic, Conn.: Twenty-Third Publications, 1984. Flemish original, 1981.

van der Meer, Frits, and Christine Mohrmann. *Atlas of the Early Christian World*. London: Nelson, 1966. Dutch original, 1958. (*Atlas*)

van Dijk, Stephen J. P. *Sources of the Modern Roman Liturgy. The Ordinals of Haymo of Faversham and Related Documents (1243–1307)*, II. leiden: Brill, 1963.

Veit, Ludwig Andreas, and Ludwig Lenhart. *Kirche und Volksfrömmigkeit im Zeitalter des Barock*. Freiburg: Herder, 1956.

Vogel, Cyril. *Medieval Liturgy: An Introduction to the Sources*. Washington D.C.: Pastoral Press, 1987.

Wagner, Johannes, ed. *Reforming the Rites of Death*. Concilium, Vol. 32. New York: Paulist Press, 1968.

Walpole, A. S. *Early Latin Hymns*. Cambridge: 1922; repr. Hildesheim: George Olms, 1966.

Waugh, Evelyn. "Death in Hollywood." *Life* 23 (1947), 73–83.

———. *The Loved One*. Boston: Little, Brown & Co., 1948.

Wegman, Herman A. J. *Christian Worship in East and West*. Trans. Gordon Lathrop. New York: Pueblo, 1985.

Weizman, Savine G., and Phyllis Kamm. *About Mourning. Support and Guidance for the Bereaved*. New York: Human Sciences, 1987.

Weller, Philip T. *The Roman Ritual* II. Milwaukee: Bruce, 1952.

Westerman, Claus. *The Psalms: Structure, Content, and Message*. Trans. Ralph D. Gehrke. Minneapolis: Fortress, 1980.

White, James F. *Introduction to Christian Worship*. Nashville: Abingdon, 1980.

————and Susan J. White. *Church Architecture: Building and Renovation for Christian Worship.* Nashville: Abingdon, 1988.

Wilkinson, John. *Egeria's Travels to the Holy Land.* Warminster, England: Aris & Phillips, 1981 (rev.).

Winstone, Harold, ed. *Pastoral Liturgy. A Symposium.* Glasgow: Wm. Collins Sons & Co., 1975.

Zandee, J. *Death as an Enemy According to Ancient Egyptian Conceptions.* Leiden: Brill, 1960.

INDEX